Resources and Man

Committee on Resources and Man

Resources and Man

A STUDY AND RECOMMENDATIONS

by the Committee on Resources and Man
of the Division of Earth Sciences
NATIONAL ACADEMY OF SCIENCES—
NATIONAL RESEARCH COUNCIL

with the cooperation
of the Division of Biology and Agriculture

W. H. FREEMAN AND COMPANY
San Francisco

National Academy of Sciences Publication Number 1703
Library of Congress Catalog Card Number 73–91928
Standard Book Number 7167–0244–4 (cloth);
7167–0243–6 (paper)

Printed in the United States of America.

9 8 7 6 5 4 3 2

Contents

Foreword

The adequacy of resources stands with peace and population control among the crucial problems of our time and the future. It places constraints both on the ultimate sizes of populations and on the level of living that populations of any density may enjoy.

The National Academy of Sciences, therefore, established a Committee on Resources and Man to evaluate national and world resources in the light of current and expected stresses and to identify problems in need of study as well as opportunities for progress. This book presents the results of two years of inquiry by that Committee. In it the Committee weighs the critical constraints, considers the time scale within which our society is likely to come against them, and recommends some steps that might improve our capability to deal with them.

The Academy is grateful for financial support for this study received from The Population Council, the Department of Health, Education, and Welfare, and the Department of the Interior.

20 June 1968

Frederick Seitz, PRESIDENT
National Academy of Sciences

Preface

No one can predict the future in detail. Past efforts to do so seem naive in retrospect. Nevertheless, we can foresee the probable consequences of some of our actions or failures to take action, and we owe it to those who will follow to look ahead as far as we can and over the broadest scope possible. The goal should be to avert the thoughtless foreclosure of options.

The problems that face mankind, however, are so numerous and so complex that it is easy to take the position that all we can or should do is work at such clearly researchable components as fall within our individual competence. Yet the larger questions will go forever unresolved if we decline to attack them merely because they appear hazy and unanswerable in our lifetimes. We must keep them under constant pressure so that they will yield the more readily to better-informed minds and more-advanced means in the future. It was in this spirit that the Committee on Resources and Man approached its task.

Peace, population, pollution, and resources are the central interlocking variables whose unsatisfactory management threatens our options. Views about this threat tend to be pessimistic or optimistic, depending on the extent to which they focus on the magnitude and ecological complexity of the problems or on the impressive technological capabilities with which we confront these same problems. In attempting better to understand the reasons for this polarization of views about resources, and to define its task, the Committee on Resources and Man examined a range of judgments and supporting evidence. During four widely spaced three-day conferences with informed persons representing a diversity of opinion, and in our discussions as a committee and as individuals over the two years during which this study was active, we sought a balanced consideration of varying views rather than a strained reconciliation. Clearly the problems we have attempted to assess will be ameliorated neither by uncritical euphoria nor by defeatist gloom but only by realistic formulation and action. The adequacy and the quality of resources, both in the near future and in the decades and generations ahead, are confining forces of major and increasing magnitude, and many of the variables that affect them are inadequately understood. Unremitting, imaginative, determined, and large-scale effort will be necessary to deal with the problems posed by these confining forces and our still inadequate understanding of them.

Although there is disagreement among informed persons as to the magnitude and specifics of our resource problems, as well as about the best solutions to them, there is no disagreement within our Committee about either their urgency or their long-range aspects. Complacency, delay, and short-range views jeopardize our chances of finding satisfactory solutions. Serious dangers beset us already, and greater ones loom in the future. People are in trouble, even around the North Atlantic—in large part because there are too many of them. Hardship can be reduced and its increase averted only by persistent efforts involving all sectors of society.

Flexible plans of long range and large scope are needed to assure the sufficiency and integrity of our environment. They must be based on informed foresight, designed to preserve a variety of choices for the future, and put into effect as soon as possible.

Precipitous haste, however, would be almost as bad as undue delay. Thus, instead of comprehensive plans, what we propose here are some steps toward their early evolution. We hope, by viewing selected critical aspects of the resource picture in an ecological context, to make clear the need for more comprehensive evaluation and wiser use of our resources. In stating this need, we recognize that without peace and population control even the most detailed knowledge and otherwise wisest management of resources are to no avail, and that a study of resources that bypasses considerations of ample pure air and water is incomplete. The latter considerations, however, are now coming increasingly into the public awareness. We wish here to focus comparable attention on resources other than air and water as equally vital components of present and future industrial societies.

Our book is intended to be evocative. We mean it to be a brief but reasonably balanced introduction to the problem of man's relation to his resources, concentrating on issues central to a rational perception of the problem rather than on detailed estimates and projections. If it expresses judgments at odds with those of others, that is part of our contribution to the continuing discussion. The important thing is that the discussion continue, and that it give rise to policy and to thoughtful action or deliberate inaction. If the future falls short of our hopes for it, we would prefer that it be because our judgment was imperfect rather than not ventured.

It is necessary to say a word about the actual preparation of this book. As our study proceeded, drafts of the various chapters were prepared by appropriate Committee members and circulated for criticism. Such drafts were subsequently discussed with the responsible author by the Committee as a whole (where feasible) or by the Chairman on its behalf. After revision, all chapters were assembled and edited by the Chairman for submission to and further review by the Divisions of Earth Sciences, Biology and Agriculture, and Behavioral Sciences of the National Research Council, and by the Committee on Science and Public Policy of the National Academy of Sciences. With the exception of Chapter 8, such review was completed and all rewriting done by June, 1968. Thus, as this book goes to press, the documentation presented may not be entirely up to date in all chapters. Since this does not affect the conclusions drawn and recommendations proposed, however, we have simply labeled all chapters with the date of receipt and final revision and published them as they were at that time.

3 May 1969
Preston Cloud, CHAIRMAN
Committee on Resources and Man

Introduction and Recommendations

"There are three imperatives: to reduce war to a minimum; to stabilize human population; and to prevent the progressive destruction of the earth's irreplaceable resources."
—Sir Macfarlane Burnet, 1966[1]

This book is about problems that confront man in seeking a durable accommodation with his natural resources. Concepts of resources, to be sure, change from time to time and from place to place, but the general notion is always of something necessary or useful, like food, clean air and water, and materials that skilled hands and discerning minds can turn to the improvement of the human lot. Various aspects of man's relation to his resources are considered in the chapters that follow. Here we state the main features of our study.

The central question is: can man approach a kind of dynamic equilibrium with his environment so as to avert destructive imbalances? Ultimately this question involves the entire globe and the distant future. We have chosen, however, to concentrate on material resources other than air and water, and on North America—although with global cognizance and in ecological context. As for time scale, we have tried to look well beyond the year 2000, but to keep the shorter term in view. In order to focus on the issues that seem to us

---

[1] In "Ecology and the Appreciation of Life," The Boyer Lectures, Australian Broadcasting Comm., Ambassador Press, Sydney, p. 29.

to block a general appreciation of the importance and gravity of resource problems, and in the interests of brevity, we have also left out much detail that might have been included in a technical report. Thus we often find ourselves dealing with methods of making estimates, and with the limitations of those methods, rather than with the commonly uncertain estimates and projections themselves. It is especially in this combination of analysis of underlying assumptions, ecological orientation, broad scope, long-range view, and relative brevity that our report differs from previous resource assessments.

In preliminary discussions we asked particularly what resources are vital to our well-being and economy now, which are likely to be vital in the future, what substitutions and technological innovations might modify resource priorities, and what limits are placed on population and material growth by resource availability. We also considered the consequences of limited supply of resources and of varying social and economic concepts that affect their use and adequacy. Such considerations bring out a major difficulty in the planning process: a series of separate decisions, each individually justifiable, can, in the aggregate, lead to results which, had they been foreseen, might have been avoided. To a degree, therefore, we have attempted to view the management of many resources simultaneously and under alternative assumptions about sociopolitical response and technological evolution, but our attempts indicate that far more extensive analysis of alternatives will be needed to develop comprehensive resource policies of long-term validity.

A prime conclusion of ecology is that species whose populations exceed or approach too closely the carrying capacity of resources in the space occupied undergo reduction. Such reductions are often severe and may lead to extinction because of disease, pestilence, predation, or aggressive competitors. Although it is true that man has repeatedly succeeded in increasing both the space he occupies and its carrying capacity, and that he will continue to do so, it is also clear that both the occupiable space and its carrying capacity have finite limits which he can approach only at great peril.

It is essential, therefore, that we carefully assess and continually reassess these limits, and that we take steps to assure that future generations, as well as people now living, will have the resources necessary for a satisfying life. These resources, moreover, must be so distributed as to exclude catastrophe as a factor in limiting population density. As Marston Bates stresses in Chapter 1, few species of animals ever really multiply to the absolute limit of their food supply under natural conditions; other controlling factors intervene, often of the sort that humans would call psychic or psychosomatic. Man also must adapt to his ecosystem—to his physical environment and its biological components. We cannot long operate as a force apart from it, for we are not. Above all, we must be wary of man's tendency to reduce the variety of components in his ecosystem, for this increases susceptibility to adverse change.

Many people outside the Atlantic community of nations are now threatened with poverty and famine as a result of population increases that locally exceed the carrying capacity of the land. To a greater or lesser degree the same potential danger threatens all people, as Malthus first clearly recognized in 1798. Wishful thinking does not banish the problem. Harrison Brown asked in 1954[2]: "Is betterment of the situation really within the realm of possibility? And if betterment is possible, at what level can the greatly increased numbers be supported? Lastly are the earth's resources sufficient to meet the enhanced demand?" The same questions haunt us with increasing intensity—an intensity as yet almost unrelieved by significant decreases in rates of population growth. By average American standards, two thirds of the world's people are still ill-fed, ill-housed, and ill-clothed, including many in North America. What can we in North America do to aid our own underprivileged, to meet the population increases that will yet precede real population control, and to help the rest of the world?

The answer is that much can be done, given sufficient effort in resource management. But other dangers arise. The quality of life, which we equate with flexibility of choices and freedom of action, is threatened by the demands of an expanding economy and population. This happens in three principal ways: (1) through the restrictive and harmful effects of pollution; (2) through the increasing frequency and complexity of unconstructive but unavoidable human contacts; and (3) through the necessary increase of regulatory measures—all in consequence of increasing use of and competition for resources, space, recreation, transportation, housing, and even educational facilities.

Thus, in addition to energy, mineral, and food resources, the quantity and quality of the human resource itself are critical components of the equation. As John D. Chapman brings out in Chapter 2, man is not only a part of his ecosystem, he is the most powerful influence in it. He is simultaneously its potentially most precious resource and its most serious threat. The gains from technological development must always be balanced in as much detail as possible against its costs. Man's own best interests plead for a more generous attitude toward the rest of nature and for less materialistic measures of well-being and success—especially in the developed countries. Such changes in attitude would make it easier to bring about dynamically balanced relations between the need for materials and the quantity available on the one hand and the quality of life and quantity of consumers on the other.

The growing quantity of people is a key factor whose future dimensions we should like to be able to estimate. Problems involved in that estimate are discussed by Nathan Keyfitz in Chapter 3. Only two things seem certain: there are going to be more people in the future and they will live in denser aggregates. The number of people to be accommodated by the end of the century, moreover, adds a new dimension to current crises. To accommodate these

---

[2] *The Challenge of Man's Future,* Viking Press, New York, p. 61.

populations, the developed world will require, by the year 2000, additional urban facilities equivalent to all of those already in existence, and correspondingly more for the underdeveloped world. This calls for an entirely different view of our cities and their resource requirements than if we think only of ameliorating specific crises step by step as they arise. Complete urban renovation, the creation of new and better living clusters throughout the country, and better and more diversified use of suburban and rural space are a big order; but it is an order that is practicable, necessary, and urgent. There is no simple "best solution." A variety of solutions must be tried, and for all of them the resource component (including clean air and water) will be central.

Somehow we must manage by the year 2000 to support a population increase in the United States from the present 200 million people to between 300 million and 340 million, and an increase in world population from the now more than 3.5 billion people to between 6 billion and 7 billion—an increasing proportion of them in cities. Failure to support that population increase would have unacceptable consequences. Population control, essential in the long run, cannot come soon enough to eliminate the challenge. To stabilize populations requires that the birth rate not exceed 14 live births per year per thousand people at the 70-year life expectancy sought as a goal for all. Only Hungary, Japan, and Bulgaria currently have such a low birth rate. This shows that a stabilized population can be achieved, but as Kingsley Davis has emphasized,[3] the inadequate measures that now pass for population control at best eliminate only unwanted births. Birth rates over most of the world cannot be brought to control levels by presently accepted measures. Steps must be taken to realize a zero rate of population increase as the ultimate goal. In the meanwhile, the increasing number of people to be accommodated will severely tax the capacity of the human ecosystem.

Nutrition is the first essential; yet problems of distribution, of local failure to exploit potentialities, and with social customs that dictate what food is acceptable are more immediately urgent than the problem of quantity of food available or producible on a global scale. If present world food production could be evenly rationed, there would be enough to satisfy both energy (calories) and protein requirements for everyone—although with drastic reductions for the now affluent. All-out effort, including the provision of ample fertilizer, and genetic, ecological, and chemical research, could probably quadruple production from the lands and double production from the waters by the end of the century. If such increased production were evenly distributed, it could keep up with population growth expected during the same time and even permit some improvement of diet. But will such all-out effort be started and sustained?

The probable ultimate increase in production of food from the sea on a

---

[3] *Science*, 1957, vol. 158, p. 730.

sustained basis is not likely to be much more than about two and one-half times the present annual production of 60 million metric tons of fish, containing 12 million tons of usable protein—an estimate that emerges from William E. Ricker's analysis of marine production in Chapter 5. An increase to as much as four times the present production is unlikely. Perhaps the most important thing to bear in mind about aquatic food products, however, is that although they are an excellent source of protein they are a poor source of calories. Only the land can supply calories in adequate quantity for the needs anticipated, an eventual increase of possibly eight times the present land production being foreseen by Sterling B. Hendricks in Chapter 4. To attain this, however, will call for maximum increases in productivity of existing lands, cultivation of all potentially arable lands, new crops, the use of more vegetable and less animal protein, continued risky use of ever-new but hopefully degradable biocides, chemical or microbiological synthesis of foods, and other innovations.

Foreseeable increases in food supplies over the long term, therefore, are not likely to exceed about nine times the amount now available. That approaches a limit that seems to place the earth's ultimate carrying capacity at about 30 billion people, *at a level of chronic near-starvation for the great majority* (and with massive immigration to the now less densely populated lands)! A world population of 30 billion is only slightly more than three doublings from the present one, which is now increasing at a doubling time of about 35 years. At this rate, there could be 30 billion people by about 2075 in the absence of controls beyond those now in effect. Hopeful allowance for such controls (Chapter 3) suggests that populations *may* level off not far above 10 billion people by about 2050—and that is close to (if not above) the maximum that an *intensively managed* world might hope to support with some degree of comfort and individual choice, as we estimate such immeasurables. If, in fulfillment of their rising expectations, all people are to be more than merely adequately nourished, effort must be made to stabilize populations at a world total much lower than 10 billion. Indeed it is our judgment that a human population less than the present one would offer the best hope for comfortable living for our descendants, long duration for the species, and the preservation of environmental quality.

Man must also look with equal urgency to his nonrenewable resources—to mineral fuels, to metals, to chemicals, and to construction materials. These are the heritage of all mankind. Their overconsumption or waste for the temporary benefit of the few who currently possess the capability to exploit them cannot be tolerated.

The nonfuel mineral resources are very unequally distributed, both as to location and as to grade. No nation is self-sufficient in all of them, even in the short term. The ultimate resources of major industrial metals such as iron and aluminum, to be sure, are very large, for their availability depends mainly on improvements in recovery methods. But true shortages exist or threaten for many substances that are considered essential for current industrial society: mercury, tin, tungsten, and helium for example. Known and now-prospective reserves of these substances will be nearly exhausted by the end of this century or early in the next, and new sources or substitutes to satisfy even these relatively near-term needs will have to be found. It is not true, although it is widely believed, that tonnages of metalliferous rock generally increase geometrically with arithmetic decrease in grade. Much of Chapter 6, by Thomas S. Lovering, is devoted to showing why this is an invalid generalization that encourages a dangerous complacency. Neither is abundant cheap energy a panacea for waning resources. Innovation of many kinds will be needed—in methods of finding ore, in mining, in extraction of metals, in substitution, in transportation, and in conservation and waste disposal. For all reusable materials in short supply, appropriate laws or codes restructuring economic incentives could facilitate conservative recovery, more efficient use, and reuse, thereby appreciably extending now foreseeable commodity lifetimes.

It is not certain whether, in the next century or two, further industrial development based on mineral resources will be foreclosed by limitations of supply. The biggest unknowns are population and rates of consumption. It is self-evident, however, that the exponential increases in demand that have long prevailed cannot be satisfied indefinitely. If population and demand level off at some reasonable plateau, and if resources are used wisely, industrial society can endure for centuries or perhaps millenia. But technological and economic brilliance alone cannot create the essential raw materials whose enhancement in value through beneficiation, fabrication, and exchange constitutes the basic material fabric of such a society.

The mineral and chemical resources of the sea (Chapter 7) will increasingly supplement those from the land—but only for a few of the many commodities we need. Information on which to base a durable assessment of such resources is not now available, but it can be expected to improve as research and exploration increase. Although ocean waters cover two-thirds of the earth, what little is known about the composition and probable history of the three quarters of the sea bottom that lies beyond the continental rises does not support the popular belief that this region harbors great mineral wealth. Beneath a thin veneer of young sediments, the floor of the ocean basins appears to consist of young basaltic rocks, only sparsely metalliferous and in constant slow motion toward and beneath the continents. Much more promising are the potentialities of the submerged parts of the continents—of oil from the sediments of the continental shelves, slopes, and rises and of mineral placers near the coast. Seawater is also an important source of some useful elements and salts, but only for a few of those needed.

On the one hand, therefore, mineral and mineral-fuel production from the sea are certainly worth going after and will increasingly help to meet needs and shortages in certain commodities. On the other hand, there is little basis for assuming that many marine mineral and chemical resources are of large usable volume or feasible recoverability or that for many essential substances there are any marine resources at all. The roughly $4 billion 1964 world production of offshore mineral resources shows clearly that profits are to be had from the sea. Whether offshore minerals will provide an adequate supplement to the mineral resources of the lands in the needed variety of products is quite another matter.

Finally, energy resources are considered in Chapter 8, by M. King Hubbert. Known or potential energy resources include power from flowing waters, tidal power, geothermal power, solar energy, and mineral fuels. Of these, conventional water power, if fully developed, would be about equal to that currently generated from fossil fuels. Important as they could be, however, especially in presently underdeveloped parts of the southern hemisphere, conventional sources of water power are erratically distributed, and reservoirs silt up. Tidal power and geothermal power are only locally available and neither represents a potential energy supply of more than about 2 percent of that available from water power. Solar energy, although daily renewable and enormous in amount, offers little promise as a major source of industrial power because of the difficulty of achieving the essential concentration and continuity of energy and because of the large quantities of metals and other materials that would be required for solar energy plants of significant capacity.

Sources of power for the future are to be sought among the mineral fuels, and above all in nuclear energy. It will take only another 50 years or so to use up the great bulk of the world's initial supply of recoverable petroleum liquids and natural gas! Recoverable liquid fuels from tar sands and oil shales, although their estimates are very uncertain, might supplement conventional petroleum fuels sufficiently to extend the total lifetime of the petroleum family of fuels as an important source of industrial energy to as much as a century from now. The remaining effective lifetime for coal, if used as the principal source of energy at expected increased demands, would be no more than two or three centuries (although the normal tapering-off in use of a diminishing resource will assure its continued production for perhaps another 500 years from the present). Moreover, we cannot simultaneously use the fossil fuels for fuels, petrochemicals, synthetic polymers, and bacterial conversion to food without going through them even more rapidly. A major side benefit from converting to nuclear energy as our main energy source, therefore, could be the adoption of measures to conserve the fossil fuels for other useful purposes and for *essential* liquid fuels.

Nuclear power from naturally fissionable uranium-235 and from fissionable isotopes obtained by neutron irradiation of uranium-238 and thorium-232 is potentially orders of magnitude larger than that obtainable from all the fossil fuels combined. The supply of uranium-235 from high-grade ores, however, is severely limited, and the production of nuclear power at a cost competitive with fossil fuels or water power, using the present light-water converter reactors and uranium-235 as the principal energy source can be sustained for only a few decades.

If the potential of nuclear power based on the fission reaction is to be realized, therefore, this can be accomplished only by an early replacement of the present light-water reactors (which can use only about 1 percent of natural uranium) by fully breeding reactors capable of consuming the entire amount of natural uranium or thorium supplied to them.

Controlled fusion has not yet been achieved and may never be. Should it be, however, the energy obtainable from the deuterium contained in 30 cubic kilometers of seawater would be about equal to that of the earth's initial supply of fossil fuels!

On a long-term basis, an achievement no less essential than a practical nuclear-energy economy itself must be the development of an adequate system of safe disposal of nuclear-fission wastes. Much progress has been made within the last decade by the U.S. Atomic Energy Commission in the processing and safe underground disposal of low-volume, high-level wastes. Less satisfactory progress has been made in the handling of the voluminous low-level wastes and solid trash. In fact, for primarily economic reasons, practices are still prevalent at most Atomic Energy Commission installations with respect to these latter categories of waste that on the present scale of operations are barely tolerable, but which would become intolerable with much increase in the use of nuclear power.

To summarize this study, Chapters 1 and 2 of our book pose the problem: since resources are finite, then, as population increases, the ratio of resources to man must eventually fall to an unacceptable level. This is the crux of the Malthusian dilemma, often evaded but never invalidated. Chapter 3 considers the possibility of a final evasion of this dilemma by population control. Chapters 4 through 8 consider the possibility of escape by increasing resources of food, minerals, and energy, each chapter dealing with essential but not coordinate aspects of the problem. The inescapable central conclusion is that both population control and better resource management are mandatory and should be effected with as little delay as possible.

We must add an elaboration, however. Studies of animal populations suggest that environmental factors other than simple limitation of material resources may act in unexpected ways to limit populations before theoretical maxima are reached. To consider whether the earth might support three more doublings of the human population is probably to consider a purely hypothetical situation. It seems more likely that further crowding, the necessary social and governmental restrictions that accompany dense settlement, and certain kinds of boredom resulting from isolation from nature in an immense, uniform, secular society may prove so depressing to the human spirit or so destructive of coherent social organization that no such population size will ever be reached. Current urban problems are perhaps premonitory of what can come in the absence of more effective attention to the broader problems of resources and man. In attempting to deal with such problems we would do well to consider the basic causes as well as the symptoms. To delay progress toward full self-regulation of population size is to play "Russian roulette" with the future of man.

More specific recommendations arising from this study will be found in the following section. The words we would choose to express the essence of our hopes for the future, however, have already been written: "Our goal should be not to conquer nature but to live in harmony with it."[4]

Recommendations

This study points to the need for better information on which to base an improved assessment, not only of the natural resources of the nation and the earth, but also of the likely future demands on them and of their deeper societal implications. Although no real physical *terra incognita* remains today, we have much to learn about what we have, how to estimate it, and how to manage it in the best interests of man and nature. The Malthusian limits are more likely to be extended by recognizing their validity and doing something about them than by uninformed ridicule. We recommend below,[5] therefore, some of the steps that should be taken by the United States to enhance the prospects of an ample world for all.

These recommendations are not intended to be comprehensive or rigorously systematic; rather, their aim is to highlight the steps that most deserve to be initiated or pursued more vigorously by reason of special relevance, timeliness, or high potential value to society. They are arranged, according to their main aspects, under four broad categories: (1) Early Action, (2) Policy, (3) Research, and (4) Organization. Listed after each recommendation, as appropriate, are the chapters in which substantiating discussion is to be found. Where no specific chapter reference is given, the recommendation emerged from the study as a whole, including discussions at our several exploratory conferences.

---

[4] Roger Revelle, 1967, p. 1 of "Introduction," in United States Participation in the International Biological Program, U.S. National Committee for the I.B.P., Rep. no. 2.

[5] Members of the Committee who are not citizens of the United States have disqualified themselves from participating in recommendations regarding specific actions of the U.S. Government. They concur in principle, however, with the recommendations made here.

EARLY ACTION

The Committee on Resources and Man urges early action to implement the following recommendations:

1. *That detailed assessment of the actual and potential agricultural and forest lands of the world and their classification into best-use categories be undertaken, together with increased technical help to the farmers of the world.*   Many parts of the world are not as productive as they could be, and others are unproductive for poorly understood reasons. Special problems arise in the tropics (Recommendation 20), where the United States should establish a laboratory and field organization for tropical agriculture. This recommendation calls for action by the Department of Agriculture, with the collaboration of the State Department and the United Nations. *Chapter 4.*

2. *That there be a large increase in the effort directed toward a comprehensive geochemical census of the crustal rocks of the nation, the continent, and the earth, including those parts beneath the sea.*   Better knowledge than we have of the distribution and abundances of the elements is needed to define the world's metallogenic provinces, to develop new exploration techniques, to identify substitutes for materials in short supply, and to designate substances with a variety of physical and chemical properties for consideration in the design of new products. A geochemical census, of course, must be done in the framework of adequate geological mapping, sequence control, and investigations into a variety of geological processes. Such studies ordinarily need lead times of a decade or more before application, but their results can be useful for many decades. The existing program of the U.S. Geological Survey should be intensified and enlarged, and new activities should be started. Global coordination calls for suitable international structures, with the Geological Survey, the Bureau of Mines, and university groups playing major operational roles. *Chapters 6, 7.*

3. *That the present Helium Conservation Program of the Department of the Interior be reevaluated.*   Helium is unique in its combination of unusual properties and critical uses. It is essential for cryogenics, superconductivity, cooling of nuclear reactors, exploration of the seabed, and the space program. According to available estimates it is in short supply, yet it continues to be wasted in the combustion of natural gases. Its recovery from these gases and conservation for the future is feasible and is already being done on a limited scale. The Helium Conservation Program should be carefully reevaluated to determine if it can meet helium needs beyond the early part of the 21st century. If such evaluation leaves any question at all about the adequacy of the

program, the program should be extended without delay to apply to lower concentrations of helium and more natural gas fields. *Chapters 6, 8.*

4. *That a new and more rigorous monitoring system for radioactive waste disposal be instituted at Atomic Energy Commission and other installations where such wastes are now or may later be produced.* Such a system must be independent of the agencies and organizations that generate such wastes, analogous to a system of financial auditing. Reports emanating from the responsible group charged with the operation of this monitoring system should be made public so that every citizen will know what is being done to protect his safety as well as what needs to be done that is not being done. The financial cost of maintaining such a system and responding to necessary safety measures must not be a limiting factor in achieving the best possible surveillance and action program. *Chapter 8.*

POLICY

The Committee on Resources and Man presents the following recommendations for implementation as matters of national policy:

General Policy

5. *That efforts to limit population increase in the nation and the world be intensified by whatever means are practicable, working toward a goal of zero rate of growth by the end of the century.* Healthy and intelligent people are man's greatest resource. If limitation of population is not eventually achieved at some reasonable level, moreover, food and other resources will surely be inadequate. With limitation of populations the objective can be shifted from combating starvation and want to the improvement of the human resource and its level of living. Although this recommendation is by no means novel, it emerges again from our study, and particularly from Chapter 2, that population control is the absolute primary essential without which all other efforts are nullified. Our Departments of State and of Health, Education, and Welfare should adopt the goal of real population *control* both in North America and throughout the world. Ultimately this implies that the community and society as a whole, and not only the parents, must have a say about the number of children a couple may have. This will require profound modification of current attitudes toward parenthood. *Chapter 2.*

6. *That innovation of all kinds to stretch out, renew, enlarge, or substitute for the components of the world's mineral-resource base, be encouraged.* An ample

energy base, more efficient long-distance transfer of energy, and better transport systems can make available the ores of remote places. Research in the properties, purification, extraction, and fabrication of metals or even nonmetals not now used, or used for other purposes, can lead to substitution. New synthetic products made from abundant raw materials should be sought as substitutes for rare or depleting natural commodities. Clad metals (as in present "silver" coinage) can stretch out rare materials and generate new combinations of properties. Man's resources may be limited but his imagination in their use and conservation need not be. Much work of this sort can and should be done under the auspices of the Departments of the Interior and Commerce. The need for a constant flow of fresh ideas and new viewpoints, however, will best be met by greater involvement of university groups through sponsored research. Such sponsorship should come not only from mission-oriented agencies, but also from the National Science Foundation in pursuance of its new charter to extend its support of selected areas of applied research.

7. *That continuing systematic programs and structures be organized to promote more pervasive interaction among the environmental sciences, and between them and the behavioral sciences, technology, and the strictly physical sciences.* We need more schools and institutes of environmental studies where ecologists, hydrologists, meteorologists, oceanographers, geographers, and geologists will work closely together, and with scholars and practitioners from other fields. Such organizations might serve as the cores of new "urban grant" universities intended to nucleate new urban centers, thereby also helping to create the scientific manpower to support the environmental and resource programs needed. More interaction among governmental agencies concerned with different parts of the environment should also be generated, as well as among them and other parts of the scientific and governmental communities. These goals should be explicitly supported by the National Science Foundation and the Department of Health, Education, and Welfare. Given the interest the National Science Foundation is now taking in the environmental, applied, and behavioral sciences, institutional structures wherein all could focus simultaneously and in concert on our deteriorating human ecosystem could be a major step toward its improvement.

8. *That formulation of natural resource policies for the nation, the continent, and the world be vigorously sought—through whatever government structures and bilateral and multilateral covenants may best serve such purposes.* Resources are not a one-state or one-country affair; they concern the whole world and all people. The international character of the formulation of resource policy clearly requires the participation of the Department of State, which must develop the necessary mechanisms to work in close conjunction

with the Departments of the Interior, Agriculture, and Commerce, as well
as with other concerned groups (e.g., Recommendation 26).

Policy with Regard to Sources of Food

9. *That the efficiency and capacity of agricultural productivity, both in the
United States and abroad be increased to the maximum levels possible.* This is
necessary not only to assure national food reserves, but also to help those
countries in need. Overproduction, as well as underproduction, of perishable
products must be controlled, for it is evidence of poor national management
and vitiates the improvement of farm production and management. The
Department of Agriculture has been working in these directions for a long
time, in collaboration with the Department of State and the United Nations.
The effort should be continued, improved, and intensified. *Chapter 4.*

10. *That there be purposeful regulation of fisheries, now declining in yield because of overexploitation, and effective control of the catch of other stocks that
will be threatened in the future.* This involves knotty problems of internal
jurisdiction and international negotiation, but they must be overcome. In this
case the Department of the Interior, with the collaboration of the State
Department and other organizations, has done what it could. But again the
effort needs to be increased, improved, and extended. *Chapter 5.*

11. *That fishing efforts toward currently underexploited stocks, both in the sea
and in fresh waters, be expanded.* In this sense "fishing" refers not merely to
fish, but to the capture of all kinds of edible aquatic organisms, plants as well
as animals. Again, the Department of the Interior is already involved and
further initiative should come from that department. *Chapter 5.*

12. *That the use of aquatic "farming" operations, not only in fresh waters, but
also in marine and brackish-water bays and estuaries, be improved and extended.* Particular attention should be given to operations that do not compete seriously with use of other resources. Examples are ponds sited in
swamps or on tide-flats, and shellfish culture either on the sea bottom or from
rafts. Responsibility for this effort could rest equally with the Department of
the Interior directly and with the National Science Foundation through its
authority under the Sea Grant Program. *Chapter 5.*

Policy with Regard to Nonenergy Mineral Resources

13. *That the re-use and better use of materials that can be recycled be encouraged, and that this be required for mineral commodities known to be in short
supply.* Incentives should be devised to encourage the optimum use of met-

als and other materials, as well as proper disposal of spent substances. Research on problems and methods of re-using or otherwise extending the lifetimes of all kinds of materials, as well as the recovery of wasted or deleterious by-products, should be supported, both for conservation and to reduce problems of pollution and waste disposal. The automobile is a prime target for improvement. The copper content of the average car should be reduced from about 1.4 percent to 0.4 percent or less of the total carcass and problems of metal recovery simplified. The metals involved could then be used repeatedly, with greatly reduced waste and with elimination of unsightly modes of disposal. New methods of combining metals in clad structures, for instance, make it possible to utilize the desired properties of special metals (such as silver and copper) with great economy, better structural properties, and reduction to levels that eliminate the adverse effects of mixing. Other targets are the wasteful disposal practices that could be improved to salvage more used metal. Military uses, of course, are especially demanding on supplies of relatively rare metals. To the many urgent reasons for seeking peace and for damping the arms race must be added the conservation of unreplaceable resources for future generations. In addition, the Departments of the Interior and Commerce should be authorized and directed to collaborate in developing and instituting a practicable and effective metal conservation program. *Chapters 2, 6.*

14. *That action should be taken to reduce the lag between the recognition of probable mineral-resource shortages and investigations intended to alleviate them.* It takes an average of about five years from the beginning of surface exploration for new deposits to be found on land and another five years of underground exploration and development to bring them into production. Even longer lead times will be needed in developing marine mineral resources. And very long lead times must be allowed for the surveys and research needed to establish an exploratory framework or to underpin long-range forecasts. Specific recommendations on such matters should be a primary function of the Department of the Interior, which should also continue and expand its exploration programs. *Chapters 6, 7.*

15. *That geological exploration of the continental shelves and borderlands be accelerated and intensified.* The continental shelves, slopes, and rises, and the inland seas, are the parts of the seabed that are most likely to contribute useful and abundant mineral commodities to supplement our depleting reserves on land. They should be studied not only for their broad surficial features, but also at depth by drilling, and in areal detail in regions that offer good prospects either of containing mineral resources or of contributing to an understanding of their origin. Contiguous areas ripe for such detailed studies include the Atlantic shelves and the Gulf of Mexico, the continental border-

land of southern California, and the Bering shelf. In emphasizing the continental margins, of course, we merely stress the logical priorities. We do not overlook, but rather consider as severely limited, the possibility of resources from the other 75 or 80 percent of the sea. Programs now in progress on the continental shelves by the Department of the Interior should be continued, enlarged, and wherever possible improved; and Interior's cooperative efforts with university groups should be increased. *Chapter 7.*

16. *That legal problems involved in marine exploration and mining be resolved with as little delay as possible, and international agreements established to facilitate underwater exploration.* Neither national nor international law is really clear as to the limits within which discoveries made may be claimed by private, state, or national interests. Clarification is needed, both to encourage exploration and to avert troublesome disputes over ownership of marine resources beyond the continental shelves. National interests beyond the continental slopes could well be submerged in favor of some workable international jurisdiction such as suggested in the "Maltese Proposition"—with gain for international cooperation and little loss of potential territorial wealth. The Departments of the Interior, Commerce, and State should work together on these problems. *Chapter 7.*

Policy with Regard to Sources of Energy

17. *That the development of high-neutron-economy reactors be accelerated, including an efficient and safe type or types of breeder reactor(s).* The development of nuclear energy is an urgent national and global goal because of the approaching depletion of fossil fuels and the need to conserve them for other purposes. But without greater utilization of uranium-238 and thorium-232 through breeding or other efficient conversion, the economics of nuclear power is such that the supply of uranium-235 from high-grade ores at current prices could become severely restricted within a few decades. The achievement of nuclear fusion, of course, would greatly extend nuclear reserves in the very long term, and fundamental research in this field should be continued. *Chapter 8.*

18. *That the fossil fuels be conserved for uses which cannot be met by other sources.* The fossil fuels (petroleum, natural gas, coal) are needed for petrochemicals, synthetic polymers, and essential liquid fuels, for which suitable substitutes are as yet unknown. They might also play a part in synthetic or bacterial food production (although such a use is also limited). They should not be spent in the generation of electricity, for heating, and for industrial purposes where substitutes can qualify. The Department of the Interior should be authorized and directed to develop and institute a practicable and effective hydrocarbon conservation program. *Chapter 8.*

RESEARCH

Research is clearly an essential component of many of the preceding recommendations, yet there are additional topics in need of intensified research which we believe deserve early attention. The Committee on Resources and Man, therefore, recommends greatly increased research on:

General

19. *The complex of nonmaterial factors that affect man's use of and demand for resources.*   Although circumstances required the present Committee to bypass most aspects of such a study, our inquiries so strongly reinforce the need for it that we urge the formation of another group to study the various social, psychological, legal, medical, religious, and political aspects of the problems of resources and man that we have been forced to set aside. What, for instance, are the consequences of man's different conceptual environments—of how he imagines things to be regardless of how they really are? What is the effect of religion and religious differences on the nature of and demand for resources? How can cultural preferences be altered so as to relieve demand on resources and reduce pollution while minimizing social disruption? What are the processes whereby regulation of family size is best achieved? How do resources and economic factors really interact? What are the resource consequences of technological development and of different densities and patterns of human settlement? As with Recommendation 7, the National Science Foundation would do well to consider this an area of major focus for its growing program in the behavioral sciences. The Department of Health, Education, and Welfare, of course, should also be involved.

Sources of Food

20. *Tropical lands and crops.*   The tropics are among the most thickly populated regions of the earth, yet they produce insufficient food for their populations. This poor productivity in food resources for humans is in part due to the unusual ecological diversity of large parts of the tropical climatic zone. It is also in part due to geologic and climatic factors which make many tropical soils (lateritic and leached soils) deficient in mineral nutrients and resistant to tilth as compared with those of the middle latitudes. It will require more than good seeds and good management to turn the Amazon Basin into another "breadbasket." Assuming it can be done, it will require enormous quantities of mineral fertilizer and a good share of creative agricultural science. These and interacting sociological and economic factors must be weighed in seeking to develop new food crops that could increase the present productivity of tropical regions without seriously impairing their

ecological stability. This is clearly a job for the Department of Agriculture, with the collaboration of the State Department; but continuation of the good works of the Rockefeller Foundation should be encouraged, and the participation of the National Science Foundation in the long-range aspects of the program through the sponsorship of private institutions is also important. *Chapter 4.*

21. *The productivity of the sea and fresh waters.*   How can aquatic productivity useful to man be increased and a larger fraction of food be harvested from the waters without endangering desirable species? The variety and quantity of food products from the sea might be increased (a) by transplantations shown to be feasible as a result of studies of the life cycles and ecological adaptivity of organisms; (b) by more widespread culture of food animals; and (c) by improved methods of capture. More intensive fishing for some species is desirable, whereas for others greater yield must be sought by restricting fishing effort under international agreement. Research alone can produce the information needed to resolve such questions. This recommendation involves a clearly defined mission of the Department of the Interior, but it could also appropriately be furthered by National Science Foundation grants in the underlying supporting disciplines such as aquatic biology and ecology. *Chapter 5.*

22. *Methods of harvesting currently unused but edible aquatic organisms.* Many species of marine organisms can be eaten and occur in quantity but are difficult to catch in large volumes. A practicable method for harvesting the larger species of animal plankton, for instance, would permit us to work closer to the base of the food pyramid and thus to utilize a larger fraction of the total stock. Although this would carry the risk of affecting other fisheries adversely, it might be done in regions where the planktonic animals are not being consumed in quantity by usable animals. The small crustaceans called krill, for example, although abundant in both Arctic and Antarctic seas (and formerly harvested by whales) are not now being utilized. This recommendation involves an established mission of the Department of the Interior, but the National Science Foundation could also play a part through support for this objective under its Sea Grant program. *Chapter 5.*

23. *The processing, marketing, and consumer-acceptance of products such as fish-protein concentrates.*   Proteins and fats from the waters could be much more widely and effectively used in human nutrition if organisms not now acceptable for food as harvested could be concentrated in palatable form. In view of their established missions, this recommendation concerns the Departments of the Interior, Commerce, and State. *Chapter 5.*

Mineral Resources

24. *The geology, discovery, and development of ore deposits.* Especially needed are studies of the genesis, localization, and discovery of ore bodies that have no surface manisfestation—"blind" ore bodies. New methods must be employed in seeking such ores, and better methods are needed in evaluting and recovering them. Concepts of metallogenic provinces also need to be clarified and extended; for they might help greatly with the intensified geochemical census urged in Recommendation 2. Equally needed is research on the geology, exploration methods, and evaluation and recovery of marine mineral resources. The U.S. Geological Survey and the U.S. Bureau of Mines should be encouraged to expand and improve their programs dealing with such problems. *Chapters 6, 7.*

25. *The geology of the sea floor beyond and adjacent to the continents.* Although prospects of specific rewards should not be called upon or required to justify exploration of the deep sea floor, *some* new mineral wealth can certainly be expected as a partial consequence. Such bonuses, to be sure, are just as likely to come from a better understanding of the processes involved in the origin of land deposits as from actual discovery of ore deposits at the sea floor. At the very least, sea floor studies will contribute to better concepts of the structure, evolution, and management of the earth. Such research can and should be undertaken by a number of different government, private, and university organizations, and all should be encouraged. The continued healthy growth of the Sea Grant program of the National Science Foundation could serve this end. *Chapter 7.*

ORGANIZATION

Because national and international welfare and harmony ultimately depend on natural resources, and since conditions affecting resources are constantly changing, it is only prudent to monitor these changes in such a way that crises of supply or environmental degradation can be foreseen and ameliorated. As an important move toward such a review and warning system, therefore, we recommend:

26. *That there be established, at an appropriate location within the United States government, a high-level group of broadly qualified resource specialists and ecologists having the following duties—*
   (a) to maintain continuing surveillance of both nonrenewable and renewable resources, particularly with regard to the future;
   (b) to inform the government and the public concerning impending short-

ages, problems of environmental deterioration, and other prospective developments affecting natural resources;

(c) to recommend to the government well in advance of crises optimum courses of action, not only for the avoidance of resource shortages and environmental catastrophe, but equally for the achievement of maximum social well being and international harmony in the uses of resources.

1 / The Human Ecosystem

Marston Bates

*"In the West, our desire to conquer nature often means
simply that we diminish the probability of small
inconveniences at the cost of increasing the probability of
very large disasters."*
—Kenneth E. Boulding, 1966, p. 14

Our planet has been aptly called "Spaceship Earth." It forms, overwhelmingly, a closed system as far as materials are concerned. Science fiction to the contrary, we have no present basis for believing that this essential isolation will be altered—that we can colonize other parts of the solar system or import from outer worlds any appreciable quantities of materials. This earth is our habitat and probably will be as long as our species survives. We would do well, then, to treat it carefully and to take thought in planning our actions.

Early men—the food-gathering and hunting peoples of the Old Stone Age—were closely interacting parts of the biological communities in which they lived. Tools and language made them unusually efficient hunters but not really different in their impact on the community from other kinds of social carnivores or omnivores. The first major change in man's relations with nature came with the deliberate making of fire. No other animal starts fires. Their frequency must have increased greatly when man began setting them, with far-reaching ecological effects.

Typescript received April 1967. Final revision, June 1968.

Man's relations with the rest of nature underwent a much greater change with what anthropologists call the "Neolithic Revolution"—although "revolution" is perhaps a poor word for changes that may have taken millenia and that occurred at different times and in different sequences in various parts of the world. The important changes, which were at least in part interrelated, involved the cultivation of plants, the domestication of animals, the settlement of villages, the making of pottery, and a series of improvements in toolmaking. Man began to alter the biological community in which he lived by removing vegetation he did not want or could not use and replacing it with crops.

Gordon Childe (1941), the British anthropologist, looked at post-Neolithic developments in terms of two further "revolutions"—the Urban, turning on the transport and storage of food, which made possible the formation of cities and the specialization of labor and knowledge, and the Industrial, based on the harnessing of power other than the muscles of men or beasts. C. P. Snow (1959) would add a recent revolution, the Scientific, resulting from the union of science and technology for the solution of practical problems—the revolution that gave rise to the dramatic and drastic increase in power available to man in the twentieth century, including the development of nuclear and electronic techniques. The Scientific Revolution in particular has the potential to bring about even more sweeping worldwide ecological changes than we have seen in the past.

The idea of looking at cultural development in terms of a few relatively abrupt "revolutions" is obviously an oversimplification. Yet equally obviously, man's history does not show a smooth and gradual increase in knowledge and power. Shifts in techniques and ideas have resulted in periods of rapid change; and there have been long periods in the history of every culture in which neither ideas nor ways of life have changed much—periods of temporary near-equilibrium, or "stagnation" as some would say. The charting and description of these developments are matters for historians; and, although they may never reach agreement, their efforts are nonetheless thought-provoking in the attempts that each of us make to understand ourselves and our world.

Whatever the history, whatever the interplay of cause and effect, the result is the curious paradox of man as a part of nature, and man as apart from nature—a force of geological magnitude changing the face of the earth. Many of the activities that we think of as peculiarly human have parallels in other animals, but man has come to work on a different scale. Compare, for instance, Hoover Dam with the work of beavers, or Manhattan Island with a gopher town. The difference in scale is so great that we can only regard it as a difference in kind. In a somewhat comparable way, the human ecosystem has become a different sort of phenomenon from anything else that we know.

The world of life—the biosphere—can be looked at as a single, interconnected though endlessly diversified system. There is no denying the diversity. A desert and a forest are different kinds of places however difficult it may be to delineate their boundaries. Yet the many different kinds of biological communities that make up the biosphere display a very real underlying unity. Life everywhere is organized on the same basic principles.

Essentially all life as we know it depends on the transformation of radiant energy from the sun into the chemical energy of hydrocarbons through the process of photosynthesis based on chlorophyll. The chlorophyll-bearing organisms of the seas are mostly microscopic floating algae of the surface waters where sunlight penetrates. Such algae are probably also more important in fresh water than are the fixed plants of the shallows. But on land the "vascular" plants, the herbs, grasses, shrubs, and trees, are overwhelmingly important. These organisms that carry on the photosynthetic process are called *producers* by ecologists. The animals that live off them directly or indirectly are the *consumers*.

The British ecologist Charles Elton (1936) has called the animals that live directly off the plants "key industry animals," because all the rest of the animal system depends on them. They can also be called "first-order consumers," which in turn are eaten by "second-order consumers," and so on. This leads to the idea of a food chain—grass, grasshoppers, frogs, snakes, hawks—which is a neat idea, but vastly oversimplified, because any attempt to diagram who eats whom in a biological community results in a complicated network of lines more appropriately called a "food web."

Most ecologists would add a third category of organisms, the *decomposers*: bacteria, fungi, and the like, that cause rot and decay, reducing the corpses of dead animals and plants to dust (or mud). The component chemicals are then available to be used again—carbon from the carbon dioxide of the air combined with oxygen from water through photosynthesis and the other necessary chemicals through absorption by plants or digestion by animals.

Most vegetable material never passes through the animal system at all, as is obvious enough in a glance at the uneaten leaves of any forest or prairie. This economy of abundance is necessary for the functioning of the biological community. When, because of some upset in the balance of the system, the forest is defoliated or the prairie overgrazed, the consequence is catastrophe for both the plants and the animals. In general, throughout nature, animal populations do not multiply up to the limit of their food supply—other controlling factors intervene. Plants, however, under favorable circumstances, may occupy all available space.

Most of the key industry animals (first-order consumers) are small, and often individuals of a given species are very abundant—insects on land, and minute crustaceans in water. Yet some of the largest of animals are herbivores

—the elephants of today and the giant mammals, reptiles, and even birds of times past. Generally, however, the herbivores are more numerous than the predators that feed on them; and various studies have shown that, with each step away from the producer plants, only six to ten percent of the available energy is transmitted. It is not possible for animals, either in terms of energy or numbers, to operate beyond the fourth- or fifth-order consumer level.

What limits the number of individuals of a given species of animal? In 1798, Thomas Robert Malthus published his little book, *An Essay on the Principle of Population as It Affects the Future Improvement of Mankind.* Concern with the human population problem can be neatly dated from the publication of this book. An enlarged and much revised edition, published in 1803, states his basic propositions thus:

1. Population is necessarily limited by the means of subsistence.
2. Population invariably increases where the means of subsistence increase, unless prevented by some very powerful and obvious checks.
3. These checks, and the checks which repress the superior power of population and keep its effects on a level with the means of subsistence, are all resolvable into moral restraint, vice and misery.

This has been called the "dismal theorem" of Malthus, and there are those who would exorcise it with ridicule. But, dismal though it may seem, its basic validity remains unaffected either by man's ingenuity in finding means for the increase of his own subsistence or the likelihood that he will continue to achieve such increases up to some limit not yet reached. The theorem, of course, was intended to apply to people: "moral restraint" and "vice" can hardly refer to any animal except man. Under "misery," however, Malthus included such things as disease and starvation, which are not restricted to humans. In any event, it is instructive to consider his propositions in the context of the behavior of animal populations in general and not just that of *Homo sapiens.* Food is certainly the ultimate limit on the population of any animal, whether we think in terms of local or global populations. Yet, as noted above, populations in nature very rarely multiply up to the limit of the food supply. What, then, are the checks that normally limit animal populations? What prevents a population from multiplying until it reaches the point at which its food supply is exhausted? The search for the answers to such questions has led to a great deal of experiment, observation, and speculation. It is clear that there is no single kind of check, no simple answer—that we are dealing with a complex system of checks and balances that we cannot yet describe completely, let alone fully understand (e.g., Dawson, 1968).

Perhaps the most general check is the so-called balance-of-nature resulting from the fact that animals not only eat but are eaten. Herbivores tend to be controlled by carnivores before they reach the point of exhausting food supply—as has been amply suggested by the damaging multiplication of such animals as deer or rabbits when man has removed their "enemies" such as pumas, wolves, or foxes. The carnivores may be limited in turn by other carnivores that live on them. The young of all animals are particularly susceptible to predation and to death through accident. And the most lordly carnivore may fall victim to parasitic disease. Disease particularly tends to be "density-dependent," becoming more prevalent as individuals of a particular host species become more common.

The whole system has a great deal of flexibility, of "play." A given predator in a particular region may concentrate largely on some one species of prey until this becomes rare and hard to find, then shift its attention to other species. More commonly, a predator may eat a variety of animals; but since the most abundant kinds would be most often caught, there is a sort of automatic limit on abundance for any given species.

The availability of food, however, is not the only factor limiting population size. A population may be limited by the availability of suitable breeding and rearing sites or by other special requirements of habitat. We are gradually learning about a variety of mechanisms that operate within a population to limit its growth. These include such things as cannibalism and failure to reproduce because of crowding, endocrine stress, and so on. Perhaps the most extensively studied of these limiting factors is territoriality. With many kinds of animals, especially fishes, lizards, birds, and mammals, an individual, a pair, or a social group may inhabit a particular area and defend it against intrusion by other individuals of the same species. Different kinds of territoriality have been described. All serve to space individuals; but where the defended area is large enough to include more food than can be utilized by the defenders, territorial behavior keeps the number of individuals below the theoretical limit imposed by the means of subsistence. The limit thus can be availability of appropriate space as well as food or other controls.

There is thus a constant turnover of individuals within a biological community, but with mortality balanced by reproduction so that the result, over a period of time, is a fairly steady state—a kind of dynamic equilibrium in the functioning of the community. This is comparable to the equilibrium that is maintained by the body of an individual: cells dying and being replaced, various organ systems working together harmoniously through an elaborate system of nerve and endocrine controls. This tendency to maintain a steady state despite environmental changes, stresses, and shocks (called *homeostasis*) is expressed in various natural population controls and the resulting balance of nature (Slobodkin, 1962; Slobodkin, Smith, and Hairston, 1967).

Ecologists find it convenient to use, as their unit of study, the *ecosystem* rather than only the biological community, thus taking into account both the living organisms and their physical environment, which together form an interacting system. Every organism is affected by the conditions of the world in which it lives, but every organism also has some effect on these conditions, however trivial. The kind of forest growing in a particular region is in part a consequence of the soil, climate, and water supply of that region; but the kind of soil is also in part a consequence of the type of forest—coniferous, hardwood, or other—and the presence of the forest has a measurable influence on local climatic conditions and water supply.

The reciprocal interactions between organisms and environment are particularly striking in the case of the human species. Our activities are influenced in many ways by the nature of the physical setting in which we live—coastal, inland, desert, mountain, or forest. But we are also capable of altering the environment with unprecedented speed and effect. We would do well, then, to think in terms not of modern man in dominant relationship with other biological communities but of the human ecosystem—of the man-altered landscape and its biological components.

Man's actions can be looked at as efforts to simplify the biological relationships within the ecosystem to his own advantage. By clearing land and planting crops or orchards a complex of mixed species of wild plants may be replaced by a single kind of plant, a monoculture, which may extend over a wide area. In living off grain or fruit or tubers, man functions as a first-order consumer. In largely vegetarian societies he is, thus, a "key industry animal," which means that a large population can be supported—but he is also a dead end, not giving support in turn to the usual predators and scavengers. With modern medicine he has even largely defeated the parasites.

Man's food web, in such societies, is thus reduced to a simple producer-consumer interaction, often with the decomposer system greatly modified as plant growth is maintained by adding fertilizers to the soil. Man also tries as far as possible to reduce or eliminate competition, controlling the insect pests of the crops and attempting to eliminate vertebrate competitors, whether crows, rats, or raccoons.

As a meat-eater, man becomes a second-order consumer, growing grain for his chickens or hogs or pasture for his cattle and then eating the animals. Again there is an attempt to eliminate competition from hawks, weasels, big cats, or wolves; again there is a vastly simplified food relationship, unique to the human ecosystem.

These simplified food relationships are efficient as long as they can be sustained, and they now support the large and expanding human population. In fact, they could be regarded (in conjunction with medical reduction of the death rate) as a cause of this population growth, in terms of the second of the Malthusian propositions. There is no doubt about the effectiveness of the system to support an exploding human population *up to a point*, but it carries the danger of inherent imbalance and some large questions of ethics and aesthetics.

The danger in the simplified ecosystem is in its liability to catastrophe (e.g., Ehrlich, 1968, p. 4). The most complex of natural ecosystems (in the sense of those including the largest numbers of different kinds of organisms) are the most stable in that they are the least liable to great fluctuations in number of individuals of a particular species from year to year. Greatest contrast observed is between complex biotas such as those of the tropical rain forest or coral reef and the relatively simple biotas of the arctic tundra or northern forests. Records of fluctuations in various tundra animals suggest either a cyclic Malthusian relationship with food supply or catastrophic physiological or psychological controls. Such cyclic fluctuations are unknown in the rain forest, where the complexity of relations makes for flexibility and results in a relatively steady state among limited populations of the many species there.

Charles Elton (1958) has summarized six lines of evidence for the relative stability of complex communities. First there is the mathematical argument: "models" of simple predator-prey population relations show conspicuous fluctuations. As Elton says, "Put in ordinary language, this means that an animal community with only two such species in it would never have constant population levels, but would be subject to periodic 'outbreaks' of each species." The second line of evidence comes from attempts to test these simple relationships under laboratory conditions. "One thing stands out from the results: it is very difficult to keep small populations of this simple mixture in balance, for not only do they fluctuate but one or both of the species is liable to become extinct." Greater stability can be achieved by arranging for complex experimental conditions that provide cover for the prey to hide and dodge about in; but it is still difficult to maintain prey-predator populations for any length of time.

"The third piece of evidence," to quote Elton again, "is that natural habitats on small islands seem to be much more vulnerable to invading species than those of the continents." Animals and plants, accidentally or intentionally brought into simple island communities by man, often undergo catastrophic population explosions. Hawaii has seen many examples of this. The efforts at cure have involved attempts to restore a steady state by increasing the complexity of the system through the introduction of parasites and predators of the invading aliens.

"The fourth point is that invasions and outbreaks most often happen on cultivated or planted land—that is, in habitats and communities very much simplified by man." Our crops are notoriously subject to damage by pests, both native and foreign, which must be kept in control by chemical means—the chemicals sometimes producing unexpected side effects.

Elton's fifth line of evidence is based on the contrast in stability between tropical and arctic communities, as mentioned above. His final point involves recent research on orchard pest control. "Orchards are especially good for testing the effects of ecological variety, because they are half-way between a natural woodland and an arable field crop—less complex than the wood but more complex than the crop, and more permanent." Attempts to control orchard pests have disclosed many unexpected relationships among the populations involved. Elton quotes an observer as remarking: "We move from crisis to crisis, merely trading one problem for another."

Analogy can be made between the value of diversified ecosystems and the value of diversified national economies: where the economy depends largely on a single crop or a single industry, the danger of disruption is always greater than in situations where the economy has a diversified base. Large areas devoted to a single crop, covered by a single species of plant, or inhabited by concentrated numbers of a particular kind of animal, always present conditions conducive to the development of epidemics. History affords many examples. One of the most dramatic and best documented involves the Irish potato blight of 1845 (Bates, 1955). The Irish population provided a neat demonstration of the validity of the Malthusian propositions within something like a closed system by growing rapidly, following introduction of the potato, to more than eight million at the time of the census of 1841. When the crop failed in 1845 and again in 1846 because of the sudden appearance of the blight, more than a million people died directly of starvation, and as many as could emigrated. The shock in this case resulted in an eventual stabilization of the Irish population, which has remained at a level of about four million for the last fifty years—half of the preblight figure. In Malthusian terms, "moral restraint" (aided by migration) has checked the tendency to multiply up to the limit of the means of subsistence again.

Modern man, thus, depends on the simplified food relations of intensive agriculture, and modern technology has been efficient in developing methods of pest control. But the danger is always there—of a new pest, of immunity to chemical methods of control, and of environmental pollution from the pesticides. It would seem most prudent, therefore, to preserve as much of the natural diversity as possible, as is done in densely settled Europe with the hedgerows—at least until we understand the system well enough to foresee, guard against, and repair the consequences of possible oversimplification.

The aesthetic argument depends on the impression that a varied landscape is more pleasing, more satisfactory for living, then a monotonous one. This may be a matter for debate; and it carries over from landscapes to the general question of the value of diversity in styles of life, in ways of thinking and acting. From diversity comes the possibility of change, of adaptive response to new conditions, of development and evolution.

There would thus seem to be a need, in planning, to maintain as much diversity as possible within the human habitat. There is also a need to preserve substantial areas in which disturbance by man is kept at a minimum—the concept of nature reservations and national parks. Such parks serve at least four different and at times conflicting purposes: the recreation function, providing the possibility of escaping temporarily from the all-encompassing man-altered landscape; the research function, allowing the continued study of natural ecosystems; the museum function, preserving for future generations adequate samples of the diversified biosphere that has developed on our planet; and, perhaps most important of all, a reservoir function, whereby are sustained the organisms from which destructively altered environments may be restored.

The ethical question has been little explored by our philosophers. We have the power to alter the landscape and to exterminate species of animals and plants that we do not like or that we do not find convenient to our purposes. But do we have the right? Geological history is, of course, in part a record of the disappearance and replacement of organic types. But the rate of extinction increased enormously following the evolution of man as an ecologic dominant—and the rate is accelerating with the growth of human numbers, human power, and human intervention. Elton mentions a remark from Albert Schweitzer's book *My Life and Thought*, pointing out that a fault of ethical philosophy has been that it has dealt only with the relations of man to man. And Aldo Leopold has decried the same oversight in terms of our need to develop an "ecological conscience."

Problems of immediate practicality and utility may override such aesthetic and ethical considerations locally or in emergencies; but the three in large measure coincide. There is need periodically to take stock of and to reconsider our behavior in terms of our own survival. As the demographers have shown, we are rapidly multiplying toward the spatial limits of our earth and toward a possibly tragic final test of the truth of the dismal propositions developed by Malthus. Our industrial society is not sufficiently aware of its needs to recycle the very materials on which its survival depends. We are changing the composition of air, water, and soil in ways that are to some extent irreversible and that have already in places reached disastrous proportions.

In very large measure, we have the knowledge we need to live harmoniously within the confines of our "Spaceship Earth" if we do not insist on the constant growth of populations and new technology. The question that looms threateningly over the future of our species is, will we gain the wisdom to use this knowledge and to generate the new knowledge needed to evaluate and to cope with the environmental consequences of advancing technology?

The following chapters will present in condensed form the main threads of what is now known and will suggest how our knowledge might be improved and used to assure a favorable variety of options for future generations. The needed wisdom must come from the people, who will demand action, and from their governments, which will enact the legislation and administer the programs needed to stabilize populations at levels that can be supported and to regulate the use of resources with the needs of the future in view.

References

Bates, M. 1955. *The prevalence of people.* New York: Scribner.

Boulding, K. 1966. *Human values on the spaceship earth.* New York: National Council of Churches of Christ in the U.S.A.

Childe, V. G. 1941. *Man makes himself.* London: Watts & Co.

Dawson, P. S. 1968. Xenocide, suicide and cannibalism in flour beetles. *Am. Naturalist* 102(924): 97–105.

Ehrlich, P.R. 1968. World population: a battle lost? *Stanford Today* ser. 1, no. 22, pp. 2–7.

Elton, C. 1936. *Animal ecology.* New York: Macmillan.

Malthus, T. R. 1798. *An essay on the principle of population as it affects the future improvement of mankind.* Facsimile reprint in 1926 for J. Johnson. London: Macmillan & Co.

Slobodkin, L. B. 1962. *Growth and regulation of animal populations.* New York: Holt, Rinehart & Winston.

Slobodkin, L. B. 1968. Aspects of the future of ecology. *BioScience* 18(1): 16–23.

Slobodkin, L.B., F. E. Smith, and N. G. Hairston. 1967. Regulation in terrestrial ecosystems, and the implied balance of nature. *Am. Naturalist* 101: 109–124.

Snow, C. P. 1959. *The two cultures and the scientific revolution.* New York: Cambridge Univ. Press.

2/Interactions Between Man and His Resources

John D. Chapman

"Resources are not; they become."
—E. S. Zimmerman, 1951, p. 15

It is the purpose of this chapter to introduce a geographer's view of the relations between resources and man. In such a context one looks upon the
elements of the physical world as having significance only in relation to the
inhabitants for whom they constitute environment. The particular elements
or combinations of elements that are significant vary according to whether
human, animal, or plant life is involved; each has its own system and sub-
systems, separately identifiable but all more or less interlocked. In the human
ecosystem, man assigns untility to various elements of his environment and
thus confers upon them the role of resources. Resources then are neither
wholly of the physical world nor wholly of the world of man but are the result
of the interaction between the two. The environmental elements that man
calls upon to serve as resources, and the nature and size of the requirements
he places upon them, depend on his numbers, his needs and desires, and his
values and skills.

Typescript received September 1967. Final revision, June 1968.

RESOURCE REQUIREMENTS

Man's resource requirements depend, among other things, on the sizes and distribution of populations. On the global scale he is faced with a relentless population growth and with increasing concentration into particular regions. Within such regions, there is further concentration into urban, metropolitan, and megalopolitan nodes. While each additional human being requires an increment of basic necessities such as food, water, shelter, and space, he also requires more. How much more, and of what, depends upon his individual tastes and desires as well as his ability to satisfy them. Mankind collectively is in the midst of a "revolution of rising expectations," involving a universal commitment to the concept of economic growth as "an irreversible and irrepressible need" (Jaguaribe, 1966).

The gap between economies characterized by massive consumption and modest population and those characterized by low consumption and massive population is seen by many as a major contributor to world instability. Large-scale efforts have been made and are being made to narrow this gap and to diffuse higher per capita consumption to an ever greater proportion of the world's population. Some realists observe that, although the minimum levels are indeed being raised, the gap is widening, not closing (Myrdal, 1965). Others speculate about world requirements for metals, fuels, and food if the per capita consumptions of the North Atlantic economies are to be approached elsewhere. Relating such requirements to their expectations for available resources, they see, in the short run, the prospect of an attractive market situation; in the long run, the specter of scarcity and exhaustion.

In economies with already high per capita economic development, further increments of growth contain smaller requirements for material input (Barnett and Morse, 1963). In such economies, reduction in the rate of growth of the required quantity of new material input (i.e., resources) is accompanied by a growing concern for the "quality of the environment" (Jarrett, 1966). There is the implication that as a society reaches some threshold of economic development, with its attendant scientific and technological capabilities, it can afford to concern itself less with materials and quantity and more with the quality of life. Whether this implication is true or not, and however we define our terms, attaching utility to the quality of environment has the effect of perceiving as resources some aspects of the environment not previously considered to be resources—the appearance of the landscape, wilderness, animal life, plant associations, and the like. A range of new problems thus emerges (Krutilla, 1967).

More serious are recently formulated questions that squarely challenge the need for and desirability of continued expansion of per capita consumption (Boulding, 1966). Does not this very expansion create indirect costs (e.g., waste disposal, health hazards) that outweigh the benefits? Is it possible that

American standards of consumption are excessive and that to accept them as world targets is a tragic mistake? Can improvements in the quality of the environment and of life be most satisfactorily achieved at a lower level of material consumption than is associated with the "average" American today?

Questioning voices, however, are rarely heard above the broad swell of belief in what is considered to be the inherent necessity for economic growth and increased per capita consumption. When coupled with an increasing population, such rising expectations seem bound to increase resource requirements at exponential rates.

RESOURCE AVAILABILITY

The availability of resources at any time is the result of the interactions among the nature and size of man's requirements, the physical occurrence of the resource, and the means of producing it. Estimates of the future availability of resources, therefore, require the assessment of: (a) the particular combination of economic and technological conditions that determines *present* production, (b) the level of production that *would* take place under different economic conditions, (c) the level of production that *could* take place under different technological conditions, and (d) the nature and quantity of the total physical stock of both "renewable" and "nonrenewable" resources. Because the relations between these physical and human variables are complex and vary with time and place, views concerning future supply need to be carefully expressed and set in a context such as the threefold hierarchy of total stock, resource, and producible reserve. These concepts are summarized below from the work of Lovejoy and Homan (1965), substituting the term *total stock* for their use of *resource base*.

Total stock is the sum of all components of the environment that would be resources if they could be extracted from it. Assessment of the total stock is largely the concern of earth and life scientists, and the state of knowledge concerning it depends on the adequacy of prevailing theory, the state of exploration and survey technology, and the extent of its application. Applied to what are conventionally referred to as nonrenewable resources, the total stock is finite and thus eventually exhaustible. Applied to renewable resources, the total stock consists of highly complex systems in a state of dynamic, delicately balanced, and only partially understood, equilibrium.

Resources comprise that proportion of the total stock that man can make available under technological and economic conditions different from those that prevail. The state of technology assumed will set the limits within which different economic and social variables can determine what proportion of the total stock can become available. Assessment of a resource involves not only physical and biological scientists but applied and social scientists as well.

They must make judgments about the directions and rate of change of technological developments (e.g., gradual increase of efficiency of extraction of a mineral deposit or yield of a crop as against dramatic, order-of-magnitude, breakthrough changes); about the impact of changed economic conditions and new alignments in international relations; and about public attitudes on such varied matters as birth and population control, transportation preferences, and clean air. In essence the question is one of judging man's potential for creating resources out of the total stock; of selecting the chief agent of change from among technological, economic, or other societal forces; and of determining the relevant time and space dimensions. Resource estimates are speculative in proportion to the extent to which they go beyond prevailing conditions and the amount by which they extend the time and space over which they apply.

Reserve refers to that proportion of a resource that is known with reasonable certainty to be available under prevailing technological, economic, and other societal conditions. This term embraces current extraction rates, yield, management practices, legal frameworks, and social attitudes. It is therefore the least speculative, shortest term, most place-specific, and smallest of the three types of estimates.

These three concepts provide a framework into which each of the many estimates of resource availability may be fitted and thus be seen in perspective. By providing a rationale that can accommodate what often appears to be starkly conflicting professional opinions, these concepts reduce the ground for misunderstanding, overoptimism, or undue pessimism. Furthermore, they incorporate the notion of resources moving from one threshold of availability to another in response to changing values of variables under human control, allow estimates to be made in physical or economic terms, and yet permit retention of the essentially "physical world" character of the materials involved.

TIME, SPACE, AND TECHNOLOGY

Among the many factors that affect the relation between the requirements for and the availability of resources, those of time, space, and technology are selected for particular mention here, because, despite their acknowledged importance, they often do not receive explicit treatment.

Time

In the discussions concerning resources and man, what time dimensions are appropriate and in what terms should they be expressed? Conservationists point to the need for thinking in terms of generations to come. Biologists are concerned with the contrast between the long time required for ecological processes to establish a dynamic equilibrium and the short time it takes man to introduce major instabilities. Statements, however, are rarely time-specific.

An exception, in an ecological context, is found in Chapter 8, in which M. King Hubbert sets out a time scale in thousands of years on either side of the present, in order to illustrate the recency of prevailing per capita energy consumption and its potentially short life unless nuclear energy becomes available in large quantities. Landsberg, Fischman, and Fisher (1963) conducted a survey of U.S. resources that specifically dealt with the interval ending in the year 2000. Barnett and Morse (1963) have used a set of schematic curves to illustrate, in economic terms, their concept of the influence, over an increment of time, of technology on resource availability.

The appropriate time scale within which to deal with questions concerning resources and man depends on whether the questions being raised have operational, planning, or policy-making implications and on what resources are involved. Some would say that one should look ahead only as far as the impact of prevailing technology and other societal arts can be discerned. The extreme expression of this view is that, because the rate of technological change is so rapid, projections concerning resources, which so intimately involve technology, are relatively meaningless. Others claim that more distant vistas must be scanned in order to demonstrate that unless change is initiated in directions suggested by such reviews, there will be insufficient time to avoid drastic consequences.

In what terms should the time dimension be expressed? In absolute numbers of years, such as decades or centuries, chosen on the basis of some bench mark (e.g., midcentury, centennial, year 2000); in relative terms, such as human generations or time to harvestable maturity; or in some more complex derived terms, such as the period required to double the population or to reach the "take-off" period in a developing economy.

Whatever the answers to the above questions, the important thing is to ensure that no question is raised and no answer offered without being accompanied by an explicit statement of the time period to which it refers and by an evaluation of the factors that have been considered. The more restricted the time scale adopted, the less intractable the resource problems can be shown to appear; and vice versa. With no time scale the way is open to diametrically opposed interpretations.

Space

The spatial context refers particularly to such matters as spatial scale, location, distribution, and interaction. These are dimensions of resource problems that, although frequently mentioned, are rarely dealt with explicitly.

As communications have improved it has become common to speak of one world. In the past, interaction across great distance was often impossible or severely limited, because of either the lack of or the high cost of transportation facilities. Today, with the advent of bulk carriers, pipelines, highways, and other transportation systems, these restraints have been, or can be, greatly reduced. As a result we see massive long-distance distribution of previously "shut-in" resources to consuming areas, which can now look farther and farther afield for supply and can consider imports as a realistic alternative to scarcity or reliance on domestic resources alone. Furthermore, the space that may be affected by some developing technologies (e.g., offshore drilling, undersea mining, weather modification, nuclear engineering) is much larger than that affected by current practices. All these developments lend support to the notion of a shrinking world in which various factors affecting resources interact more and more complexly.

Despite these strong tendencies, the fact is that the physical environment, the cultural values, the political systems, and the levels of economic development continue to exhibit marked areal differentiation. Since these are the variables that determine the relations between resources and man, and since they differ strikingly from place to place, it becomes difficult to say anything useful about this man-resource relationship on the global scale.

In fact, there is not just one world of resource requirements and availabilities but many. The access of a particular area of consumption or potential consumption to one of supply (and vice versa) is not necessarily assured. Although reduced, physical problems of transportation and cost still exist, as do additional institutional and cultural barriers to spatial interaction, such as political alignments, trade policies, and their manifestations in tariffs. As a result, even when a strong complementarity exists between a "world of surplus" and a "world of want," they remain two world economies, not one. Between them very real barriers may prevent spatial interchange.

What, then, is an appropriate areal framework within which to deal with resources? In general, it is the size of the area over which the variables determining resource requirements and availabilities have been or can be made to have some considerable degree of homogeneity. An obvious example is the nation state. Within it the variables can be brought into focus and, for short- and medium-range intervals of time, statements concerning resources can be made with a high degree of confidence. Thus, for Canada one can specify a number of metals, fossil fuels, and renewable resources, whose availability will continue to exceed domestic requirements until the year 2000. In this statement Canada is the unit of reference—nothing larger, nothing smaller—and the dimensions of this unit determine which factors are internal and which are external.

In general, it might be said that the more restricted the space the more severe the resource problems become, the more rapidly they develop, and the greater is the chance that effects of resource operations will extend beyond the area in which they are initiated. The corollary to this, of course, is that the greater the area involved the greater the variety of potential resources and opportunities for spatial substitution and dispersion, with attendant decrease of problems and a longer lead time before they emerge. The ecology of resources thus reflects the principle stressed in Chapter 1—the more diverse systems are the more stable ones.

An important element of the spatial context is the degree of concentration or dispersion. Many problems of resources and environment arise as a result of areal concentration of consumers (for example, spillover effects of wastes produced in urban areas and resulting pollution of water, land, and air). There is not much indication, however, that the pattern of distribution of population will change drastically in the near future on the world or national scale. Rather it appears likely that there will be an increased concentration of population as a result of the coalescence of present nodes. If this occurs, then the resource implications of spatial concentration of population should receive as much attention as those of a nonspatially explicit increase in total numbers. Among other things, we must ask how massive intercontinental migration can be restrained as the pressure of population on resources rises locally. And how shall we resolve the agonizing confrontation between rising ethical standards in the developed world and the needs of the rapidly increasing underprivileged and undernourished for space as well as food?

What are the resource implications of concentration versus dispersion of population? Is there convincing evidence that the forces bringing about concentration will necessarily continue to outweigh the forces causing dispersion? From a resource point of view, should public policy seek ways of accommodating to the seemingly ever-increasing concentration, or should it seek to bring about dispersion? Does society prefer increasing technological complexity, population control, social revolution, or some combination of these things? The spatial scale at which questions such as these are posed and the assumptions made about spatial distribution and interaction will have a significant influence both on the nature of the answers and on the range in space to which they can be extended.

Technology

One of the most fundamental societal factors involved in the interaction between man and nature is the technology that man has at his disposal for discovering, producing, processing, and using the materials of his environment. The range of technology available changes rapidly with time as the total stock of skills and understanding grows, as a result of both many small incremental gains and larger breakthrough advances. This continuous growth and changing capability of technology contributes greatly to the dynamic state of resource issues.

The impact of technological advance upon resources is usually interpreted positively, optimistically, and enthusiastically, for it provides the means of "creating" resources out of environmental material, of substitution, of increased extraction rates, and of greater efficiency of use. On the other hand, the enormous requirements of some technologies in themselves contribute greatly to the depletion of resources and to the production of waste in unprecedented quantities. Furthermore, technology provides the means by which man may ever more effectively challenge nature (White, 1967) and thus be increasingly capable of unbalancing the systems of which it is composed.

In recognizing technology as one of the most powerful forces impinging on the resource scene, one is led to ponder whether, and in what directions, its development is influenced by interactions between resources and man. New technology arises from research and development programs that are themselves started and directed by social, political (including military), and, most frequently, market forces. But there are questions to which the market does not yet know how to react (Krutilla, 1967) and other questions concerning relationships that are expected to exist sufficiently far into the future so that they produce no signals in the marketplace of today. Where technology is the limiting factor, the question is whether the desired technological development will arise. Where scarcity of particular resources may become limiting, the question is whether the market will react far enough ahead to provide time for substitutes to be sought or technological solutions to be devised. (For discussion of such matters see U.S. Department of Commerce, 1967; Nelson, Peck, and Kalechek. 1967.)

The ability to invent and the receptivity to innovation and dispersion of new techniques vary with the degree of development of a society with respect to a range of cultural characteristics, of which education is often seen as the most important. As a consequence, pronounced geographical differences need to be taken into account when evaluating the role of technology in resource development and use. An international corporation may be able to disperse technological change to all its plants regardless of their location, but the dispersal of new varieties of crops to millions of independent users, or the introduction of such users to the use of artificial fertilizer, may face severe spatial limitations. It must be stressed again that in practice there is not one technological world but many, and that to extrapolate from experience in one area to expectations in another is hazardous.

FRAMES OF REFERENCE

Many formulations of the relation between man and resources have evolved over the years. Each of these tends to emphasize a particular factor or group of factors as determinant, and each has been, or is, sufficiently plausible to receive wide acceptance.

The Malthusian Doctrine

Malthus (1798, p. 13–14) wrote that "the power of population is indefinitely greater than the power in the earth to produce subsistence for man. . . . Population, when unchecked, increases in a geometrical ratio. Subsistence increases only in an arithmetical ratio."

This initial statement of the Malthusian doctrine, or more sophisticated versions, lies at the root of most of society's anxieties about the relations between man and resources. Specific predictions based on such relations, however, must examine the relevance of the underlying assumptions to a particular space and span of time.

Conservation

The meaning of the term *conservation* varies from person to person and time to time, although it is generally associated with resource scarcity and has its roots in the Malthusian formulation (Barnett, 1959; Krutilla, 1967). The conservation idea, however, is often associated with political and emotional overtones. Over the last half century it has been associated with a number of identifiable viewpoints (Herfindahl, 1961). The first of these was probably the concern to define the "limits" of resources by means of inventories and surveys. Second, in order to avoid the problem of approaching the limits of resource availability, the notion of deferring production developed and became the interpretation of conservation generally adopted by economists. A third viewpoint, recognizing that use is unavoidable, emphasizes the need for constant efforts to reduce waste and encourages multipurpose use whenever feasible. A fourth, closely associated with the conservation tradition, calls for the preservation of nature from the ravages of development.

The Ecological Approach

A more recent formulation of the man-resource relationship, with some antecedents in the conservation idea but owing its full development more to biologists than to laymen, is the ecological approach. This approach sees the natural world as a series of interrelated systems in a state of dynamic equilibrium into which man intrudes as an unbalancing factor. The study of these complex, interrelated systems by proponents of this approach has led to support for multiple-path, multiple-choice, and systems-analysis methodology in dealing with resource problems rather than "linear chain-reaction determinism" (Weiss, 1962).

The Technological Fix

During the last decade the Malthusian doctrine and other positions of conservationists have come under attack by economists. The doctrine of scarcity (in economic terms) has been discounted, and at least the part of the conservationist's position that supported the deferment of use has been challenged. The key process supporting such challenge is technological change, particular emphasis being placed on such developments as will permit far-ranging chemical synthesis and offer the prospect of more massive and cheaper supplies of energy than man has ever had at his disposal before. The essence of this view is expressed by Barnett and Morse (1963, p. 10) as follows: "Few components of the earth's crust, including farm land, are so specific as to defy economic replacement, or so resistant to technological advance as to be incapable of eventually yielding extractive products at constant or declining cost."

The position taken is that given mobilization of enough highly trained personnel, money, and equipment, solutions to problems of foreseeable resource scarcities will become available. Some proponents of this view claim that to bring about the necessary technological development is, in the long run, easier than attempting to change social attitudes toward resources and environment (Weinberg, 1966).

The Quality of Environment

In many respects the quest for environmental quality, and the measurement of other goals in relation to this, is closely allied with the ecological approach; but it draws increasingly wide support from physical and social scientists, as well as from the public and government (Jarrett, 1966). Clean air, clean water, beautiful landscapes, and the like are said to become the goals of society when the benefits of technology release it from an overriding concern with material resources.

CONCLUSIONS

Each of the formulations identified above has its proponents in high places and its following in the citizenry at large. Adherence to one or another of them is basically determined by which combination of variables is given the greatest weight, the terms used (e.g., physical, economic, qualitative), and the temporal-spatial context assumed. The differing assumptions from which they depart may lead to such contrasting statements as:

> The notion of an absolute limit to natural resource availability is untenable when the definition of resources changes drastically and unpredictably over time. (Barnett and Morse, 1963, p. 7.)

and

> That such rates of growth are essentially ephemeral, and cannot be continued into the future indefinitely, can be seen by noting that the earth on which we live is finite in magnitude; whereas no physical quantity, whether the human population, the rate of energy consumption, or the rate of production of a material resource such as a metal, can continue at a fixed exponential rate without soon exceeding all physical bounds. (Hubbert, 1962, p. 125.)

Which of the many variables are the determinants, which of the several perspectives the most germane? There is no one answer for all time and all places. Reality requires that account be taken of variations both in time and space together, and that is where the greatest difficulties and contradictions arise.

The commitment of highly respected individuals and groups to particular perspectives, and the resulting variety of positions, is both confusing and troublesome. If policy makers, managers, and the public at large become committed too far to one outlook, the danger arises that some insights of the others will be lost or that debate will center on the polemics of the bias in vogue. Preferable is a continuing balanced appraisal of the complex and dynamic interaction between man and resources, set explicitly in the context of the range of perspectives available and varying with the times and places involved. Perhaps the most helpful thing that could happen would be for students of the problem to agree on a few models in time, space, population density, and level of living that would become frames of reference for the unambiguous evaluation of resource sufficiency.

References

Barnett, H. J. 1959. *Malthusianism and conservation—their role as origins of the doctrine of increasing economic scarcity of natural resources.* Resources for the Future, Reprint no. 12. Washington, D.C.

Barnett, H. J., and C. Morse. 1963. *Scarcity and growth.* Baltimore: Johns Hopkins Press.

Boulding, K. 1966. The economics of the coming spaceship Earth. In *Environmental quality in a growing economy*, H. Jarrett, ed. Resources for the Future. Baltimore: Johns Hopkins Press.

Darling, F. F., and J. P. Milton, eds. 1966. *Future environments of North America.* New York: Natural History Press.

Herfindahl, O. C. 1961. *What is conservation?* Resources for the Future, Reprint no. 30. Washington, D.C.

Hubbert, M. K. 1962. *Energy resources.* National Academy of Sciences—National Research Council Publ. 1000-D. Washington, D.C.

Jaguaribe, H. 1966. World order rationality, and socio-economic development. *Daedalus*, Spring 1966, pp. 607–626.

Jarrett, H., ed. 1966. *Environmental quality in a growing economy*. Resources for the Future. Baltimore: Johns Hopkins Press.

Krutilla, J. V. 1967. *Conservation reconsidered*. Resources for the Future, Reprint no. 67. Washington, D.C.

Landsberg, H. H., L. J. Fischman, and J. L. Fisher. 1963. *Resources in America's future*. Resources for the Future. Baltimore: Johns Hopkins Press.

Lovejoy, W. F., and P. T. Homan. 1965. *Methods of estimating reserves of crude oil, natural gas, and natural gas liquids*. Resources for the Future. Baltimore: Johns Hopkins Press.

Malthus, T. R. 1798. *An essay on the principle of population as it affects the future improvement of mankind*. Facsimile reprint in 1926 for J. Johnson. London: Macmillan & Co.

Myrdal, G. 1965. The United Nations, agriculture, and the world economic revolution. *J. Farm Econ.* 47(4): 889–899.

Nelson, R. R., M. J. Peck, and E. D. Kalechek. 1967. *Technology, economic growth and public policy*. Washington, D.C.: Brookings Institute.

U.S. Department of Commerce. 1967. *Technological innovation—Its environment and management*. Washington, D.C.

Weinberg, A. M. 1966. Can technology replace social engineering? *Bull. At. Scientists* 22(10): 4–8.

Weiss, P. 1962. *Renewable resources*. National Academy of Sciences—National Research Council Publ. 1000-A. Washington, D.C.

White, L. 1967. The historical roots of ecologic crises. *Science* 155(3767):1203–1207.

Zimmerman, E. S. 1951. *World resources and industries*, revised (2nd) ed. New York: Harper.

3/United States and World Populations

Nathan Keyfitz

"The gravest problem facing man in a peaceful world is the establishment of a reasonable harmony between a stabilized world population and the environmental resources upon which that population depends."

—U.S. National Committee for the International Biological Program, 1967, p. 1

The likely limits of future population and demand are central to problems of the adequacy of resources, yet such limits are difficult to predict. In this chapter we will look at some of the reasons for this difficulty, give some estimates of expected future populations, and discuss some aspects of the increasing concentration of people in cities.

MAKING POPULATION PROJECTIONS

The simplest but not the most realistic set of assumptions for population projections is that the age-specific birth and death rates of a given year will persist without change into the future, and that net migration is zero. Figure 3.1 shows population predictions for the United States in the years 1970, 1980, 1990 and 2000, based on such assumptions and starting from data for different years between 1920 and 1965. For the year 2000, the range in predictions is considerable—146 million people when we start from 1935 up to 360 million people starting from 1960, a difference of 214 million

Typescript received July 1967. Final revision, June 1968.

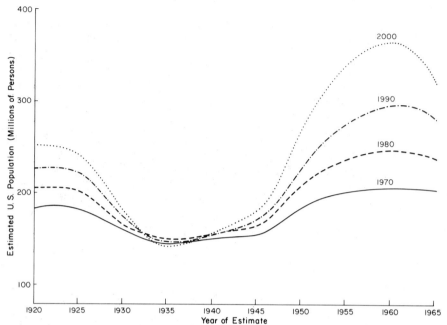

FIGURE 3.1
Comparison of population estimates for the United States. Curves for the four terminal years indicated are generated by connecting points predicted on the assumption of simple constancy of trends, starting from the years indicated on the horizontal axis. Births are adjusted for underregistration.

people. Projections to a given year are generally low when made from times of low birth rates and high from times of high birth rates. Moreover, the prospect can change sharply. The projection for the year 2000 fell by 60 million people in the five years from 1960 to 1965.

Variation in the forecasts ought to be diminished by projections in which, at each period, allowance is made for future changes in birth and death rates. Yet Table 3.1 shows that such projections based on the judgment of good demographers between 1931 and 1956 were not much better than estimates based on fixed age-specific rates from the same dates.

It is obvious from Table 3.1 that:

1. *Short-term projections are more likely to be correct than long-term projections.*
2. *The ranges of the projections tend to be too narrow to have a reasonable chance of including actual numbers later observed.* To have said in 1943 that the 1960 population of the United States would be between 147.7 million people and 156.5 million people is not much better in relation to the observed figure of 179.3 million people than to have said it would be 153.4 million people. If, on the other hand, limits

are made wide enough to be sure to include numbers of people actually counted at some distant future date, they are likely to be too wide to seem useful.

3. *When allowance is made for birth control, variations in logical projections for the future are considerable.* Such projections depend largely on the prognosis of births, rather than on the other two components, death and migration.

A fourth conclusion might be that predictions of future populations are getting better as we learn more, but this is not certain. A. L. Bowley's 1924 estimate of the population of Great Britain by 1961 was 48–49 million people, which compares very well with the 1961 census of 51.4 million people. This highly successful estimate, however, contrasts with others made in the 1930's. They predict a falling population for Great Britain that by 1960 would have plunged below 45 million people. The observed trend in Bowley's time just happened to predict a nearly accurate number.

FACTORS AFFECTING BIRTH RATES

The pattern of population growth in the United States since World War II suggests that internal efforts are currently limiting population growth, although, as Davis (1967) has made clear, this by no means supports the hope that population control is imminent. From the Depression rates of well under 20 births per thousand of population in the 1930's and early 1940's, the birth rate rose to a plateau of 23.4 per thousand in 1945–1949,

TABLE 3.1
Projected and observed population of the United States for 1960 (in millions of people).

Projected by	Low	Medium	High	Projected by fixed age-specific rates from given dates	Observed
Scripps, 1931		143.9		152.1	179.3
Scripps, 1935	137.1	149.4	159.5	145.4	179.3
Scripps, 1943	147.7	153.4	156.5	149.7	179.3
Scripps, 1947	149.8	155.1	162.0	157.8	179.3
U.S. Bureau of the Census, 1949		160.0		166.5	179.3
Organization for European Economic Cooperation, 1956		180.0		177.4	179.3

Sources: Scripps projections from Dorn, 1950, p. 318; OEEC, 1961, p. 140, adjusted back one-half year.

and from there it increased to 25.0 per thousand in 1954 and 1957. In 1957 it started to fall, and it fell in every year and in every age group, declining to 19.4 births per thousand people in 1965 and 1966 (it must fall to 14 births per thousand in order for population to stabilize where mean life expectancy is 70 years). Meanwhile, European rates have tended to be low. The postwar "baby boom" there was relatively small and of short duration.

This configuration of events could be attributed to limitations of space and crowding, not in a physical but in a social and economic sense. Where schools at all levels are crowded, as they only now are in the United States, launching one's children in a desired career is not easy. This crowding and competition for places is very well known in Europe and taken for granted there. Ever since the Revolution, French peasants have not wanted to subdivide their lands, and they have had limited confidence about being able to find employment for their sons in the city. The sentiment that results seems to make for a birth rate of about 16 to 18 per thousand people. Such a sentiment is new in America, but some signs suggest its arrival here. The difficulties encountered by large numbers of young people, born in the late 1940's and now seeking to enter good colleges and to find good jobs, are visible enough to have an effect on prospective parents.

The ecology of reproduction is very different in the less developed countries. Birth control materials and information are generally not available, especially among the illiterate. Subsistence, rather than careers, education, or leisure, is the aim of the greatest drive. Children are valued to help work the land—sons in particular, for prestige and as a form of old-age insurance. Reduction of juvenile mortality, moreover, is too recent to have overcome the belief that many children are needed to assure that some will survive. All of these and other difficulties, customs, and prejudices must be overcome before significant depression of the birth rate can be expected in the underdeveloped countries. Given universally available birth control facilities and old-age insurance, many unwanted births might be eliminated. And if, through genetic engineering, assurance could be given that the first child would be a male with a high chance of survival to maturity, many unwanted female births could be averted. Real population control, however, is quite another matter.

PREDICTED FUTURE POPULATIONS

United States

Recent official projections to the year 2000 are now available from the Bureau of the Census (1964; U.S. Department of Commerce, 1966). Four sets of projections were made, based on different sets of assumptions. Series A supposes that the completed fertility of women moves gradually to an average of 3.4 children; Series B that it moves to 3.1; Series C, to 2.8; Series D, to 2.5. Only minor changes in mortality are assumed. The resultant numbers are given in Table 3.2.

Effects of Immigration. That there will be immigration to the United States in the years between now and the end of the century is certain. Gross immigration during the decade 1941–1950 was 1,035,000, and during 1951–1960 it was 2,515,000 (U.S. Department of Commerce, 1966, p. 94). The corresponding net figures, including unrecorded migration, are somewhat higher. For the years 1960–1965, net immigration was estimated to average 367,000 per year. Projections of Table 3.2 include, from 1965 to the end of the century, an average annual increment of 400,000 immigrants. Though the number is higher than actual past immigration, it does not in fact greatly affect the projection. The higher figures, moreover, seem likely, on the assumption that, under its liberalized immigration laws, the United States will attract new citizens in greater numbers. The continuing movement of talent and skill from the less developed to the more developed countries appears inevitable.

Effects of Age Distribution. A stable age distribution is that which a population (say of females) would approach if the age-specific birth and death rates of a given period remained constant. Existing age distributions are usually different from the stable configuration, largely because of past changes in birth rates. The significant difference is in the proportion of women in the childbearing ages, sometimes greater in the actual than in a hypothetical stable structure, and sometimes smaller. In considering the future it is interesting to calculate the number of females in a population of stable age distribution that would be the reproductive equivalent of those in an actual population.

The estimated female population of the United States in mid-1960 was 91,348,000. But the curve of reproduction by ages was not symmetrical, because of the general decrease in births during the 1930's. With 76,840,000

TABLE 3.2
Four alternative U.S. population projections for 1965 by the U.S. Bureau of the Census.

Projection	Children per woman	Population in millions			
		1970	1980	1990	2000
A	3.350	208.9	249.4	298.1	356.1
B	3.100	207.1	241.9	284.4	331.6
C	2.775	205.5	233.6	268.8	304.4
D	2.450	204.1	226.0	254.0	280.1

Source: U.S. Department of Commerce, 1966, p. 6, 8.

females of stable age distribution, and the same age-specific rates of birth and death as actually existed in 1959–1961, the ultimate population to be expected would be the same. It is in this sense that we will call 76,840,000 the stable or reproductive equivalent of the observed 91,348,000. From this we can estimate future populations. Given a value of 0.02115 for the intrinsic rate of natural increase, r, for 1959–1961, the future female population in t years after 1960 (if age-specific rates remain fixed) would be $76{,}840{,}000e^{0.02115t}$, where e is 2.7183. Figure 3.2 shows the close comparison between this and the conventional projection by the year 2000. To use the observed population as the coefficient in the above equation would result in an overestimate of nearly 20 percent for any future date.

Between 1960 and 1965, however, some of those females born during the postwar "baby boom" reached childbearing ages, and the age distribution became more nearly balanced, to the point where the stable equivalent and the observed totals practically coincided (Figure 3.3). More than offsetting this effect was a drastic decline in birth rates, so that the intrinsic rate fell to 0.01267. Hence the future population estimated from data for 1965 would be $98{,}645{,}000e^{0.01267(t=5)}$ if t is still measured from 1960.

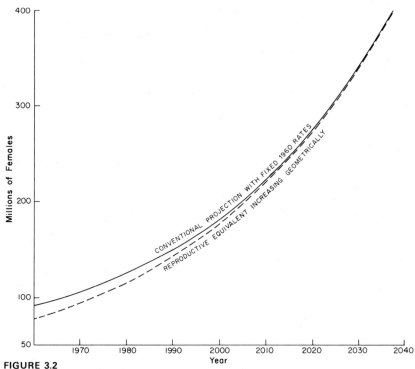

FIGURE 3.2
Growth of female population in the United States as estimated by two different methods projected from 1960.

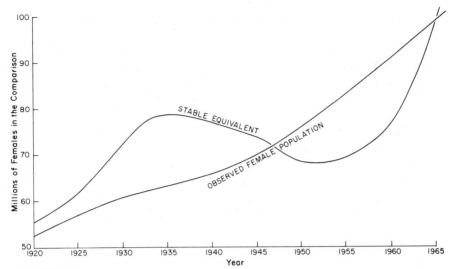

FIGURE 3.3
Observed female population of the United States compared with stable equivalent
number. Data summarized are three-year averages from 1919–1921 to 1954–1956, plus
figures for 1960 and 1965.

The spread in estimates of future populations thus tends to increase as
the projection interval grows longer. When we project from 1960 rates we
obtain 419 million females for 2040, as against 256 million when we project
from 1965. The sex ratio is not likely to be far from unity in either instance,
so we are discussing the prospect of a total population of 500–800 million
for the United States in the year 2040. If the birth rate could fall enough in
five years to change the prospect this much, however, then it could fall
further. The answer may be lower than either figure.

Europe

The future seems somewhat more determinate for Europe. Here birth control
is even more widespread than in the United States and aimed at more con-
stricted norms. Thus postwar fluctuations have been smaller. The total
population of Europe west of the USSR, 430 million in 1961, is now increasing by about 35 million per decade. Thus the year 2000 should show
about 560 million, assuming persistence of the 1961 rate of increase.

More precisely, the 1961 female population for Europe west of the
USSR was 219,803,500 (1961 information was incomplete for Northern
Ireland and Albania). The stable equivalent number of females was not
very different: 217,270,000. A projection from this base, using the intrinsic
rate 0.00643, gives, after 39 years, 279 million females. If Europe recovers
from its war losses to the point where males (in 1961 fewer than females

by 14 million) become equal in number to females, then we can estimate a total for the year 2000 of 558 million people, or, with Northern Ireland and Albania, about 570 million. For 2040 the corresponding figure is 740 million. These figures are less arbitrary than we shall be able to turn up for any other continent. They agree closely with the United Nations 1966 "High" variant which stands at 563 million for the year 2000.

Other Developed Countries

Aside from the United States and Europe, populations of the remaining countries generally considered to be developed—Canada, Australia, New Zealand, Japan, and the Soviet Union—constitute another 360 million. (A United Nations report (1966) includes with the developed countries the 36 million people of Argentina, Chile, and Uruguay, because of the low birth rates there.)

The populations of Canada and Oceania will probably continue to grow somewhat faster than that of the United States; Japan's population appears almost stationary; the Soviet rate of growth has been almost identical with that of the United States. These countries offer somewhat the same difficulties to prediction as does the United States, and uncertain data for the Soviet Union create some additional problems.

The crude birth rates for the Soviet Union closely resemble those of the United States. The United States started down from 25.0 births per thousand of population, the upper edge of the postwar plateau, in 1957, while the Soviet Union started down from 25.4 in the same year. By 1965 the United States reached 19.4; the Soviet Union reached 18.5. Both seem to be continuing downward. If there is any difference in fertility, the United States is higher, for the crude rate in the Soviet Union is affected by a somewhat more favorable age distribution. Intrinsic rates of natural increase, as far as they can be compared, were about 10 per thousand of population for the Soviet Union as against 18 for the United States toward the end of the 1950's. This is partly accounted for by lower mortality rates in the United States.

If the increase of one percent per year for the Soviet Union continues to hold, its 209 million inhabitants of 1959 would increase to a little over 300 million by the year 2000 ($209e^{0.01t} = 315$, where t is 41 years). The United Nations (1966) "Low" variant estimates 316 million Russians at the end of the century.

The Underdeveloped Countries

The above consideration of the developed countries accounts for about one billion (10^9) of the 1965 world population of 3.3 billion. What happens to the populations now making up the remaining 2.3 billion is all-important. For reasons mentioned, our remarks about this must be even more provisional than those above.

The standard work on India, by Davis (1951), gave a population of 465–550 million for India and Pakistan by 1970, and 560–790 million by 2000. The United Nations (1966, p. 67) "Medium" population estimate for India is 543 million for 1970 and 981 million for the year 2000. Even on the lowest United Nations estimate, Indians and Pakistanis together will total 1,163 million at the end of the century. This exemplifies the persistent tendency of forecasts to be revised upward as the dates on which they are based become more recent. Demographers have no way of knowing the exact course of upward movement of population in the latter half of the twentieth century.

If the future of North American populations depends importantly on the changing sentiments of parents, in some degree influenced by economic fluctuations, the future of the underdeveloped world depends on quite different circumstances—whether parents will adopt birth control and what proportion of parents will use it effectively. This, of course, transcends the realm of individual whim to become a vast dilemma for all humanity. Only when a demographer has some basis for judging the probable prevalence and pace of birth control measures can he predict in a rational way, and only when such measures finally result in real population control can mankind relax the effort to relieve the population pressures on the already overcrowded "Spaceship Earth."

Mortality is sure to decline still further if sanitation and medicine continue to spread. Health measures that have brought certain otherwise underdeveloped countries around the rim of Asia (Ceylon, Singapore, and Taiwan, for example) close to European levels of mortality are likely to move inland. Whether fertility will decline as much or more or less is what we need to know.

The future birth rate in most new countries is thought to depend on the effectiveness of government action. Governments of such countries as India, Pakistan, the Philippines, Colombia, and Chile, have declared that the birth rate must decline. They have helped in some degree by offering sterlization, loops, pills, and other contraceptives. In Europe, however, the birth rate fell most in the presence of governments advocating population increases. This gives rise to the following conjectures:

1. If people reduced their families in France when the government was urging them to have more children, how much more, and more quickly, will they reduce them in India now that the government advises such reduction.

2. The underlying social structures and the peasants' wish to keep their farms intact, not government advice, determined family size in France.

At best, people disregard the urgings of governments to do what their social perceptions indicate to be inadvisable; on the other hand, people may simply do the opposite of what governments urge them to do.

Governments may be less influential than the first conjecture assumes, but people could start to practice contraception because means are available. If they do not, then something must be done to provide incentives. The incentive to birth control in nineteenth-century Europe was that life was hard for children and for parents of children and much less hard for those with few children than for those with many—so much so that birth control was effective even though the principal method was coitus interruptus. But humane governments in the new nations have done much for children in the way of education and the provision of food. The pivot of the incentives approach is to find a way to discourage new births without hurting children already born. Governments that have an uncertain position with their people are especially unlikely to withdraw expected benefits from families in the interest of such a long-run goal as national economic development, even where they recognize that nothing less than development is at stake.

Some of the more advanced countries of Asia show the best net progress in fertility reduction to date (Figure 3.4). By contrast, examples of increasing birth rates are plentiful, including such Asiatic countries as Thailand and such Latin American countries as Jamaica. The countries of declining fertility graphed in Figure 3.4 include total populations of only 60 million people and are of interest mainly as indicators of what could happen elsewhere. Whether the trend they show will spread, and how fast, no one knows. Nor should it be overlooked that populations are still increasing at the rate of approximately 2 percent per year even in these countries.

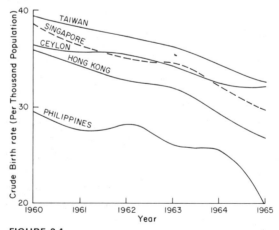

FIGURE 3.4
Declining birth rates in selected Asian countries, 1960–1965. (After United Nations, 1966, Table 12.)

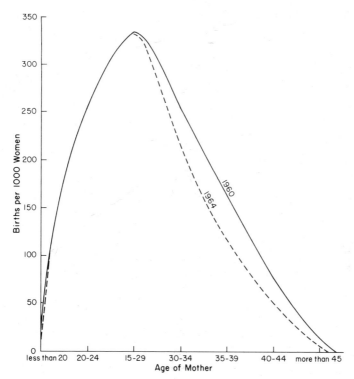

FIGURE 3.5
Taiwanese birth rates by age of mother, 1960–1964.

One aspect of the decline in fertility shown in Figure 3.4 suggests that it will not continue indefinitely. This is the ages of mothers at which the decline occurs. Figure 3.5 shows age-specific birth rates for Taiwanese females for 1960 and 1964. No decline in fertility is shown for mothers in their twenties, who are responsible for more than half of all births (263,000 out of 417,000 in 1964). Substantial decreases, however, are shown for women past the main ages of childbearing. This does not make the decline between 1960 and 1964 any less real, but it raises the question of how far into the future it will continue and whether it will affect the younger and most fertile mothers. Younger couples apparently have yet to change their views of the problems associated with child-rearing and population increases.

Expected Total World Populations

World population in mid-1965 was estimated by the United Nations at 3.25 billion people. It is relatively safe to estimate that the world will contain 3.5 billion people by about the end of 1968. The 1965 population distribution by continents is shown in Figure 3.6. This figure also shows the United

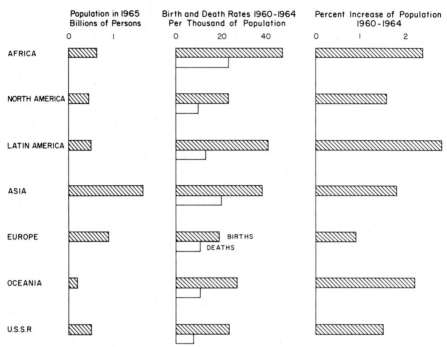

FIGURE 3.6
Some facts about world populations.

Nations estimates of birth and death rates for the interval 1960–1964, their net result being a population increase of 1.8 percent per year. That these figures for population increase are optimistic is suggested by their attributing to mainland East Asia (mostly China) an increase of only 1.4 percent per year. The growth of China's population has been estimated at as high as 2.5 percent per year. The birth rate everywhere exceeds the death rate by a factor of two or more (Figure 3.6). By 1968 a rate of annual population increase of 2.0 percent or higher was presumably reached for the world as a whole.

A rate of 2 percent applied to a population of three and one-half billion people gives an annual increase of 70 million people. Only eight countries have populations as large as 70 million people. Such a rate of increase amounts to a new United States every three years, a new Chicago every two weeks. If the greater metropolitan area is equated with Chicago, a month would suffice for world reproduction to equal it!

Figure 3.7 shows six projections of world population starting from 1965. Differences by 1970 are negligible, being probably less than the range of ignorance about present population. Even for 1980 the spread is only from 4,061 million to 4,551 million people, which can be counted as close agreement in view of the varied possibilities. However, by the year 2000 the spread is very wide indeed—between Bogue's optimistic estimate of about 4.5 billion and the United Nations "High" estimate of about 7 billion people. Even this high estimate, however, supposes an appreciable decline in fertility. The estimate with fertility constant is over 7.5 billion. This dismal prospect is not impossible, since fertility actually does increase as an immediate effect of industrialization under some circumstances, and one does not know how to weigh the weakening of such traditional controls as the nonremarriage of widows in India against the introduction of birth control.

While the notion that future changes will exactly offset one another is rarely justified, a projection has been made at the present increase of 2 percent per year. To continue this figure into the future supposes that the

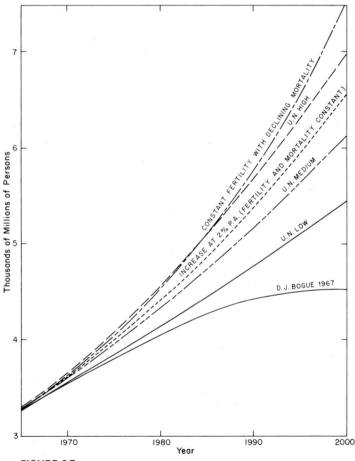

FIGURE 3.7
Six estimates of world population, 1965–2000.

present age distribution is approximately stable, a relatively innocuous assumption. More important, it supposes that declines in mortality will be matched by declines in fertility. Despite its tenuous base, the 6.5 billion that results as a prediction for world population in the year 2000 is as convincing a figure as any. It happens to be almost exactly midway between the United Nations "Medium" and "High" results.

The United Nations "Medium" estimate could well turn out to be conservative, although it would be unwise to count on that. It implies an increase of very nearly 1.8 percent per year, which is almost exactly what we saw in Figure 3.6 to be the world increase for 1960–1964. Figure 3.8 shows the breakdown of the United Nations "Medium" estimate by continents, and Figure 3.9 shows it for developed and underdeveloped regions. Attention is drawn especially to the increase in the proportion of the total world population expected in the underdeveloped regions—from 68.5 to 76.5 percent. This will inevitably place severe pressures on the developed regions.

Conclusions About World Populations

The foregoing analysis leads us to suggest the figures listed in Table 3.3 as the most likely United States and world populations for the years up to 2000 A.D. For the United States the C level of Table 3.2 seems justified.

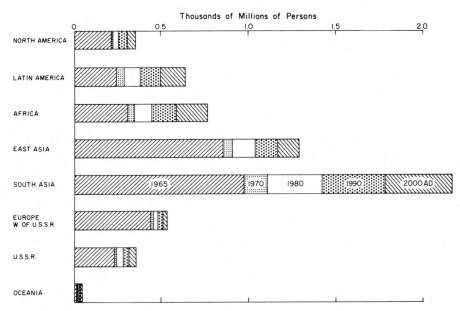

FIGURE 3.8
Expected populations of major divisions of the world, 1965–2000. (Based on United Nations Medium projections, 1966, p. 134.)

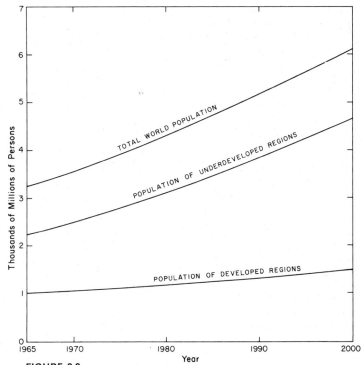

FIGURE 3.9
Population and development, 1965–2000. (Based on United Nations
Medium projections, 1966, p. 134.)

For the remainder of the world, the "Medium" estimate of the United
Nations (1966, p. 134) is taken.

For the first half of the twenty-first century such formal, weighted indica-
tions are not available. A relatively "optimistic" basis for further projection
can be found in the average rate of increase postulated by the United Nations
"Medium" variant between 1970 and 2000. Thus, we subtract 3,592 from
6,129 and divide by 30 to find an average increase of just under 85 million

TABLE 3.3
**Provisional estimates of future United States and world populations (in millions
of people).**

	1970	1985	2000	2050
United States (official estimate)	205	251	304	470
United Nations "Medium" variant				
Total developed countries	1,082	1,256	1,441	2,040
Total underdeveloped countries	2,510	3,490	4,688	8,320
World total	3,592	4,746	6,129	10,360

people per year. Projected over the 50 years between 2000 and 2050 this amounts to 4,230 million people. When added to the estimated world total of 6,129 million for the year 2000, this gives a world population of approximately 10.4 billion people for the middle of the twenty-first century.

Since the number of females of childbearing age increases with the total population, however, the actual increase in numbers per year will almost certainly be greater after the year 2000 than before, without great interim progress toward population control. Our estimate can be realistic only if the annual rate of population increase for the world as a whole is steadily reduced to arrive at a rate of 0.8 percent by 2050. This is about half the rate of increase that has been typical of the United States during the postwar period; and it is about the same as the present rate of increase for Europe. The present underdeveloped countries, now increasing in population at three times this rate, will have to achieve far greater success in bringing down their birth rates in the 80 years after 1970 than they are having in the present "Decade of Development." This will not happen without large-scale, determined, and persistent efforts. If current rates of population increase do not abate, world population in 2050 could approach 18 billion people—well over half the number the world can ever hope to sustain, even at a level of chronic near-starvation for all. Moreover, as Davis (1967) has pointed out, the essential ultimate goal of real population control will require something more effective than merely eliminating unwanted births.

URBAN GROWTH AND THE QUALITY OF LIFE

Increasing populations place increasing demands on resources of all kinds—on food, on water, on air, on mineral resources and construction materials, on space for a variety of purposes, and on the human resource itself. Here we shall consider the latter, borrowing almost verbatim from an earlier paper by Keyfitz (1966), with the permission of the American Institute of Biological Sciences.

The increase of cities, especially the increase of very large cities, is to be seen on all continents. The cities are expanding not only in the rich countries, as foci of industry and trade, but in the poorest, to which industry has hardly come. During the 1950's the urban populations of developed countries increased by 55 percent. The increase of dense poor populations was twice as rapid as that of dense rich ones (Bourgeois-Pichat, 1966).

How could such an increase occur? The surplus food of the Asian peasantry did not increase greatly in the 1950's; it hardly increased at all. How can Djakarta be five times as populous as it was before World War II and three times as populous as ancient Rome at the highest point of its imperial power? Djakarta has not much more industry than Rome had. Its weak civil or military domination of an island territory, in some degree democratic, cannot compare in extractive power with the iron rule of Rome. The answer, of course, is that it draws food from foreign territories, including the United States—some of it paid for with the export of raw materials, some of it borrowed, some as gifts.

Unable or unwilling to exploit its own peasantry, the large contemporary nonindustrial city more and more bases itself ecologically on the fields of America, together with the ships and harbors that link those fields with its massive populations. Population growth in the Asian countryside is growing beyond food supplies; far from having a surplus to ship to the city, the peasant himself is hungry.

When the inhabitants of the local countryside can no longer produce enough food for themselves, they must be supported by foreign food. The people then tend naturally to gather into such seaport cities as Djakarta, Calcutta, and Rio de Janeiro, as close as possible to the spot where the ships will discharge cargoes of American, or occasionally Burmese or Cambodian, grain. If people are to be fed from abroad, it is cheaper to have them at the seaports than dispersed throughout the countryside. In 1966 the United States was shipping about 800,000 tons of grain per month to India alone. At the Asian standard of about one pound per person per day, this is enough for about 40,000,000 people to live on; a number that happens to be about equal to all the citizens of India living in the seacoast cities. If population continues to increase in the countryside and food does not, further flight to seacoast cities is certain.

Much could be said about what further increase in density and size will do to the dependence of those cities. We know that their inhabitants tend to perform services rather than make goods. The services have the function of distributing the claim to the food shipments, the ideal being to give employment rather than to get work done. Some studies have indicated that the new migrants to the cities retain links with the countryside. Others show that the simple and traditional patterns of association in the countryside are transferred to the city, which thereby resembles a number of contiguous villages, lacking only their fields and crops. These dense cities of rural culture are a new phenomenon in the world.

For some quite different concomitants of density, shown in their most accentuated form, we must go to those world cities of the nineteenth century that were ecological consequences of the railroad and steamship—New York, London, Paris, Berlin. In the twentieth century West a process of dispersal has occurred; cities produced by the automobile are less dense than those produced by the railroad and street car. We are getting strip cities, of which the best known is Megalopolis, the name Gottmann (1961) gave to Boston-New York-Washington.

The industrial city of the nineteenth century as well as the strip city of the late twentieth century intensifies competition on many levels. We must not only find a livelihood, we must find a life, each of us for himself, in the crowded city. This search for a tolerable physical and moral existence pre-occupies every city dweller, and it has far-reaching consequences for urban society as a whole. Just as Darwin saw the animal or plant adapting to a niche in which it is partly sheltered from competition, so the sociologist Durkheim (1960) sees the city man restlessly searching for, and adapting to, a niche constituted by a specialized occupation and specialized personality. If one had to face daily the direct competition of millions of people, the struggle would so weigh on each of us that existence would be impossible for our spirits as well as our bodies. One's niche may be teacher, stockbroker, or truck driver; it requires skills that others lack or involves work that others do not want to do. It gives each a place with a certain minimum of predictable security.

The electronics engineer in Chicago, say, has to concern himself, at most, with the competition of other electronics engineers. He does not even have to cope with all of them, at least in the short run. There are a hundred specialties within the field of electronics, and within each of these recognized specialties an individual practitioner, through his own tastes and capabilities, can make himself unique. People in a particular plant come to depend on him. If the city is, on the one side, a jungle of potentially infinite and destroying com-petition, it shows, on the other side, a nearly infinite capacity of its members to differentiate themselves, to become useful to one another, to become needed.

Such a basis of respect is characteristically metropolitan. In a society of smaller volume such as a village, each gets to know all about the few score or the few hundred people with whom he will have contact in the course of a lifetime. He knows them as whole people, is concerned with literally every-thing about them.

Individual city people may have contact in a day with as many individuals as the villager meets in the course of a lifetime. This includes store clerks, bus conductors, fellow passengers, public officials, co-workers, restaurant em-ployees, and so on, not to mention those we pass as we walk or drive along the street. It would destroy us if we had to react fully to every one of them as whole people. We need to know about each of them only enough to cover his particular relationship with us. We care only that the bus conductor is an authorized employee of the company and will take our fare and drop us at the corner of Madison and 42nd Street. Whether he is happily married with two children or a debauched bachelor, whether he is Presbyterian or Catholic, we never inquire. His uniform tells us everything about him that is important to us. It is mere whim on our part if we even look at his face. The imperson-ality of the great city is preservational and pervasive.

Whereas constant full exposure to what the city offers and demands would weary and frustrate the urban dweller, by protecting himself sufficiently against stimuli he survives and may even live a happy well-adjusted life. This is the nature of urban contacts, suggestively portrayed by Simmel (1964). Note that this characterization applies only to those members of the city who have adapted to city life over two or three generations and, as a result, are suitably educated and are productive enough to command the facilities of the city. It does not apply to the recent migrant to Chicago from the rural south or to Calcutta from inland Bengal.

The ultimate refuge against the pressures of the metropolis is flight. A quiet place in the country becomes the ideal of all, and, in one form or another, the seasonal recuperation of many. But with the acceleration of population growth, and especially with the prevalence of the automobile, that quiet place in the country, most precious of resources, is bound to become scarcer.

Simultaneous with the increase of numbers, the advance of technology makes each of us in the developed countries more mobile and requires more space—especially highways—to be set aside merely for facilitating our movement. Nearly 10 million new vehicles are put on the road each year in the United States, offset by only two-thirds that number of scrappings. This fact alone would tend to crowd us even if we were the same number of people. Year by year we are both more in numbers and are moving faster, always within a fixed people-container, the terrestrial area of the United States or the globe. The result is rising pressure and temperature, apparently under the operation of laws analogous to those governing the behavior of gases.

How shall we respond? Will we build up higher capacity for discretion and reserve? Will we develop the sort of etiquette of noninterference with our neighbors—silence, dignity, and good humor—that helps make life tolerable on a long submarine voyage?

In fact, the response of society to higher density is usually the very opposite of reserve and respect for the privacy of individuals; it is usually interference and planning. The frontier had no traffic lights or parking regulations. People did not have to regulate their activities by the activities of others. If the clocks and watches of frontier families were randomly in error, little inconvenience would have resulted; but if those of a modern city were out of phase, or if the electricity went off, most of the city's usual activities would be disrupted. Everything we do interlocks with what others do. The frontier needed nc zoning bylaws or building standards. The necessity for all these forms of planning has come with density. Meier (1962) describes an arrangement of the city of Madras in southern India, one of the growing harbor cities mentioned above, such that 100 million people could live in it; but life would have to be planned in the most excruciating detail. People would not even be allowed to own bicycles, simply because parking individually owned bicycles would tie up the streets. Movement would be restricted, and all that was necessary would be provided by mass transportation.

The density continuum from the frontier to Meier's imaginary Madras is also a planning continuum; density and planning seem to be positively correlated.

Our picture now is of two dense agglomerations of mankind facing one another across the oceans, both urban, one rich and one poor. America takes its cities into the countryside—it becomes an urban society through and through. Asia remains rural, even to parts of the dense agglomerations at the seaports—it brings rural culture into the cities. In a sense, the rich city has called the poor one into existence, first by insecticides and medicine, which lowered the death rate of India, for instance, from perhaps 35 per thousand to 20 per thousand, and then by the provision of food.

In a quite different sense, Europe had earlier contributed to Asian population. The industrial revolution of Europe and America demanded raw materials, and this demand was translated into a demand for people who would produce its goods. The needs of Europe for sugar, spices, and rubber brought into existance large populations, for example, in Indonesia, where the population of Java grew from under 5 million people in 1815 to 40 million by World War II. And when our technical advance, especially western synthetics, enabled us to make the things that formerly could only be produced by tropical sunshine and tropical labor, those populations were left high and dry. They are functionless in relation to the Western industrial machine which brought them into existence, but they keep growing nonetheless.

Western governments and electorates sense the tragic state of affairs and, at least vaguely, feel responsible for this aftermath of colonialism. Therefore, we provide food and other kinds of aid. But such are the dilemmas of doing good in this difficult world that each shipment of food draws more people to the seaports, and we arrive at nothing more constructive than a larger population than before dependent on shipments of food. If the need for food is a temporary emergency, philanthropy is highly recommended, but the conditions of tropical agriculture and population seem to be chronic rather than acute—fertilizer plants and technical assistance and training are needed rather than ever-larger quantities of wheat.

The only escape, other than ultimately moving the people to where the food is, is through the economic development of the countries of Asia, Africa, and Latin America. With increase of income arises the sort of communication system through which people can receive and act on signals in regard to the size of their families. Americans since 1957 have begun to understand that families had been too large—signals reach them to this effect through the price system and through the difficulties of placing children in college and in jobs. For underdeveloped people such a signaling system of prices and costs is not in existence, and messages that create a desirable feedback and permit automatic control do not carry. The control of population must be tackled directly. Each point by which the birth rate falls makes the process of development that much easier.

A number of countries are achieving development today, including Hong Kong, Taiwan, Mexico, Turkey. On the other hand, no grounds can be seen for the facile optimism that declares that development is imminent for all.

Is the hardship of life in the crowded and poor city itself a stimulus to effective action? Do density and poverty make for greater sensitivity to the real problems and greater judiciousness in their treatment? Not for the miserable newcomers, the first ill-adapted migrant generation to the city. In the slums of first settlement, whether in nineteenth-century London and Paris or twentieth-century Chicago, Los Angeles, Calcutta, or Paris, city mobs can be readily aroused by their troubles to action and to violence, but they do not necessarily see the root of their frustrations and the way to overcome them. Penetrating analysis does not guide mob action. The crowd, mobilized by some incident, acts with a violence out of all proportion to the event that excited its anger. It streams through a city street, stops to throw bottles or paving blocks at the police who reply with tear gas, overturns automobiles, and is finally dispersed by armed troops. Far from being a disappearing relic of the past, city mobs are with us both in the temperate zone and in the tropics, in wealthy countries and in poor ones. Food riots occur in Bombay and civil riots in Newark, Memphis, and even Washington, D.C. This ultimate manifestation of population density, which colors the social history of all continents, is a challenge that can no longer be deferred. It will not cease until population control is a fact and the rising expectations of the underprivileged everywhere have been met or come into balance with the capability of the world's resources to meet them. This will place monumental demands on collective social wisdom, on technological innovation, and on the earth's material resources.

References

Bogue, D. J. 1967. *The prospects for world population control.* Univ. of Chicago Community and Family Study Center.

Bourgeois-Pichat, J. 1966. Population growth and development. *International Conciliation*, no. 556 (Jan.), pp. 5–79. New York: Carnegie Endowment for International Peace.

Bowley, A. L. 1924. Births and population in Great Britain. *Econ. J.* 34: 188–192.

Davis, K. 1951. *The population of India and Pakistan.* Princeton, N.J.: Princeton Univ. Press.

Davis, K. 1967. Population policy: will current programs succeed? *Science* 158: 730–739.

Dorn, H. F. 1950. Pitfalls in population forecasts and projections. *J. Am. Statist. Assoc.* 45: 311–334.

Durkheim, E. 1960. *De la division du travail social*, 7th ed. Chap. III, La solidarité due à la division du travail ou organizue. Paris: Presses Universitaries de France.

Gottmann, J. 1961. *Megalopolis—The urbanized northeastern seaboard of the United States.* New York: Twentieth Century Fund.

Hawley, A. H. 1950. *Human ecology—A theory of community structure.* New York: Ronald Press.

Keyfitz, N. 1966. Population density and the style of social life. *BioScience* 16(12): 868–873.

Meier, R. L. 1962. Relations of technology to the design of very large cities. In *India's urban future*, Roy Turner, ed., pp. 299–323. Berkeley and Los Angeles: Univ. of California Press.

Organization for European Economic Cooperation (OEEC). 1961. *Demographic trends 1956–1976 in Western Europe and in the United States.*

Simmel, G. 1964. The metropolis and mental life. In *The Sociology of Georg Simmel,* Kurt H. Wolff, ed. and trans., p. 409–424. New York: Free Press of Glencoe, Collier-Macmillan.

United Nations. 1966. *World population prospect as assessed in 1963.* U.N. Population Studies, no. 41, ST/SOA/Series A/41. New York.

U.S. Bureau of the Census. 1947. *Forecasts of the population of the United States, 1945–1975.* Washington, D.C.

U.S. Bureau of the Census. 1964. *Population estimates—Projections of the population of the United States, by age and sex (1964 to 1985).* Bureau of the Census Series P-25, no. 286. Washington, D.C.

U.S. Department of Commerce. 1966. *Statistical abstract of the United States, 1966.* Washington, D.C.

U.S. National Committee for the International Biological Program. 1967. *Program statement of the Subcommittee on Productivity of Freshwater Communities and Subcommittee on Productivity of Terrestrial Communities*, Jan. 1967. National Research Council. Washington, D.C.

4/Food from the Land

Sterling B. Hendricks

"The answer to the world food problem does not lie in increasing still further the productivity of the rich, industrialized nations, however necessary this may be—it lies in increasing the per capita food production of the underdeveloped countries and in reducing their rate of population increase."
—E. J. Underwood, 1967, p. 396

People in many regions of the world are hungry. While we share our plenty with them, their plight raises specters of a possible destiny for us. Both to help them and to protect our own future, we are introspective about our present well-being and look ahead to what the obvious wants of others portend. To do this, we need to assess the material resources of the world for producing food and fiber, as well as the ways for best using these resources. The main resources are arable land, mineral fertilizers, and water supply.

There would be little cause to be concerned with these matters if populations were not rapidly increasing (see Chapter 3). The numbers of people already encroach on the means of living in many regions. The banishment of pestilence from the apocalyptic four—war, pestilence, famine, and death—has loosened the bonds for further increase. No matter what the ultimate size of population, the time is upon us to face the elementary demands for food in deprived regions now and in the world as a whole over the long term.

Typescript received July 1967. Final revision, June 1968.

Food and vegetable fiber are renewable materials. They can be harvested year after year without exhausting the means for renewal. Some fields have been farmed for millenia and still are moderately fertile. Even misuse of the land, which is to be deplored, is not irreparable except in small areas of greatest erosion. The real threat to potential worldwide adequacy of food is a demand for twice as much, or more, food than is now available. Still larger areas than there are now might then suffer drought and disaster or approach the Malthusian limits (see Chapter 1).

When food supplies become limited, social structures are apt to break down. The loss of supply may then be accelerated as a consequence of man's failure to apply existing technology. A starving person is ignored in central China or on the streets of Calcutta. If a semblance of social structure remains, however, limited food supplies can be extended through knowledge of nutrition. A few trained people in large populations can apply this knowledge. In better times, the knowledge can be spread, despite politico-religious barriers and inadequacies of government, just as pestilence can be suppressed. Table 4.1 shows the dietary facts for different nations. Later we will look more closely at some possibilities.

THE ARABLE LANDS

Production of food can be increased even though facing some of the realities strains or exceeds the powers of existing organization. The bases for increase are five: (1) new lands, (2) enhanced productivity of land now in use, (3) prevention of loss (of tithing to rats, fungi, and insects), (4) innovation, and (5) change in the economic base. The greatest immediate hope is to enhance productivity of land now farmed, for this can be done at a moderate pace without displacing people. Each farmer can add a little to what he knows.

TABLE 4.1
Estimated calories of food and grams of protein in the average daily diets for various nations.

Country	Prewar calories	1951/53 calories	1957/59 calories	1963/64 calories	Protein, grams
U.S.A.	3280	3130	3110	3110	92
France	2880	2840	2940	3070	100
Sweden	3120	3020	2930	2980	84
Spain		2490	2590	2850	78
Brazil	2190	2380	2590	2850	69
Japan	2020	1930	2170	2280	73
India	1950	1750	1910	1990	50
Philippines		1690	1760	1990	46

Source: United Nations, 1966.

TABLE 4.2
Land-use capability classes.

Class		Best Use[a]
	Arable Lands	
I.	Few limitations on use.	cultivation
II.	Some limitations on use, reducing the choice of crops or requiring some conservation practices.	cultivation
	Grazing Lands	
III.	Severe limitations on cultivation.	pasture, forest
IV.	Severe limitations on cultivation, reducing the choice of crops or requiring special practices.	pasture, forest
	Limited-use Lands	
V, VI, VII.	Soils are severely limited—generally unsuited for cultivation.	pasture, range, or forest
VIII.	Soils are severely limited and do not give satisfactory returns for management input.	

[a] Forest now occupy some lands of all classes.

Innovation, though, will shape the future for the more advanced countries, and some of the new methods can be extended to others. Change in the economic base to give the farmer a better life is most important for underdeveloped countries (Schultz, 1966) and will be increasingly necessary in advanced countries to ensure continuing development of farm production. The requirement is for greater return of amenities to the producer of food so that he may share in a full economy. This interplays with the other four factors as a leading incentive for effort. The best lands have long been preempted. In general, their soils contain minerals capable of producing plant nutrients when they break down under weathering. In favorable climates for agriculture, this implies that rocks have been degraded to form soil within the last few thousand years. Included are postglacial, volcanic, and recent alluvial areas and weathering uplands. More than 80 percent of the world's food is produced on these lands.

About one-fourth of the world's 32 billion acres are potentially arable, that is, suitable for cultivated crops. Another fourth can best be used for grazing; it would yield little additional food in crops. The remaining half, which includes wastelands, tundra, desert, and mountains, is forested in part. This half can be of only very limited use in production of food, however, even under the most optimistic outlook on innovation.

Somewhat less than half of the world's potentially arable land (3.5 billion acres) is now cultivated, and more than half of the grazing land is used. These lands are the chief sources of food for the present 3.5 billion people of the earth—an average of an acre of cultivated land and somewhat more than an acre of range land per person. Land-use capability classes are indicated in Table 4.2.

TABLE 4.3
Percentage of potentially arable land now cultivated, and acres cultivated per person, on different continents.

Continent	Percent cultivated	Acres cultivated per person
Asia	83	0.7
Europe	88	0.9
South America	11[a]	1.0
Africa	22[b]	1.3
North America	51	2.3
U.S.S.R. (Europe-Asia)	64	2.4
Australasia	2[c]	2.9

[a] Tropical limitation.
[b] Desert and tropical limitation.
[c] Desert limitation.

In Europe and Asia, 80 to 100 percent of the potentially arable lands are in use, and population densities are as great as six persons per acre. The densities are three or more persons per arable acre in Egypt and New Jersey. In the United States as a whole, the average figure is about one person per three acres. The percentage of potentially arable land now cultivated on the different continents and acres cultivated per person are shown in Table 4.3. Note that much of the world's vacant land is in tropical South America and Africa. The vacancy is not without reason.

Can, or will, the swelling population expand into the unused part of the potentially arable land? The answer is an eventual "yes," but only over a long period and to an extend beyond our poor powers of prediction. The people are concentrated in the now utilized areas, and many barriers to emigration exist.

THE TROPICS

Broad generalizations about land are hazardous. Although the world population is concentrated in the more favorable middle latitudes, many tropical areas also have very fertile soil and support dense populations. They are favored by long or continuous growing seasons, allowing growth of several crops per year. The best of the lands are in volcanic regions at moderate elevations, as in Costa Rica, Madagascar, Kenya, and the Rift Valley of Africa. Low-lying volcanic areas of Java and Bali, as well as alluvial regions such as the valleys of the Nile, Ganges, Irrawaddy, and Mekong, are also highly cultivated. Moderate production is possible with primitive technology, and this production can be enhanced.

Wide areas of vacant tropical lands are suitable for cropping and are well watered (Table 4.4). A third of all arable and potentially arable land is included in the humid tropics. Some of this land is reasonably fertile, but most is leached of the mineral nutrients necessary for plant growth—potash, lime, magnesia, phosphate, sulfates, and nitrogen compounds. Average populations are on the order of 10 people per square mile in such regions of Africa. Because of the soil properties and the low nutrient levels, these lands are now widely used for bush-fallow—variously known as shifting agriculture, swidden, milpa, or kaingin (Nye and Greenland, 1960). Bush-fallowing is based on the slow gathering of scarce nutrients and on the protection of the soil by organic matter. When the trees are cut, killed, or burned, some of the gleaned nutrients are available for a crop. A patch is used in rotation for one or two years after cutting and is then returned to fallow for a decade or more—as was a common practice in colonial America. Small populations now exist by this bush-fallow, but if population pressure shortens the fallow, fertility decreases. Grasses and other shallow-rooted plants of poor gleaning capacity take over, and potential for supplying organic matter is reduced (Maher, 1949).

Many other lands of the tropics have lateritic soils of high iron content that harden irreversibly in use—West Africa, India, Southeast Asia, Australia, and parts of South America afford examples. These were the "problem soils" of colonial agriculture—intractable and giving only a low return.

Population pressures have long existed in the tropics. Peoples on the alluvial and volcanic areas suited for rice culture have increased in numbers, to encroach on the surrounding high lands. Famine pressure in ancient India along the Ganges Valley forced emigration to the more hazardous region to the south, where even the infertile lateritic soils are tilled. Because of drought, the Mayan civilization of Yucatan fell, giving way to a sparsely peopled dry land. But the uncultivated vacant lands have remained vacant even under these pressures.

TABLE 4.4
Area of potentially arable soils in the world's tropical zones compared with the total areas now cultivated (in millions of acres).

Region	Now cultivated	Tropical Soil Type			
		Base rich[a]	Alluvial	Highly weathered	Other
Africa	390	160	105	1200	110
Asia	1280	80	285	270	145
N.A. + S.A.	780	50	40	1135	35
Australasia	40	40		40	50

Source: U.S. President's Science Advisory Committee, 1967.
[a] Assuming irrigation.

Extremes of well watered tropical lands of favorable lay but of very contrasting fertility are illustrated by Java and Borneo. Java has a total area of
40 million acres of which about 25 million are arable. Its population is
about 80 million, or more than three people per arable acre. Borneo, in an
equivalent climatic zone 250 miles to the north of Java, has four times the
area but a population of only 3 million people. About two-thirds of the
people of Borneo live on one-seventh of its area along the Java Sea, no more
than one person to 10 acres. The remaining area has only a few people per
square mile.

The difference between Java and Borneo is the soils (Mohr, 1944; Dames,
1955). Seventy-five percent of the soils of Java between 106° 38′ and 108° 8′
east longitude, for example, are derived from recent andesitic volcanic materials, or from alluvium and solifluction debris (lahars) containing volcanic
materials—all of which, upon weathering, yield soils rich in mineral nutrients
(Figure 4.1). The remainder of Java's soils come from limestone and marl
with an input of volcanic ash. More than 87 percent of the area is cultivated,
about one-third being in terraced rice fields. On the young soils formed from
volcanic ash of the Merapi plain of central Java, population densities exceed
six persons per acre. The Merapi volcano, the dominant one of the region,
has been very active since 1006.

Borneo, in contrast to Java, is essentially an old alluvial region derived
from weathering of siliceous shales and sandstones (Mohr, 1944). The small
amounts of volcanic effusives have high silica content (from rhyolites and
dacites), which leads to infertile soils. The rainfall over much of the area exceeds 100 inches per year, without a dry season. This is a condition of soil and
climate similar to the Congo and Amazon basins. Where igneous rocks of low
silica content are present, long weathering and continued reworking of
weathered material has resulted in formation of extensive and notoriously
infertile laterite. The better soils along the coast are derived from relatively
recent marls and, in Western Borneo, from weathering of granite, which
produces moderately fertile soils. This coastal area has the highest population
density on the island. Throughout most of Borneo, the clays in the soils are
less than 5 percent saturated with bases—in contrast to the 70 percent needed
for a moderately productive soil. Mohr (1944) writes that "drainage and
generous fertilization will produce a harvest from this land. But if we stop to
figure out how much calcium, potassium, magnesium, and phosphorus we
would have to add—it would be quite impossible to develop an agriculture
which would pay."

A limited-paying agriculture does exist in Borneo, nevertheless. It is rubber
production, which persists despite inroads of synthetics. Such tree culture in
Borneo, Malaysia, Liberia, Ghana, and the Congo Basin really is a hope for
the vacant humid tropics. The African oil palm was the basis of a Belgian
development in the Congo. These are examples of effective use of the

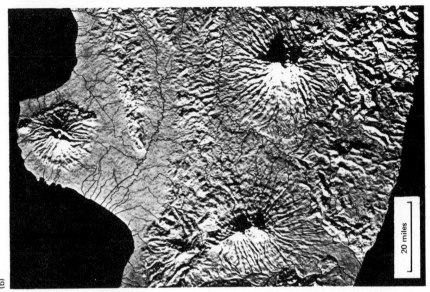

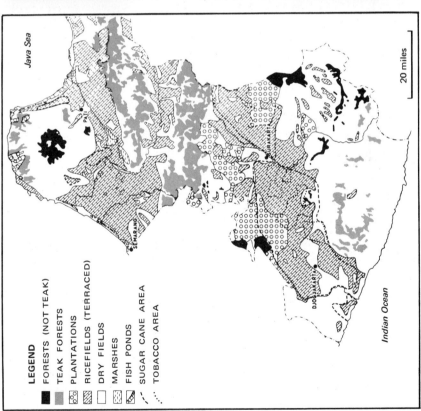

FIGURE 4.1
Land use and relief in east central Java. Note correspondence of map and relief model. (After Dames, 1955.)

LEGEND

FORESTS (NOT TEAK)
TEAK FORESTS
PLANTATIONS
RICEFIELDS (TERRACED)
DRY FIELDS
MARSHES
FISH PONDS
SUGAR CANE AREA
TOBACCO AREA

Java Sea

PATI

SEMARANG

SURAKARTA

DJOGJAKARTA

Indian Ocean

20 miles

(a)

(b)

20 miles

71

generally infertile tropics. Population densities supported by tree-dependent agriculture are low, however, and development times of the crop are long.

An end result is serious overpopulation of Java while nearby Borneo remains vacant. Bali and western Irian are an equally contrasting pair.

Guyana, which is nearer to us (just a few hours from New York to Georgetown by plane) has some soil contrast, but follows the general pattern of Borneo.

Guyana, with a total area of about 50 million acres, has about 3.5 million acres in a coastal plain, of which about 1 million acres are potentially arable. The arable land is the littoral, built up by the Orinoco, the Amazon, and the local Essequiobo and Courantyne rivers. Only about 300,000 acres of the geologically recent low-lying areas are cropped, chiefly in rice and sugar, which require the modern technology of land diking, flooding, and drainage. About 400,000 acres are used for unimproved pasture. The older marine terraces are not considered arable. Infertile areas underlain by highly siliceous rock begin about 30 miles from the coast and extend several hundred miles to the southern boundaries with the Rio Negro Basin of the Amazon region in Brazil. This vast hinterland is practically unused except for sparse grazing on the southern Savannahs (Simonson, 1958).

The low-lying soils of Guyana and neighboring Surinam have been renewed in recent times by alluvium. Clay content and base saturation are moderate. Some salinity from the sea maintains a soil structure suitable for rice and sugar cane cultivation without excessive demands for heavy plowing. The population of about 650,000 is restricted almost entirely to this low-lying, coastal land, with practically no encroachment on the vacant backcountry. Guyana is a large exporter of food. An increase in population will decrease its means of livelihood from the land.

TECHNOLOGY AND THE LAND

What can technology do about the vacant lands? The answer is much—*an academic much*. The first essential—nutrients—can be supplied, in theory, but usually at the cost of haulage of immense tonnages from great distances and often by impractical import from other nations. But nutrients are not enough for a crop. Soils and their use must be *understood*. Plants, particularly in the tropics, need protection from insects and disease. Transport, machines, improved seed, credit, and many other things are required. In short, *maintenance of the soil* and *organization of technology* are as important as the technology itself. Lacking technology and even the rudiments of fertility, the vacant lands remain vacant except for sparse self-subsistent populations. Barriers against technological progress are high, and the most optimistic hopes cannot meet short-term needs. Even the middle-term outlook is questionable.

So famine is a continued certainty for the hot countries. Some can be named—Haiti, India, Egypt, and many others that might better heed Malthus than Hymen. The "advanced" countries—themselves backward in the matter of population control—can still gain time through technology and give some help to the technologically "backward" ones.

What about technologically advanced countries—the United States and others? Greater productivity of land now in use is their immediate source of new food (Table 4.5). The pressures are not so great as to force unprofitable haste in raising productivity except to help in feeding the hungry nations. Changing patterns of food use, by shifting from animal products to direct consumption of pulses and grains, can prolong the middle term—to a dimly forseen century hence. This possibility is not open in the tropics, for animal products have always been secondary in volume there.

In the United States all the many technological factors come into play when productivity is to be raised. The main quantity requirements beyond land itself are water and fertilizer (Table 4.6), i.e., the supply of plant nutrients. Both can be increased with favorable return under existing economic conditions, either directly or by subsidy if the economy cannot otherwise remain balanced.

Fertilizers are made from nonrenewable materials. The manufacturing technology involved is not complex but does depend heavily on energy sources for nitrogen fixation and, eventually, for phosphate treatment. Mining and transport are important. The tonnages distributed are large and involve global trade. Supplies of the raw materials—potassium compounds, sulfur and sulfates, phosphate rock, limestone, natural gas or coal, and air (for nitrogen)—are adequate and would be at present or moderately increased rates of use even beyond the middle term. Increased fertilizer costs, however,

TABLE 4.5
Indexes referred to 1950–1952 production in yield per acre for several crops in the United States during the period 1950–1964.

Years	Wheat	Rice	Corn	Cotton	Soybeans
1950–1952 Production	17.0 bu	2,360 lb	39.0 bu	273 lb, lint	20.9 bu
Index	1.00	1.00	1.00	1.00	1.00
1953–1955	1.08	1.13	1.04	1.32	0.93
1956–1958	1.36	1.34	1.27	1.54	1.10
1959–1961	1.41	1.44	1.44	1.64	1.15
1962–1964	1.50	1.66	1.66	1.83	1.15
Maximum attained	12.2	4.00	7.8	7.3	4.5

Source: U.S. Department of Agriculture, 1966. Maximum attained—calculated from diverse sources.

TABLE 4.6

Indexes referred to 1950–1952 fertilizer consumption in the
United States[a] during the period 1950–1964.

	Nitrogen	Phosphate	Potash
1950–1952 Consumption (in tons)	1,420,000	2,190,000	1,560,000
Index	1.00	1.00	1.00
1953–1955	1.33	1.13	1.19
1956–1958	1.66	1.09	1.30
1959–1961	2.15	1.23	1.42
1962–1964	3.02	1.52	1.72

Source: U.S. Department of Agriculture, 1966.
[a] Hawaii, Alaska, and Puerto Rico included.

would come quickly if the manyfold greater needs of the underdeveloped areas were to be met. Only the richest and best situated deposits of raw materials are now competitive. Fertilizer input, while vital to the result, is only a small part of the crop cost at this time. A severalfold increase in cost could be tolerated.

Water is one of the several basic supports of agriculture. Most of it is evaporated by the sun and wind, thereby cooling the plants. The demands for water are clearly evident in desert regions, where it is the first requirement. This is no less the case for maximum productivity in well watered regions when droughts come. Inadequate water, even for a few days, sharply curtails yield. The gaining of high productivity—a doubling of the average yield—is predicated on a means of supplying water during the random droughts. This is now practiced for crops of high value per acre—vegetables on Long Island, for example—but seldom for the staple ones. It can give good returns for a reasonable increment of costs. Sources of the water are near at hand for many humid regions. Distribution of water for occasional use is the real question—a solvable problem, but at a cost, much like rural electrification and telephone service. The flower bed in the city seldom wants for water though the crops on nearby farms are wilting.

Water for irrigation in dry and desert regions is quite another matter. Here the source becomes important. Even with complete gathering, all the water of many regions would not be enough to supply the potentially arable land—for example, in Spain, Israel, Central China, and the Colorado Basin of North America. The Salt River Valley of Arizona has a water deficit of more than 2 million acre-feet per year. Additional sources must be sought. For some regions with adequate technology and near the sea, atomic power for multistage distillation now is approaching possibility (Weinberg and Young, 1967)—a phase in which the costs can be paid by valuable crops, and associated industry can absorb the power output. For other regions, transport from sources at great distances is entirely feasible if we wish to make the effort and pay the price—from Alaska or Canada to Arizona, for example, or from Siberia to the Don River and The Steppes. But ample lead time is needed from the inception of plans to the supply of food in the market place.

As population pressure increases, we become increasingly aware that productive land is beyond value. The gain of an acre at fifty or more times its annual product value can be quite feasible where amortization of the initial cost is over centuries. The Insel-meer operation in the Netherlands is highly economical, even though the dikes might break in unusual storms, as they did on Walcheren Island.

Enough water now falls on North America to supply all its needs (Figure 4.2). Growing populations will not change this fact. We are slow, however, in realizing our charge, slow in coming to grasp with planning for the best use of all river basins. Political controversy, reflected in political inaction, exists where action is needed, as for the Delaware, the Colorado, the Arkansas, and the Potomac. In contrast, the Sabine, the Yazoo, the Tombigbee, the Chatahoochee, and the Savannah are not even mentioned when planning is considered, although they could water much of the coastal plain— enough to multiply its productivity severalfold.

As technology is put to wider use and population pressure increases, greater productivity can also come from intensive use of lands. Emphasis

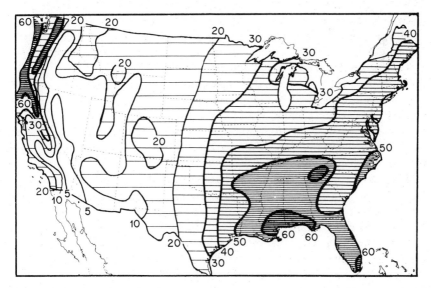

FIGURE 4.2
Annual precipitation in the United States in inches of rain equivalent.

can change from maximum output per man, as now practiced in the United States, to maximum output per acre. This is the pattern in the Ukraine, in Belgium, in Japan, and in Java. The waste in use of land in Kansas would be intolerable in Java.

More land can be cropped—land now grazed or in forests in the less populated advanced countries such as the United States (Figure 4.3 and 4.4). With necessity, ingenuity, and suitable regional plans, areas can be claimed from the deserts and swamps. This pattern can be seen in the most densely populated regions (e.g., the low countries of Europe) and in primitive ones. The Ifagao people in northern Luzon terraced steep forest slopes to gain security. The Fen district of England was once a swamp, no more promising than the Dismal Swamp and others in our Coastal Plains.

GRASSLANDS AND FORESTS

Grasslands and open bush, used as grazing and browsing areas for wild animals, are deeply interwoven with the developments of man. These are areas from which populations condensed as civilization came and into which expansion took place as the need arose for more arable land. This reserve is now practically gone. Present grazing lands are generally less watered, steeper, at higher elevation, or more stony than the arable ones. Most are sparsely inhabited, and many are still roamed by nomads with their flocks, as in Central Asia, or by sheep herds, as in our western mountains. They play an important part in the animal component of food production.

Grazing areas are apt to remain rather constant, gaining from forests and losing somewhat to cultivation. Fertilizers can help animal productivity on many grazing areas, but water or some other factor is apt to be limiting. Management to prevent overgrazing, control of bush, and animal care and breeding are more likely first factors in production. Range plants, too, can be improved.

Grasslands are subject to degradation through unintelligent use by man much as are arable lands. They suffer erosion by wind (the Great Plains, Gobi) and invasion by bush (Western Texas, Mexico) or degradation to desert (Utah, Southwest Africa). Water, too, in infrequent storms on an open landscape, can be a very severe erosional force. But man, himself, has been the greatest enemy of the land. Shantz and Turner (1958) remark:

> In the grazing areas of South Africa, white settlers have transformed grasslands into bushlands and semi-desert: so complete and widespread has this grassland deterioration become that serious controversy has arisen as to whether the alarming changes have been due to excess grazing pressure. . . . Native population has increased greatly . . . this increase has placed a great strain on the more produc-

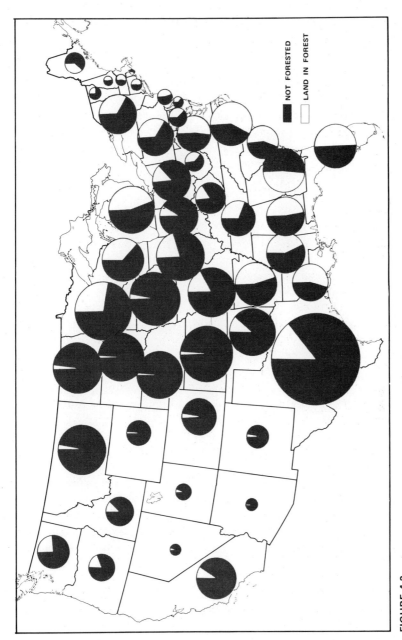

FIGURE 4.3
Proportion of cultivatable land (Classes I–IV) in the United States now in forest. (After Wadleigh and Klingebiel, 1966.)

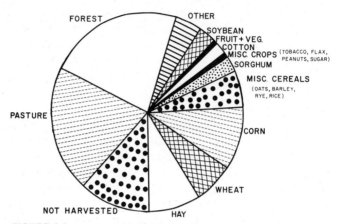

FIGURE 4.4
Use of privately owned land in Classes I–IV
in the United States in 1959.
(After Wadleigh and Klingebiel, 1966.)

tive lands and in many instances the native has had to extend his cultivation into distinctly submarginal areas.

Shantz and Turner (1958) further comment about African development in a broader sense:

> European civilization with its knowledge of medicine, agriculture, urban develop-ments, etc., has induced changes which have increased native populations to such a degree that severe pressures have been brought to bear upon a land that was already heavily taxed with production and food demands.

The value of grazing lands is that the harvesting is done by herbivores, which are able to use plants that are otherwise wasted to man. These herbi-vores, or cellulose utilizers, supply about a fourth of the protein need of man. The concern here is with the animal component of nutrition in terms of the use made of land. Animals are one step further along a food chain from plants to man—representing a factor of eight away from the plant. When population pressure is high, they are of value because of their protein quality and their use of potential food materials that otherwise would be wasted. Goats and deer can browse, and swine can forage for almost any waste. Where luxury exists, grains are efficiently converted by chickens and by swine, although for greatest efficiency, an animal protein input is also used with chicken feeds. The land animal, however, is surely a diminishing factor in food consumption per person in advanced countries, even though the grazing lands are improved and are still being grazed.

Proteins, however obtained, must amount to no less than about 36 grams of *high-quality* protein per day for adults if proper nutrition is to be maintained, or 57 grams of *total* protein, including about two-thirds from vegetable materials, chiefly grains and pulses—the difference between the Philippines and India in Table 4.1 is in the quality of the protein. The plant fraction can be increased, particularly if the quality of grain is changed by breeding and amino acid additions. Both are practical, and both are advocated and pursued.

Even where total food is adequate in amount, the nutritional needs can best be met by intelligent use of existing supplies rather than by greater pressure for more food, for more land, or for better use of land.

Forest lands are like the grasslands in being a component of the total land area subject to some encroachment for food production. This is equally true for the humid tropics, the middle latitudes, and the northern zones. In Java, the teak forests on the lower mountain slopes (see Figure 4.1) are an essential part of the economy. The Philippines export mahogany and veneer logs. In the Pacific Northwest, continued tree cropping is under way, as practiced in Europe, although harvesting of old growth is now the basis of the economy. In Borneo and Amazonia, a more difficult but probably not impossible situation exists with respect to use of forests in the economy. Diversity in kinds of trees in the forest hinders use, however.

Use of wood, and thereby of forest land, is more open to simple innovation than is production of food. The per capita consumption of timber products in the United States has been essentially constant for 30 years though changing in the relative sizes of its components of lumber, plywood, and pulp (U.S. Department of Agriculture, 1965). A forest-product economy based chiefly on pulp and reworked fiber as wood products is realizable. Construction materials, however, continue to be modified toward increase in mineral products. Cellulose from wood, cotton, hemp, henequen, flax, and other plants diminishes in competition with synthetic fibers based on hydrocarbon resources. These changes release land for food production. Such innovation though is not apt to shift significantly the ratio of forest to other land uses, for this is determined more by the nature of the land than the needs of man.

INNOVATION

Innovation of various kinds can enhance the supply and the quality of food. Synthetic amino acids—lysine, methionine, and threonine made from abundant raw materials—can provide protein supplement to grains. Fermentation products, while long used, still undergo much change. Monotonous diets, where meat and dairy products are excluded or impractical, are augmented by fermentation-induced flavors. Contents of riboflavin and niacin or other vitamins can be increased. Also, food that otherwise might be lost can often be preserved by fermentation. Many fermented products are now eaten: sauerkraut, tempeh, ragi, sufu, shoyu, ang-kak, tea fungus, and mizo.

In addition to increasing the productivity and quantity of cultivated land, innovation now appears to offer a faint glimmer of hope by the production of protein (or amino acids) and fats. One possible advance might be bacterial conversion of petroleum products for human consumption, which, however, depends on a wasting nonrenewable resource (see Chapter 8). Also, yeast (torula) growing on vegetable wastes can supply a limited amount of nutritious food supplement for man. Urea is now widely used in the United States as a nitrogen supplement for ruminants. In the end, it affords another method for making proteins from nonproteinaceous materials.

Water distillation by nuclear energy is a recent innovation. Nuclear energy, though, is likely to have its greatest influence on the more conventional uses of power with respect to land. Solar heaters and the use of solar energy are applicable in some places, even as water power has been developed.

More telling innovations than these are continued plant breeding and the use of synthetic chemicals for control of such pests as weeds and insects. The impact of these innovations is already great throughout agriculture (Table 4.7). They enhance productivity of land and thereby mitigate population pressure on the land. They can be distributed to even the most distant farmer.

Innovation in fertilizer production also is very effective (Table 4.7). It is reflected in a continued decrease in the production costs of nitrogenous

TABLE 4.7
Effects of plant breeding (hybrids), management improvement, and use of fertilizer on maize (corn) production in the United States, 1933–1963.

Year	Acres harvested (millions)	Production (millions of bushels)	Yield (bushels per acre)	Percent in hybrids	Plant food[a] used (1,000 tons)
1933	106	2,400	22.6	0.1	
1938	92	2,550	27.7	14.9	
1943	92	2,970	32.2	52.4	28
1948	84	3,600	42.5	76.0	
1953	80	3,210	39.9	86.5	294
1958	64	3,360	52.8	93.9	
1963	60	4,100	67.6	95.0+	821

Source: U.S. Department of Agriculture, 1966.
[a] In Illinois.

materials with increase in the size of the synthetic unit. It is displayed in the discovery of new sources of fertilizer components and in the beneficiation of poor sources. These innovations have delayed man's excessive pressures on plant nutrient supplies in North America for a long time to come—the so-called foreseeable future.

POLLUTION

Agriculture, grazing, and forestry are surely first elements in the use of land. The need for food and fiber, however, can be matched with other requirements. Man is concerned about fouling of the environment with his wastes, for reasons of both health and aesthetics. Sewage, garbage, mining, and industrial wastes are difficult to deal with, but they need not, and in fact do not, encroach seriously on land resources. The first Japanese emissaries to the United States, in 1868, were appalled by the unkempt country between Washington and Baltimore. It is still unkempt compared with the region near Tokyo. The "honey bucket," which has now disappeared from Tokyo, is matched by the garbage scow on the East River. Pigs are kept near the heart of Manila; they are only slightly less removed from the heart of New York. A difference is that the garbage is boiled for the New York pigs.

The streams of central Java, with its population density of three persons per acre, afford fish for the diet. Though malaria is often endemic, the country is beautiful beyond description. Bali still serves as the aesthetic ideal of many dreams—nor is reality there so bad except for an insufficient quantity of food and the occasional volcanic eruption.

Most forms of pollution, though shameful and unnecessary, are fleeting compared to other adverse variables. They can be handled when pressure demands that something be done. Even solid wastes and stripped and dredged areas present no unsolvable problems of refill and leveling, with trapping of drainage waters where necessary. They are the accompaniment of a technology that is more than adequate to handle them, provided there is a will or a demand expressed by laws. Attention to pollution should never be relaxed, however, for pollution is cheaper to handle by increments than by crash programs, cheaper to correct in its early stages than after serious conditions arise and have irreversible effects.

Pollution of the environment from agricultural sources is of serious current concern in the highly developed countries. Particular attention is focused on insecticides and other toxicants as well as on animal wastes. Closer controls are needed. To accomplish these controls is a test of a society's capacity to avoid despoiling the environment. More attention must be given to methods of biological control of pests, and to the problems of making pesticides biodegradable, more pest-specific, and less toxic to man. Pesticides are one of the most effective innovations of our time. Without pesticides, the future of food production in the tropics would be most unpromising. To use them correctly in controlling a pest without undue contamination of the environment is not an insuperable problem but demands constant vigilance.

Sewage, man's main aquatic contaminant, is more effectively returned to agricultural use in the Orient than in the industrialized West. The difficulty is that sewage is a very dilute source of plant nutrients and contains agents deleterious to man. It cannot compete with more concentrated materials as a real factor in agriculture. Farms, however, can be used as parts of sewage disposal systems or places for animal wastes where the need and cost for such disposal is part of the system.

THE FUTURE

"If you can look into the seeds of time and say which grain
will grow and which will not, speak then to me."
—Macbeth, Act I, Scene III

The major fact about man and land is that the best land resources are now occupied, and all resources are known to some degree. No hidden paradise is to be found beneath the sea or in some remote niche of the earth. Aesthetically pleasing places can be spoiled. Worldwide increased productivity of food to keep pace with growing populations is the goal. The immediate pressures in the underdeveloped countries may be met by a better mix of agriculture and industry. But the danger signals are up with respect to excess population demands for food supply as much as for other resources. It is folly to ignore them.

Four extreme types of regions are recognized in regard to food and land:

1. highly developed with adequate land and technology to increase food production severalfold—the United States and the Union of Soviet Socialist Republics;
2. malthusian within their boundaries, but highly developed and drawing on external sources for food at an increasing rate—England and Japan;
3. poorly developed, but with extensive land resources—Argentina and the Philippines;
4. malthusian within their boundaries and poorly developed—Indonesia and Haiti.

Countries in the fourth group are in immediate want of food, as are some nations intermediate between the second and fourth—for instance, India,

Spain, and perhaps China. The intermediate group matches increasing demand and necessary production only with difficulty. Access to new land by countries in this group is low, but improved technology and social reorganization offer hope. Such nations can be aided by the highly developed countries, but the Malthusian limit is clearly evident.

Some time can be begged even for the fourth group at the Malthusian limit by just a little technology, in the form of plant selection and pest control. It is here that the Rockefeller and Ford Foundations are acting so effectively, as in their program for Mexico (Table 4.8) and in the work of the International Rice Research Institute (Rockefeller Foundation, 1967) in the Orient.

By how much can world food production be increased before the pinch is hopeless? The average annual productivity of organic matter on fertile lands of all regions gives a sort of upper limit (Westlake, 1963). If this is taken (optimistically) as 3 tons/acre/year, the total production is 100 billion tons per year—or about 30 tons per person for the present world population. Not more than a fourth of the organic matter can be considered as possible human food, including that derived from animals. This 7 tons of primary production is about 16 times the present food requirements of a person; but it is of more academic than practical interest.

The facts warrant neither optimism nor pessimism about considerable eventual increase in food production. Whether all men can have enough food depends on what man does about both food and population. The question of food production, however, involves fewer intangibles (Figure 4.5) than does an estimate of the future course of world population (see Chapter 3). Information for an answer is extensive and many estimates have been made for components of the food supply. We adhere to a "rule of two" for food increases in the world; twofold by new lands, twofold by increased productivity, and twofold by innovation. The new lands will be of lower quality than those now used, which will make it difficult to double

TABLE 4.8
The impact of the cooperative program of the Rockefeller Foundation and the Mexican Government on wheat production in Mexico.

Year	Area (1,000 hectares)	Yield (kg/hectare)	Production 1,000 metric tons	Factor
1945	500	750	330	1.0
1950	625	900	600	1.8
1955	790	1,100	850	2.4
1960	840	1,417	1,200	3.6
1964	846	2,600	2,200	6.7

Source: Borland, 1965.

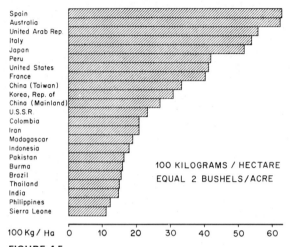

FIGURE 4.5
Comparative rice yields per hectare, 1961–1963 average.
(After United Nations, 1966.)

their productivity relative to the present farmland. Productivity can be increased almost everywhere, however, by better use of fertilizers. The final twofold factor of innovation would be impressed on the other two— a doubling from four to eight. This would have to come in part from *great changes in food habits toward use of the primary grains for human consumption.*

While the total factor of eight is possible for the United States, it would impose severe demands on rational use of water. Other nations will have to struggle to obtain even a twofold increase, being limited by fertilizer supply in inadequate economies. Perhaps one or another of the twofold factors is somewhat wide of the mark, but neither so high as to dismiss the original question for the coming century nor so low as to cause immediate despair.

References

Borland, N. E. 1965. Wheat, rust and people. *Phytopathology* 55: 1088–1098.
Burnet, M. 1966. *Ecology and the appreciation of life.* The Boyer Lectures, 1966. Australian Broadcasting Commission. Sydney: Ambassador Press.
Dames, T. W. G. 1955. The soils of East Central Java. *Balai Resar Penjl.*, no. 141, Bogor Djan.

Maher, C. 1949. Study of the farming systems in their relation to soil conservation. *Agricola du Congo Belgique Bull.* 40: 1543–1548.

Mohr, E. C. J. 1944. *The soils of equatorial regions with special reference to the Netherland East Indies.* Ann Arbor, Mich.: Edward Bros.

Nye, P. H., and D. J. Greenland. 1960. *The soil under shifting cultivation.* Commonwealth Agr. Bur. Burnham Royal England, Tech. Comm. no. 51.

Rockefeller Foundation. 1967. *Toward the conquest of hunger.* Progress report, program in the agricultural sciences, 1965–66. New York.

Schultz, T. W. 1966. Increasing world food supplies—the economic requirements. *Proc. Natl. Acad. Sci. U.S.* 56: 322–327.

Shantz, H. L., and B. L. Turner. 1958. *Vegetational changes in Africa.* Univ. of Arizona, College of Agriculture, Report no. 169.

Simonson, C. S. 1958. *Reconnaissance soil survey of the coastal plain of British Guiana.* College Park: Univ. of Maryland.

Underwood, E. J. 1967. Man, land, and food. *Australian J. Sci.* 29(11): 395–401.

United Nations. 1966. *The state of food and agriculture, 1966.* Report by Food and Agriculture Organization of the United Nations. Rome.

U.S. Department of Agriculture. 1965. *Timber trends in the United States.* Forest Resource Report no. 17. Washington, D.C.

U.S. Department of Agriculture. 1966. *Agricultural statistics.* Washington, D.C.

U.S. President's Science Advisory Committee. 1967. *The world food problem.* Report of the Panel on the World Food Supply, vol. 2. Washington, D.C.

Wadleigh, C. H., and A. A. Klingebiel. 1966. An inventory of land and water resources. *Am. Soc. Agron. Special Pub.* no. 7, pp. 1–23.

Weinberg, A. M., and G. Young. 1967. The nuclear revolution—1966. *Proc. Natl. Acad. Sci. U.S.* 57: 1–15.

Westlake, D. F. 1963. Comparison of plant productivity. *Biol. Rev.* 38(3): 385–425.

5/Food from the Sea

William E. Ricker

"They who plough the sea do not carry
the winds in their hands."
—Publilius Syrus, ca. 42 B.C.

Food supplies can certainly be increased by more intensive development of the world's fisheries. The question is, by how much? And will these supplies suffice, when land and sea products are taken together, to feed the world's growing billions? In this chapter we discuss organic production from the sea, the recent and potential growth of world fisheries, and the possibilities for increasing recovery of food from the sea.

We find that, contrary to wide belief, the quantities of food available from the sea are not "unlimited." Food production from the sea can probably be increased to not much more than about 2.5 times that being produced in 1968—an eventual total of perhaps 150–160 million metric tons annually of fish that contains about 20 percent of usable high-quality protein. The sea, therefore, can be said to be an excellent supplemental source of proteins, but it is an unimpressive source of calories. If the estimated attainable production of food from the sea could be achieved by the year 2000, it would suffice to supply about 30 percent of the world's *minimal* protein requirement for the population then expected (see Chapter 3), but only a little over 3 percent of its biological energy requirements.

Typescript received September 1967. Final revision, June 1968.

ORGANIC PRODUCTION FROM THE SEA

Primary Production

The area of the world's oceans is about 361 million square kilometers, of which 40 million comprise the more-or-less-separate neighboring seas (Bering, Japan, Black, Mediterranean, Red, Caribbean, and others). Biological production[1] in the ocean is almost as varied as on land, including areas of both high and low productivity. In general, clear blue water indicates a low density of plant plankton and small production per unit volume. However, there are compensating factors. Clearness of the water means that the zone of photosynthesis extends much deeper, and hence the production per unit of surface *area* is not so small as might be expected offhand. In addition, tropical waters, which are often clear, tend to have a more rapid turnover of the plankton because of higher temperatures. Nevertheless, direct measurements do show that annual primary production per unit area tends to be greater in cool-temperate waters than in tropical waters. Figure 5.1 shows this for the Pacific Ocean in terms of amount of carbon fixed per unit of surface area per day and per year.

On land, lack of water is often the factor that controls vegetation, but in the lighted regions of the ocean, mineral nutrients are usually the limiting factor—that is, substances other than water and carbon dioxide. Regions of large production occur in cool-temperate latitudes, as well as in the tropic seas, wherever there is upwelling of deep water that contains abundant mineral nutrients. By measuring rates of photosynthesis at a series of depths at stations scattered over the oceans, a number of estimates of net plant production have been made. The most recent is 13 billion (10^9) metric tons of carbon fixed per year (Koblenz-Mishke, 1965), or about 130 billion metric tons of organic matter; possible limits of error are given as plus or minus 50 percent. Koblenz-Mishke's figure is in the same range as an earlier estimate based on a much smaller body of data—12–15 billion metric tons of carbon per year (Steemann-Nielsen and Jensen, 1957).

One hundred and thirty billion metric tons of plant production per year is a very large quantity, but, of course, nothing like this amount of material is on hand at any one time. The plants die or are eaten, decompose, and

---

[1] *Production* is defined here as the quantity of organic matter (of a particular type) evolved during the course of a year, regardless of whether it survives in that form to the end of the year. Production can be measured in material units (wet or dry weight, weight of carbon or other elements) or in energy units. Primary production involves conversion of carbon, from the carbon dioxide and carbonates dissolved in the water, into organic substances. The organic material produced is usually measured in terms of the element carbon. For our purposes a good enough conversion is that 1 gram of carbon is equivalent to 10 grams wet weight of organic substance (typically animal protein; plants are more variable in water content).

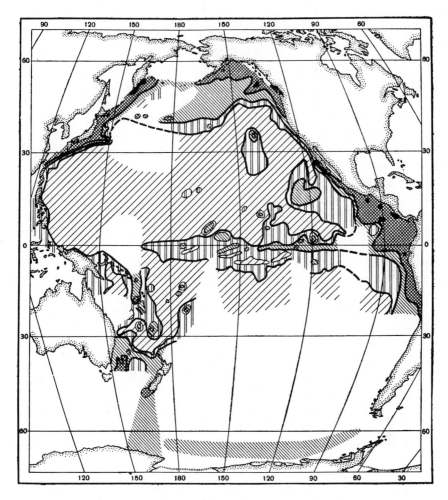

In the total water column

Milligrams of carbon fixed per day per square meter		Grams of carbon fixed per year per square meter
100	///	36
100 - 150	|||	36 - 55
150 - 250	///	55 - 91
250 - 650	▓	91 - 237
650+	■	237+

FIGURE 5.1
Gross primary production per unit area in the Pacific Ocean. Net production of plant material is about 60% of the figures shown. (From Koblenz-Mishke, 1965, Figure 2.)

become "mineralized," either directly or by a circuitous route, and the minerals released are then available for a new cycle of production. Thus some of the same actual atoms take part in production many times over during the course of a year. Bogorov (1967) estimates the average standing crop of phytoplankton in the world ocean as 1.5 billion tons wet weight, not much more than 1 percent of the annual production. This makes a striking contrast to the situation on land: the quantity of terrestrial vegetation in sight at a particular time may be of the same order of size as the annual production (grasslands and crops), or it may be many times as large (forests and shrubby deserts).

Can we look forward to harvesting plant plankton directly? The above estimate of the standing crop amounts to 4 tons per square kilometer. If it were all present in the top 10 meters, the average density of material would be less than half a gram per cubic meter. Up to 100 times this concentration of plants can occur in fertile areas at certain times, but even so, the expense of filtering or centrifuging it from the water makes its recovery uneconomical. Nor is the raw material obtained a particularly good one. Plankton flavors are not attractive, the high salt content is undesirable, and some of the dominant species have siliceous skeletons that present a serious problem in processing. Furthermore, if plant materials were to be removed from water on a large scale as quickly as they are produced, the surface water in most regions would soon become depleted of its mineral nutrients, in the same way as soils can be, and fertilizers would be required just as in agriculture. For all these reasons, direct harvesting of plant plankton has no promise as a major source of food or fodder.

Food Products from the Waters

In contrast to phytoplankton, many seaweeds and other large aquatic plants are useful raw materials; although some of the large algae are built from pentosans (5-carbon carbohydrates) and so are not easily digested by most mammals. A few seaweeds, though, can be eaten directly; in fact some are cultivated for table use in Japan. Large kelps are also processed into a variety of products, some of them edible.

Unfortunately, as most large seaweeds are attached to the bottom, they live only in rather shallow water. Hence the total food obtainable from this source is not great. The world's seaweed harvest for all purposes is now about 700,000 tons a year. It can probably be increased severalfold but will still make only very small contributions to human food supplies.

Like the sea plants, the herbivorous animals in the water are not a really large resource directly usable by man—though their contribution is not insignificant. Oysters, clams, and mussels filter plankton from the water and include a good deal of primary plant material in their food. There are also surface grazers like abalones and some fish (the ayu, for example). More important are the tropical anchovies that use a lot of plant plankton in their diet, notably the Peruvian anchoveta. The milkfish of tropical brackish waters consume filamentous algae and are extensively reared in ponds. In freshwaters the Asian silver carp and bighead consume plant plankton. Some useful animals browse on the large aquatic plants—the Chinese grass carp, some of the large turtles of warm seas, various ducks, geese, and other birds, and, among mammals, the manatees. It is also true that many of the mainly carnivorous fishes, such as the carp, various sunfishes, and the rainbow trout, eat a certain quantity of plant food.

Other examples could be added, but only about a fifth (by total weight) of animals being harvested from the water feed mainly on plant materials. On land, all the major sources of animal protein get most of their nourishment from vegetable sources. Thus, in order to assess the potential yield of the world's aquatic pastures, we must consider the several steps in the food chains that lead to the dominant useful animals—principally fishes.

The Food Pyramid—Consumption, Production, and Recycling

What are the quantitative aspects of the production processes of consumers? The usual representation of a food chain is in the form of a pyramid, such as is shown in Figure 5.2. For converting plant material into animal tissue there are two general routes. The plants can either be consumed, alive or dead, by animals, and so move directly up the pyramid; or they may first be decomposed by bacteria, followed by consumption of the bacteria by animals. The latter, indirect, route is often referred to as *recycling*—as indicated on the right side of the figure. Although recycling gets part of the dead plant material back into the line of ascent to large animals, it cannot do this very efficiently. The bacteria are typically much smaller than the plant plankters they decompose, so it is likely that there are, on the average, about two stages on the route from dead plankton algae back to an animal more or less the same size of the alga, with corresponding energy losses as described below. Bacterial recycling can, of course, also involve dead animal material, from any level of the pyramid.

When an organism serves as food for another organism, there is a loss of matter and energy in the process. Each such transformation is characterized by a certain *transfer efficiency*, defined as the percentage of the prey's annual production that is incorporated into the body tissues of the consumer species. This, in turn, is compounded of two processes characterized by separate coefficients:

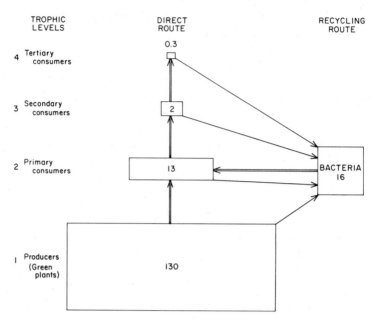

FIGURE 5.2
Simplified aquatic food pyramid, illustrating direct and "recycling" routes
for conversion of plant material into animal tissue. Areas of the rectangles
are proportioned to the estimated production (*not* the standing crop) of
material at each trophic level; production figures are in billions of metric
tons of organic matter per year.

E, the *ecotrophic coefficient*—the fraction of a prey species' annual
production that is consumed by predators (trophic referring to
nutritive or food levels);

K, the *growth coefficient*—the predators' annual increment of weight
divided by the quantity of food they have consumed (= gross growth
efficiency of Conover, 1964).

The growth coefficient, *K,* has been measured for a variety of animals, but
nearly always under experimental conditions. Ivlev (1945) found that it
reaches a maximum of 35% for well-fed specimens of fish and the larger
bottom animals (worms, molluscs, arthropods); then it declines continuously
as they grow older, reaching 10%, 5%, or even less.

For our purposes, laboratory observations on *K* are not very illuminating
except as maximum values, because so much depends on the abundance of
food available to the consumer (short rations mean little food available
above energy requirements, hence a small *K*). Among studies in nature,
Kevern (1966) estimated *K* = 8% for yearling carp in a lake where they fed
mainly on algae and detritus. This seems to be the only available estimate for
a wild fish, but, since these carp grew rather slowly, the *K* value is probably

below average. Among plankters, Lasker (1966) estimated an average K of 9% for a euphausid in the northeastern Pacific and higher values in cultures. In the Black Sea, Petipa (1967) obtained K values in nature that averaged about 15% for different life stages of one copepod, and 25% for another; while Pavlova (1967) obtained values from 12% to 16% for adults of three cladocerans and 40% for the young. In freshwater, Richman (1958) obtained values from 4% to 17% for *Daphnia* fed on algae in the laboratory. All these figures apply to the warm growing season, whereas winter conditions are certain to be less favorable. Taking this into account, an over-all average growth coefficient for plant eaters could scarcely exceed $K = 15\%$. For fish and other animals that eat animal food, the average growth coefficient is likely to be somewhat higher, say $K = 20\%$. This is particularly likely to be the case among exploited stocks in which the average age has been reduced by continuous cropping.

Information about the ecotrophic coefficient, E, is even harder to come by, but it is also less critical. If *all* consumers of a given food base be considered, including bacteria that "feed" on dead bodies or even on organic matter that goes into solution after death, then the ecotrophic coefficient must be large—approaching 100%. If we consider only larger organisms on the direct route up to a product useful to man, the percentage consumed is considerably lower. In aquaria or tanks the grazing of algal cultures by small animals is sometimes efficient enough to keep down the number of algae present in spite of rapid reproduction. In other aquaria, algae will bloom expansively in spite of various grazers and eventually die and decay, to the annoyance of the owners. Both situations have also been observed in lakes and in the sea, but what the average picture may be is not yet clear. The larger measured values for photosynthesis may come, at least in part, from regions or times in which plants are *not* being consumed very effectively and so have accumulated a large biomass.

Considering average figures for the whole "level" of marine *primary consumers* (excluding bacteria), the figure 80% would likely be a top value for the ecotrophic coefficient E, or it might be as low as 30%. Perhaps 55% could serve as a mean. The other 45% would for the most part be "consumed" by bacteria and converted into cells comparable in size to the smallest green plant plankters. Let us assume they do this with 25% efficiency, so that the above mean grazing figure of 55% would be augmented by $45\% \times 25\% = 11\%$ for a total $55\% + 11\% = 66\%$.

The most typical *secondary consumers* in the sea are pelagic fishes, such as herring, sardines, and the midwater lanternfishes, that eat mainly animal plankton. E-values up to 80% or 90% would seem possible from the collective efforts of pelagic fishes, if they alone did the harvesting. However, there are invertebrate competitors such as jellyfish and the Portuguese man-of-war; and, in shallow water, there are such things as anemones, corals, and barnacles, which are "dead-end" products from man's point of view—not directly useful and largely inedible or unavailable to useful fishes. These competitors reduce the percentage consumption of plankton by fish, so that the average E-value could scarcely be more than 70%. The adjustment for bacterial recycling is here $30\% \times 20\% \times 70\% = 4\%$, so that the total is $70\% + 4\% = 74\%$ or, say, 75%. The same percentage can serve for higher consumer levels.

The estimates developed above can be summarized as follows:

	Growth coefficient K	Ecotrophic coefficient (with recycling adjustment) E
Primary consumption (grazing on green plants)	15%	66%
Higher consumption levels	20%	75%

What then are some average values of the product KE, the over-all transfer efficiency of production from one trophic level to the next? From the figures above we get average values of roughly 10% (15% of 66%) for the primary consumer stage and 15% (20% of 75%) for subsequent stages, both figures including the necessary "recycling" adjustment. The combination gives $10\% \times 15\% = 1.5\%$ as the two-stage transfer efficiency for the combined process. This means that about 1.5% of 130 billion, or 2,000 million tons, of organic matter, largely protein, are produced at the level of secondary consumers (trophic level 3 in Figure 5.2). Transfer upward to level 4 reduces the figure to 300 million tons; and at the next level above (the largest marine predators), which we designate as level 5, it is about 45 million tons. These results are summarized in Table 5.1.

Trophic Levels and Ecological Levels

A distinction must be made between *trophic levels* (successive steps on a food pyramid) and *ecological levels* (groups of animals of generally similar size and habitat). The four major pelagic ecological levels shown in Figure

TABLE 5.1
Estimated productivities at different trophic levels, in millions of metric tons.

Primary production	130,000
Trophic level 2	13,000
Trophic level 3	2,000
Trophic level 4	300
Trophic level 5	45

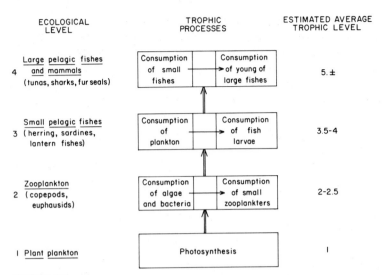

FIGURE 5.3
Diagram illustrating the relation of ecological levels to trophic levels in the
pelagic environment (not to scale). "Cannibalism" (indicated by the
horizontal arrow) within each ecological level increases the average distance
of the members of that level from the primary plant food. For simplicity, the
bacterial "recycling" shown in Figure 5.2 has been omitted here.

5.3 have sometimes been treated as trophic levels. It is certain, however,
that this tends to underestimate the true trophic position of the various
ecological categories (quite apart from incomplete consumption and recycling). As indicated in Figure 5.3 there is much within-level predation,
which decreases the net biomass produced by any ecological level; that is,
it raises the average position of its members on the food pyramid. At
ecological level 2, for example, intralevel consumption is essential in order to
convert an important block of primary production by the tiny nanno-
plankton, as well as the recycled bacteria, up to a size that can be utilized
by the larger copepods and euphausids. Thus the trophic position of the
successive ecological levels, as indicated in the right-hand column of Figure
5.3, becomes cumulatively higher than their ecological rank shown at the
left.[2] A comparable analysis of bottom-dwelling organisms indicates similar
relationships.

Fish and other products captured by man are only to a minor extent on
ecological level 2 (most molluscs and a few species of fish). To a major
extent they are on ecological level 3 (many flounders, haddock, small cod,
herring, sardines, shrimps, whalebone whales), while some of the preferred
species are on ecological level 4 (halibut, tunas, most salmon, large cod,

---

[2] A compensating factor at ecological level 4 is that many of the large pelagic fishes (tunas,
for example) consume quite a lot of zooplankton, that is, they partly bypass ecological level 3.
But for this, the estimated trophic level for this group would be greater than 5.

swordfish, seals, sperm whales). The "average" edible product harvested would be between ecological levels 3 and 4, probably closer to 3. But because of the "cannibalism" within the ecological groups, the average *trophic* position of man's harvest is likely close to trophic level 4.

At trophic level 4, the world production suggested in Figure 5.2 is 300 million tons annually.

Direct Estimate of Transfer Efficiency

Another approach to transfer efficiency is that of Steele (1965), who compares the actual biological harvest of the North Sea with its primary production. The harvest during 1955-1960 was fairly steady; it averaged 1.43 million tons a year over an area of 0.55 million square kilometers. This corresponds to 0.26 gram of carbon per square meter per year. For the net photosynthetic production of the North Sea we may use the figure 150 grams of carbon per square meter per year.[3] On this basis the transfer rate from plant production to fish *yield* is about 0.17%. In terms of fish production it would be somewhat larger, but not a great deal, because the North Sea is fished intensively and natural deaths are the exception among fish of usable sizes. Estimating average rate of utilization at 70%, the transfer rate from primary production to fish *production* becomes 0.25%.

These observations agree fairly well with the analysis given earlier. The figure 0.25% is close to the estimated percentage transfer of material up to trophic level 4 in Figure 5.2 (0.3/130 = 0.23%). Hence the average ecological position of the catch is at or somewhat above ecological level 3 in Figure 5.3. This level includes the fishes that eat invertebrates mainly, and the big-tonnage items from the North Sea are of this type (herring, haddock, small cod, plaice, sand lance).

On this basis the production of usable materials by the whole ocean would be 0.25% of its primary production of 130 billion tons, or 320 million tons.

Potential Harvest

The two methods of estimation used above agree closely for production at currently used ecological levels—300 and 320 million tons. Although this must be partly fortuitous, it at least suggests that we are operating in the right "ball park."

What fraction of this production is harvestable? For the North Sea the figure 70% was used above, and such a figure seems appropriate for most shallow seas. However, it is unquestionably much too large to be applied to

---

[3] Steele's figures are somewhat different. He uses too small a value (0.33 million square kilometers) for the area of the North Sea, so his yield per unit area is larger. He also uses 100 grams of carbon per square meter per year as a mean value for primary production (range 50–150), whereas Gessner's (1959) map puts most of the North Sea in the zone of 100–200 grams of carbon per square meter per year.

the ocean generally. For one thing production over most of the world ocean is low, and the average density of fish is much lower than in shallow water. Fishable schools of even the commoner species are farther apart and are harder to find. For some species they may not exist.

More important than this sparseness, probably, is the fact that there is no effective bottom to the open-water habitat. In a shallow sea nothing can get away from us. Plankton and detritus that reach the bottom are mostly eaten by such creatures as clams, worms, and crustaceans, some of which are directly usable, while others serve as food for bottom fish. These fish, shrimps and so on, all lie within range of our fishing apparatus, and bottom species make up about a third of the total yield of the North Sea and other shallow regions. Of all fish caught today, 80 to 90% are taken at depths of less than 200 meters, and the usual limit of commercial trawling is 600 to 800 meters. It seems unlikely that this limit could be extended much beyond 1,000 meters in the future. Apart from technical difficulties, catches at such depths have usually been disappointing.

As the depth of the water column increases, the deepwater pelagic fishes and squids tend more and more to be small, luminous, bizarre in shape, and difficult to catch. The total quantity per unit area is probably large, but it is scattered through so tall a water column that usable concentrations are unlikely to occur. One useful animal, the sperm whale, feeds on large deepwater squids and so brings material from the profundal region back up to the surface, but this is only a minor feedback. By and large, once organic material has sunk below the shallow-water levels of the open ocean it is lost to man. If we assume this loss to be similar to the proportion of bottom fishes taken in shallow seas, then a third of the usable production of the open water is not available.

For the above reason the potential rate of utilization of the sum total of fishes and other large organisms of the high seas probably averages not much more than half of that in shallow water, say 40% for the deep water as compared with 70% for the shallow. About two thirds of the ocean's primary production occurs over water more than 400 meters deep and one third in shallower water. Hence a weighted average potential rate of utilization is close to 50%. Applying this figure to the two estimates of usable production— 300 and 320 million tons—gives potential yield estimates of 150 and 160 million tons.

RECENT HISTORY OF WORLD FISHERIES

Increased Catch

The world fishery since World War II has been characterized by a rapid increase in number and size of vessels and great improvements in equipment. Along with this has gone a fairly steady increase in catch (Figure 5.4). The

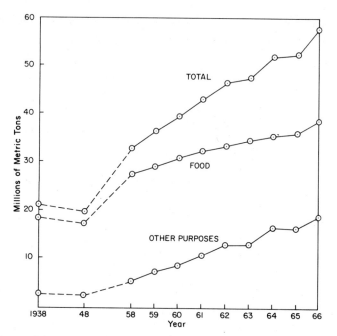

FIGURE 5.4
Reported total world catch of aquatic products (except large whales) in recent years, the portion of this used directly for human food, and the portion used for other purposes. The figures are in terms of whole weight. (Data from the FAO *Yearbook of Fishery Statistics*, vols. 22 and 23.)

increase amounted to 4.5% per year from 1952 to 1957 and 8% per year from 1957 to 1962 (Schaefer, 1965). The 8% figure reflected mainly the rapid rise of the new Peruvian anchoveta fishery. Since 1962 the rate of increase has returned to about 4%. The 1965 total catch was 52.4 million metric tons (Table 5.2), plus about 1.5 million tons of whales.[4]

New Fisheries

Important features of the postwar expansion in the use of the world's water for food supply have been the opening up of major new fishing grounds and

---

[4] Whaling statistics are given in numbers of animals, and since average sizes differ among species and have changed with time, tonnages can be estimated only very approximately. During the Antarctic whaling peak of the 1930's about 4 million tons a year were taken, but from part of this only the oil was used. Since then utilization has improved, but catches and stocks have decreased greatly. An International Whaling Commission has existed for many years, but not until 1967 did it prove possible to secure the agreement of all member nations to catch limits that would put the harvest in balance with production at the existing level of stock and, possibly, initiate a slow return to a more productive level.

the extension of fishing effort to species formerly neglected. Some important new or much-expanded fisheries of recent years include:

> Peruvian anchoveta
> Alaska pollock (N. America and Asia)
> Bering Sea flatfishes and herring
> East Pacific rockfishes
> Pacific hake (N. America and Chile)
> Pacific sauries
> Tunas, swordfish, sailfishes
> North Pacific mackerel
> South African hake and horse mackerel
> West Atlantic menhaden
> West Atlantic silver hake
> West Pacific squids
> North Atlantic redfish
> North Sea sand lance

Most of these fisheries are still flourishing, and some are still expanding. Others have passed a peak of production, but this is not necessarily a distress signal. A newly exploited population, if it contains fish of several ages, will pass through a rather brief period of "fishing-up the accumulated stock," comparable to the first harvest of a stand of timber. During this time the take may be considerably greater than the sustainable yield, so that an early decline in landings does not necessarily mean that overfishing has occurred, although it is likely to mean that take will at best decline to some lower sustainable level.

TABLE 5.2

The 1965 yield of fish from the world's major bodies of water.

Body of water	Area[a] (millions of km^2)	Yield[b] (millions of metric tons)	Yield per unit area	
			(kg/km^2)	(lb/acre)
Atlantic and Arctic Oceans	106.2	19.8	187	1.66
Indian Ocean	74.9	1.9	25	0.23
Pacific Ocean	179.7	24.1	134	1.20
Saltwater Totals	360.8	45.8	127	1.14
Inland water		6.6		
Grand Total	—	52.4	—	—

[a] Areas taken from Dietrich and Kalle, 1957.
[b] Catches include only those reported to FAO; yields given include those from neighboring seas and adjacent parts of the Antarctic Ocean.

More Fish Used for Meal and Oil

Another aspect of the postwar boom in fishing is that the take of "industrial" fish has increased much more rapidly than that of fish used directly for food (Figure 5.2). Species that are small, not very flavorful, difficult to keep fresh, or distant from markets can be utilized only indirectly at the present time. Most of them are eventually converted to animal protein in the form of meat or fowl. There is, of course, some transfer loss, but much less in terms of protein than in terms of energy, because the consumers get adequate energy from their plant foods.

In any event, as time goes on, we may expect more and more of the currently less desirable species to be used directly for food. One possibility is the wide use of fish-protein concentrate to fortify flour consumed by protein-deficient populations. At the moment the cost of preparing it is still rather high, though it is cheaper than alternatives such as dried skim milk.

Smaller Yields of Favored Species

A less desirable feature of the postwar fishing boom has been a major decline of certain species, largely due to overfishing. These tend to be species of exceptionally good flavor or keeping quality, or such as can or could be caught in massive numbers close to reduction plants. For a few species, overfishing had begun prior to 1940, and a number of others (most salmon, Pacific halibut, certain seals) were and are being maintained only by rigid restrictions on the catch.

Some of the major fisheries whose take has declined importantly are listed below; the dates indicate (approximately) the beginning of a major slump from which there has been no important recovery as yet:

Antarctic blue whales	1935
East Asian sardine	1945
California sardine	1946
Northwest Pacific salmon	1950
Atlanto-Scandian herring	1961
Barents Sea cod	1962
Antarctic fin whales	1962

Species now showing signs of strain include the Newfoundland cod, North Sea herring, menhaden, British Columbia herring, Bering Sea flatfishes, and yellowfin tuna in the eastern Pacific. Even if these are not yet being fished to the point where sustainable yield has been reduced, there is little prospect of their yield being increased appreciably.

Future of Traditional Fisheries

Possibilities for expansion of fisheries by traditional methods still exist. In general, southern hemisphere fisheries are weakly developed: in 1963 the temperate and cool parts of the southern hemisphere produced 2.7 million tons of fish, while the similar (but much smaller) northern area produced 25 million tons (Table 5.3). The southern hemisphere oceans, of course, have some serious physical disadvantages: rather small continental shelf areas, remoteness from present major population centers, and a vast area of cold stormy water that seems to lack major pelagic fish species. Considerable expansion, nevertheless, will be possible, especially around South America. Such expansion, in fact, is currently under way. The Indian Ocean is at present a small producer, but fisheries in its northwestern regions of upwelling are being expanded actively. Even in fairly heavily fished regions of the world there are still some little-used stocks that seem abundant: for example, grenadiers in the northwest Atlantic; sand lance, anchovies, and sauries in the east Pacific; capelin and small sharks (the dogfish *Squalus*) in both areas.

New or Improved Techniques

Another approach to increased food from the sea will be the development of techniques to harvest products now inaccessible. Some of these new techniques should not involve any very great qualitative changes. For example, all seas contain pelagic lantern fishes of many species. These are luminous fishes related to the smelts, typically 6 to 8 cm long. By day they are at moderate depths, concentrated in layers that can be located by an echo sounder; at night some of them rise to near the surface, but they are then more dispersed. Lantern fishes have been taken with ease in experimental

TABLE 5.3
Reported 1962 catch in millions of metric tons, of sea fish, invertebrates, and other products except large whales.

Northern seas		Southern seas	
Pacific	12.5	Atlantic	2.2
Atlantic	12.5	Pacific	0.5
Tropical and subtropical seas		Inland waters and migratory	6.7
Pacific	9.0		
Atlantic	3.1		
Indian	2.3	Total	48.8

Source: After Martinsen, 1966, Figure 3, based on FAO statistics.

fishing with trawls, but a commercial model has yet to be developed. One difficulty is the present low value of the product.

Another possibility, more distant and less certain, is that we may use products like the Antarctic pelagic crustacean *Euphausia superba*, the "krill" that was the main food of the former great whale stocks. The Soviet Union has had a ship in the Antarctic experimenting with harvesting and processing krill, but no economic success has been claimed. Similar but smaller euphausids occur in other cool seas, while in the tropics there are such species as the pelagic "red crab" *Pleuroncodes,* a staple food of tunas in the eastern Pacific. Harvesting resources such as these means tapping lower levels of the food pyramid, somewhere between trophic levels 2 and 3 (Figure 5.2). The resources at these levels are large, but to date the amount of energy and equipment required to harvest the crop has made them unavailable. Whether they will ever be competitive with other protein sources is still a question.

The most radical suggestion so far is that of inducing "artifical upwelling" over appreciable areas of ocean. As this would require massive quantities of very cheap energy, it is usually considered impractical for the near future, but it is a real prospect for the longer term. Its big attraction lies in the idea of increasing the actual primary production, as is done when we fertilize the land or fish ponds, rather than merely extending our utilization to less accessible and less attractive objects.

Fisheries of Inland Waters

Fish production reported from freshwaters and inland seas is included in the total of Figure 5.4. It amounted to 6.6 million tons in 1965, and an additional 2 million tons was probably produced in mainland China. The harvest has increased substantially since World War II, though not very much during the 1960's. Average yield per unit area is greater in inland waters than in the sea; but estimates of the area of the inland waters of the world (including rivers) are very unreliable. If 4 million square kilometers is taken as a possible figure, however, the 1965 estimated take of fish (including China) was about 2.3 tons per square kilometer or 20 pounds per acre. Part of the reason for this high rate of production as compared with the sea is that the statistics include large quantities of freshwater fish grown in ponds under intensive culture, sometimes with supplementary feeding. In addition, natural inland waters are somewhat more fertile than ocean waters on the average, and their products are more accessible.

Large areas of freshwater are underutilized in North America, either because of remoteness or because commercial fishing is prohibited or because of prejudice against the "coarse" fishes they produce. The Great Lakes and some of the large rivers, however, are or have been intensively fished. In the "old world" fairly intensive utilization is the rule.

It has been suggested, perhaps not entirely seriously, that if all freshwaters were to be intensively managed their absolute yield might equal that of the oceans. This has a certain plausibility, because in warm-temperate and tropical regions well-managed ponds readily produce 10 to 30 tons per square kilometer. To produce 52.4 million tons from existing freshwaters would mean an average yield of about 13 tons per square kilometer, which is five or six times the present average rate of yield. Moreover, good yields from ponds depend on favorable conditions of such phenomena as depth, fertility, flow, and climate, which very few natural waters possess. For example, the important lake areas of Canada and Eurasia are mostly low in nutrients and have a very short growing season (which might be increased locally, however, by using them for the disposal of waste heat from nuclear reactors). Even in more salubrious locations the excessive depth (from this point of view) of most lakes, and the flooding and general muddiness of most rivers, make artifical increase of their production a haphazard proposition at best. Heavy fertilization of small- to medium-sized lakes also has two undesirable side effects: oxygen depletion below the thin photosynthesizing layer and excessive growth of weeds in shallow water. In large lakes, the wind will maintain a thick aerated layer, but the water near the bottom loses its oxygen and fish cannot survive there. Lake Erie, unintentionally one of the most heavily fertilized large bodies of freshwater, yields no more usable fish today than when it was in a comparatively unfertilized condition—though this may be partly a result of too intensive fishing.

In summary, the world harvest of freshwater fish can be increased, but there is little likelihood of its increasing more rapidly than that of marine fish, unless there is a change in attitudes toward utilization in some regions and intensified culture in others.

Fish Culture

Two general types of operation are included under the term "fish culture." In the commoner type a complete ecosystem is set up in a pond or small lake. Typically, fertilizers are used to promote the growth of phytoplankton and larger plants—which are consumed by zooplankton and bottom animals, and these in turn are consumed by fish. Man's contribution is limited to providing the environment and, usually, mineral or organic fertilizers. In temperate climates the carp is the most popular fish for this kind of operation, and annual yields of up to 30 tons per square kilometer or more can sometimes be obtained. In Africa, China, India, and southeast Asia various local fishes are also cultivated in ponds. Some of these are primarily plant-eaters, and it is these fish that theoretically can be expected to give the largest yields.

Often a combination of species is used. In tropical regions where growth can continue all year, yields up to 50 tons per square kilometer or more are reported.

Pond culture of this type is somewhat comparable to grazing stock on fertilized pastures, and its effectiveness can be assessed on the same basis as any similar animal-husbandry operation. In many places the ponds compete with agricultural uses for the same land, though elsewhere they are constructed in low areas not normally used for agriculture or even in the otherwise useless tropical mangrove swamps. The yields quoted are in terms of the water area of the ponds, but additional space is needed for dikes, roads, and canals. There seems to be no great advantage or disadvantage to fish culture as compared to animal husbandry, though the yields of both vary greatly. In many countries fish is the preferred protein food, and everywhere it adds variety to the diet. However, we cannot expect any startling increase in world protein supplies as a result of converting pastures to ponds.

A transition to the second type of fish culture occurs when supplementary foods are supplied to fish in rearing ponds, much as cattle are fattened on a feed lot. This can double or triple the yield per unit area of water, depending on the amount and kind of foods used (Lin, 1951).

In a wholly artifical operation the fish are held in ponds or tanks and are fed organic foods, mainly of animal origin. The ponds may be freshwater or saltwater, and rather large numbers of fish can be crowded into them, so the total area and water supply required are not too great. This procedure can add to the human protein supply insofar as waste materials are used for food. In tropical Asia a family may feed table scraps and other wastes to a few "pet" fish, and in Japan surplus silkworms are a commercially important food for fish. However, the great bulk of the material used to feed fish today is other fish—mostly low-value species or undersized individuals too small to market. For example, in 1965 Japan used about 130,000 metric tons of fish (round weight basis) plus 26,000 tons of other materials to produce 31,100 tons of freshwater fish—a conversion efficiency of 20%. The species reared were mainly carp, crucian carp, rainbow trout, and eels. Saltwater fish are also raised in Japan; but for yellowtail, the principal species used, the conversion efficiency is only 13%, and the product is correspondingly expensive. About 18,000 tons were produced in 1965.

Thus today's commercial fish-rearing establishments are mainly a means of converting low-priced fish into a much smaller quantity of high-priced fish. They are wasteful of protein, because it is the main source of energy for the fish reared as well as being used for their growth. Unfortunately, plant foods can be incorporated into the diets of most fish to only a limited extent, though carp show some flexibility. It is possible that, in the future, some of the primarily herbivorous species may be reared on vegetable foods in crowded ponds. Such an industry might strive to equal the efficiency of a modern chicken ranch, but it could scarcely surpass it.

WHAT IS THE LIMIT?

Catch Predictions

Since World War II, predictions of potential fish yields have twice been surpassed. A 1949 forecast was for 22 million tons of marine fish, 4 million tons more than the prewar yield (Thompson, 1951). Only a few years later a larger quantity than this was being taken (Figure 5.4). Sights were quickly raised, and during the middle 1950's 50–60 million tons were usually forecast, twice the catch level at that time (for example, Walford, 1958). More recently a number of writers (such as Meseck, 1962; Kask, 1963; Schaefer, 1965) have predicted a yield of about 100 million tons a year without any radically new technology. This again is about double the current rate.

Will this figure also quickly be reached and exceeded? A reason for hesitation is that the forecasts are now approaching our estimates of what is biologically possible. One hundred million tons of fish is, however, less than the sustained-yield estimates developed earlier—150–160 million tons. Although these estimates might prove too high, there is little reason to doubt that 100 million tons a year will be possible. But another doubling, to 200 million tons, becomes more questionable.

Others have hinted that several hundred or perhaps up to 1,000 million tons of organic material may eventually be obtainable from the sea (e.g., Pike and Spilhaus, 1962; Chapman, 1965). Such figures seem far more dubious. They are realizable, in theory, if the average level of utilization is pushed down well below ecological level 3 in Figure 5.3 and to a little below the trophic level 3 of the food pyramid shown in Figure 5.2. In other words, the product obtained would be mainly animal plankton. However, the possibility of actually harvesting massive quantities of usable plankters at any reasonable cost has yet to be demonstrated; preliminary trials have not been encouraging. If, moreover, yields of this size were achieved without increasing primary production, it would mean that many of the currently popular food fishes and useful mammals would no longer be available in quantity, because *their* food was being harvested out from under them.

Rate of Development

To take even 100 million tons of aquatic products per year will, of course, require continued major new investment in fishing equipment, from which the return will become less and less per unit, because the additional fish to be caught will be more distant or more dispersed and, on the whole, less valuable. At a guess, the total physical investment in ships and gear might have to be three times that of the present. To reach 150 million tons might require five or six times the present equipment, provided it is feasible at all.

Processing facilities would have to keep pace as well, but these would be more or less proportional to landings.

If 100 million tons a year is taken as an interim objective, how quickly can it be achieved? The present rapid rate of increase seems unlikely to last very much longer, depending partly on whether this is considered to be 7 percent per year (1958–1965) or only 4 percent (1962–1965). Even 4 percent per year means doubling in 18 years. Many important fish stocks have already reached or passed the limit of their sustainable yield, however, and new stocks available for exploitation are becoming progressively fewer. If the world catch is 100 million tons by 1990, that will represent very good progress; but if it takes until the end of the century to reach that figure we should not be too surprised. Either target will require concerted efforts by many nations, as well as international agreements to regulate the take of many species that today are still exposed to unlimited fishing.

Meeting Man's Protein and Energy Needs

Protein.   The material harvested from the waters is mostly protein, so it can be related first of all to man's protein requirements. About 36 grams of *high-quality* protein per day (including fish protein) is enough for an adequate diet (U.S. President's Science Advisory Committee, 1967, p. 53). This comes to 43 million metric tons a year for the present population. The 60 million tons or so of fish landed in 1968 contained about 12 million tons of usable protein (including what was processed to fish meal) or 28 per cent of what is required. Losses in processing, however, and in the conversion of meal to an acceptable animal product, would reduce this to about 10 million tons, or 23 per cent. This is an important fraction of the *animal* protein requirement, because in most diets plant materials can supply up to two-thirds of the protein needed.

However, the above requirements would represent adequate subsistence only if there were worldwide rationing of protein supplies. They make no provision for expansion of the geographical bounds of the good life insofar as this concept presupposes an abundant supply of tasty natural protein foods in the diet. To supply such a demand, a large per capita increase in production of animal protein, including fish, would have to take place. The North American consumption of animal protein, for example, already averages 64 grams per person per day (U.S. President's Science Advisory Committee, 1967, p. 262).

The estimates of future fish catches indicated above suggest that, with sufficient effort, the ratio of landings to population might be improved up to the end of the century, but only moderately at best. Landings of 150 million tons by the year 2000 would mean a 37 percent increase in fish protein per head (given a population of 6 billion, see Chapter 3). If landings increase to only 100 million tons, however, that will mean a decline of 8 percent in fish protein available per person. What happens beyond 2000 A.D. will depend mainly on whether human populations have become stabilized.

Energy. Some popular writers have pictured the ocean as a limitless reservoir of food energy—one that could support any conceivable human population. Nothing could be farther from the mark. The 1968 yield of about 60 million tons a year from the waters is equivalent to about 60×10^{12} kilocalories. The annual food energy requirement for the 3.5 billion people then present was about 3×10^{15} kilocalories—50 times as much. Even *if* cheap energy and unpredictable technology were to bring annual landings of edible materials up to 1,000 million tons by the end of the century, this would still be only about 20 percent of the biological energy requirements of the 6–7 billion people then expected. The maximal *expected* production of 150–160 million tons would supply only about 3 percent of these energy requirements.

In summary, the world's ocean and inland waters cannot even begin to supply a complete ration for the world's peoples. What they can do is to make an important contribution to the protein requirements of populations up to not more than two or three times the present size. This will always be their major role in man's biological economy.

References

Bogorov, V. G. 1967. Problems concerning the productivity of the ocean [in Russian]. *Gidrobiol. Zh.* 3(5): 12–21.

Chapman, W. M. 1965. *Potential resources of the ocean.* San Diego: Van Camp Sea Food Co.

Conover, R. J. 1964. Food relations and nutrition of zooplankton. Univ. of Rhode Island, Graduate School of Oceanography, Occasional Paper, no. 2, pp. 81–91.

Dietrich, G., and K. Kalle. 1957. *Allgemeine Meereskunde.* Berlin: Borntraeger.

Gessner, Fritz. 1959. *Hydrobotanik: Die physiologischen Grundlagen der Pflanzenverbreitung im Wasser,* vol. 2, Stoffaushalt. Berlin: VEB Verlag der Wissenschaften.

Ivlev, V. S. 1945. The biological productivity of waters. *J. Fisheries Res. Bd. Canada* 23(11): 1727–1759.

Kasahara, Hiroshi. In press. *Food production in the ocean.* Proc., 7th International Congress of Nutrition, August 1966, Hamburg.

Kask, J. L. 1963. Fisheries in the year 2000. *Canadian Fisherman,* June 1963, pp. 42–45.

Kevern, N. R. 1966. Feeding rate of carp estimated by a radioisotope method. *Am. Fish. Soc. Trans.* 95(4): 363–371.

Koblenz-Mishke, O. I. 1965. The magnitude of the primary production of the Pacific Ocean [in Russian]. *Okeanologiya* 5(2): 325–337.

Laevastu, T. 1961. Natural bases for the fishery of the Atlantic Ocean, its present characteristics and future possibilities. In *Atlantic Ocean fisheries*, Georg Borgström and A. J. Heighway, eds., pp. 18–39. London: Fishing News (Books) Ltd.

Lasker, R. 1966. Feeding, growth and carbon utilization by a euphausid crustacean. *J. Fisheries Res. Bd. Canada* 23(9): 1291–1317.

Lin, S. Y. 1951. *Pond culture of warm-water fishes*. United Nations Scientific Conference on the Conservation and Utilization of Resources, Wildlife and Fish Resource Sec., Proc., pp. 131–135.

Martinsen, G. V. 1966. *Present-day world catches of fish and organisms other than fish (from FAO data)* [in Russian]. Moscow: Pishchevaya Promyshlennost' Press.

Meseck, G. 1962. Importance of fisheries production and utilization in the food economy. In *Fish in nutrition*, pp. 23–27. London: Fishing News (Books) Ltd.

Pavlova, E. V. 1967. Food requirements and transformation of energy by *Cladocera* populations in the Black Sea [in Russian]. In *Struktura i Dinamika Vodnykh Soobshchestv i Populyatsii*, pp. 66–85. Institut Biologii Yuzhnykh Morei, Akademiya Nauk Ukrainskoi SSR.

Petipa, T. S. 1967. On the efficiency of utilization of energy in the pelagic ecosystem of the Black Sea [in Russian]. In *Struktura i Dinamika Vodnykh Soobshchestv i Populyatsii*, pp. 44–65. Institut Biologii Yuzhnykh Morei, Akademiya Nauk Ukrainskoi SSR.

Pike, S. T., and A. Spilhaus. 1962. *Marine Resources*. National Academy of Sciences—National Research Council Publ. 1000-E. Washington, D.C.

Richman, S. 1958. The transformation of energy by *Daphnia pulex*. *Ecological Monographs* 28: 272–291.

Schaefer, M. B. 1965. The potential harvest of the sea. *Am. Fish. Soc. Trans.* 94(2): 123–128.

Steele, J. H. 1965. Some problems in the study of marine resources. *Int. Comm. NW Atlantic Fish. Special Publ.* 6: 463–476.

Steemann-Nielsen, E., and E. A. Aabie Jensen. 1957. Primary oceanic production: The autotrophic matter in the oceans. *Galathea Reports* 1: 49–136.

Thompson, H. 1951. *Latent fishery resources and means for their development*. United Nations Scientific Conference on the Conservation and Utilization of Resources, Wildlife and Fish Resources Sec., Proc., pp. 28–35.

U.S. President's Science Advisory Committee. 1967. *The world food problems*. Report of the Panel on the World Food Supply, vol. 2. Washington, D.C.

Walford, L. A. 1958. *Living resources of the sea: opportunities for research and expansion*. New York: Ronald Press.

Westlake, D. F. 1963. Comparisons of plant productivity. *Biol. Rev.* 38: 385–425.

6 / Mineral Resources from the Land

Thomas S. Lovering

"A great obstacle to happiness is to expect too much."
—Bernard de Fontenelle

Estimating the capabilities of the earth to supply mineral and chemical resources involves a far greater number of uncertainties than does assessment of its biological productivity—difficult and uncertain though that may be (see Chapters 4 and 5). Analysis of ore deposits is complicated by the factor of geologic time, involving many opportunities, by a variety of processes, for both enrichment and dispersal. Reliability comparable to that of estimates of biological resources is obtainable only for the relatively few important dissolved salts in well-mixed oceans of known dimensions (see Chapter 7), and perhaps for fossil fuels and a few other sedimentary mineral deposits (gypsum and salt, for example). Estimates of the quantities and locations of the other, and far more numerous, useful materials that might be obtained from the solid crust of the earth are not as reliable— especially those for most metals. Such estimates depend not only on the accuracy of averages calculated for the often erratically varying concentrations of elements or minerals in particular kinds of rock but also on our very incomplete knowledge of the usually concealed and highly irregular surface boundaries of the host rocks and their extensions at depth.

Whether a particular type and grade of mineral concentrate at a particular

Typescript received December 1967. Final revision, June 1968.

location in the earth's crust is or can become an ore (a deposit that can be worked at a profit), moreover, depends on a variety of economic factors, including mining, transportation, and extractive technology. Even if comprehensive information were available on the geochemistry and configuration of the earth's crustal materials, we could still not assess the likely eventual reserves of ore for specific mineral commodities at the level of confidence we might like.

Thus, until more and better data become available, estimates of eventual reserves and of lifetimes of current mineral commodities and their potential substitutes will certainly contain inaccuracies such as have discredited many past estimates. What is more to the point at this time is to discuss some important characteristics of mineral deposits, to illustrate some of the difficulties and misconceptions that affect the estimation of regional metal reserves, to consider the order of magnitude of probable demand, and to suggest some actions and cautions that might improve the future outlook for our mineral-based economy.

GENERAL FEATURES OF MINERAL RESOURCES

The total volume of workable mineral deposits is an insignificant fraction of 1 percent of the earth's crust, and each deposit represents some geological accident in the remote past. Deposits must be mined where they occur—often far from centers of consumption. Each deposit also has its limits; if worked long enough it must sooner or later be exhausted. No second crop will materialize. Rich mineral deposits are a nation's most valuable but ephemeral material possession—its quick assets. Continued extraction of ore, moreover, leads, eventually, to increasing costs as the material mined comes from greater and greater depths or as grade decreases, although improved technology and economics of scale sometimes allow deposits to be worked, temporarily, at decreased costs. Yet industry requires increasing tonnage and variety of mineral raw materials; and although many substances now deemed essential have understudies that can play their parts adequately, technology has found no satisfactory substitutes for others.

Relative abundance and local distribution of the elements play a crucial role in their continued availability to industry through various "stretching" devices, making it hazardous to generalize from one type or group of ore deposits to others. Production of several of the scarcer metal "vitamins" essential to the life of industrial giants is concentrated in a few major deposits in very small areas of the world (although minor production may come from a large number of small deposits intermittently worked). Mercury belongs in this group. The clarke, or average crustal abundance, of mercury is at most 400 parts per billion (0.000,04 percent); this is four orders of magnitude less than in ore, which commonly contains from 0.2 to 0.5 percent mercury. A similar range exists for other important industrial metals such as tungsten (clarke less than 2 parts per million), tantalum, silver, tin, and molybdenum.

At the opposite extreme, aluminum ore formed by residual enrichment (bauxite) commonly averages 20 to 25 percent aluminum, whereas the average aluminum content of most igneous rocks, as well as of shale, is about 8 percent. Sedimentary iron ore now mined contains 20 to 30 percent iron, and a few special types of ore contain much less; while the average iron content in such common rocks as basalt is 8.6 percent, and even ordinary shales contain 4.7 percent iron on the average. Under unusual conditions very low-grade sources of iron can be mined economically—the Soviets report mining black sands containing less than 4 percent iron, which can be magnetically concentrated in a ratio of 15 to 1.

Several metals are intermediate in abundance between the iron-aluminum group and the scarce metals of the mercury-tungsten group. Among them is copper, having a workable ore grade (in 1968) of approximately 0.4 to 0.8 percent and a clarke of 87 parts per million in basic igneous rocks. In some igneous rocks, however, the clarke averages several hundred parts per million, only an order of magnitude below the present cutoff grade for some porphyry coppers. Cobalt, nickel, and vanadium are similar to copper in terms of ratio of clarke to ore grades. Both zinc and lead approach this group, but currently their ratios of ore grade to crustal abundance are higher than those for cobalt, nickel, or vanadium.

Some elements are found in minor amounts in complex ores exploited chiefly for some other metal. Molybdenum is a valuable by-product of the concentrating processes used for getting copper from porphyry coppers. Tin and tungsten are valuable by-products of some molybdenum deposits that have all the characteristics of the porphyry coppers except that copper is present only in trace amounts. Most of the silver and antimony produced in the United States comes as a by-product from the treatment of ores mined for some other metal. Processing of greater amounts of complex ores would provide additional, though limited, supplies of by-product metals at a sufficient increase in price, but at the risk of flooding and depressing the market for the major constituents. Should this happen, most such deposits would become uneconomic.

A look at procedures and assumptions commonly employed in estimating regional reserves and at some of the geological limitations that affect such estimates will illustrate the problem. In this discussion, primary attention is given to the metal resources; fuel will be discussed in Chapter 8. Shortages of nonmetallic mineral resources are not discussed, because they are less likely to occur and are more readily met by substitution and recycling.

Estimation of Metal Reserves

Once a mineral deposit is located, the reserves of minable ore contained in it can be estimated to any needed precision by drilling enough exploratory holes and analyzing each segment of each hole. Estimating reserves not yet found or known to be available is more difficult, because the answer depends on economic and technological factors as well as on geological ones. Since the emphasis of this report is on the longer term, estimates of absolute geological availability of future ores would be appropriate. The information on which reasonably accurate estimates of reserves of future ores might be based is, unfortunately, not now available. What we can do, however, is to consider how estimates of regional reserves have been made in the past and to review the geological limitations that affect their reliability and underscore the need for more and better data.

Mathematical Models.   Analysis of the relation of reserves to tonnage and average grade of ore produced in copper porphyries led the geologist Lasky (1950) to formulate a principle now widely employed outside its field of validity by mineral economists; it is known as the A/G (arithmetic-geometric) ratio, the grade-tonnage ratio, or the Lasky ratio. This ratio is generally taken to mean that reserves increase geometrically as the average grade to be mined decreases arithmetically, or, as Lasky (1951) expressed it: Average Grade $= K_1 - K_2 \times$ log cumulative tonnage.

In referring to his equation and the curve it generates, Lasky (1950) said, "It fits the porphyry coppers . . . and apparently also other deposits of similar type in which small quantities of ore minerals are scattered through great volumes of shattered rock." Lasky stated as a general principle that "in many mineral deposits *in which there is a gradation from relatively rich to relatively lean material,* the tonnage increases at a constant geometric rate as the grade decreases." A typical curve for a porphyry copper plots as a straight line on semilogarithmic paper, for which the decrements in grade are represented by the arithmetically spaced vertical lines and the increments in tonnage are scaled by logarithmically spaced horizontal lines. The straight-line plot represents the cumulative production or tonnage of ore—not metal—in a porphyry copper with decreasing average grade of total tonnage extracted as ever leaner ore is mined. This constraint is a very important one, well understood by Lasky but apparently misunderstood by many economists.

Lasky averaged the characteristics of the eight major porphyry copper deposits known in the United States in 1950 and noted that for such an average deposit there would be, at the start, about 60 million tons of 2 percent copper ore and somewhat more than 600 million tons of ore averaging about 0.6 percent of copper when it has been mined out—down to and including zero cut-off grade. In this average deposit, the tonnage of mineralized rock increases at a rate of about 18 percent for each decrement in grade of 0.1 percent. Most of the copper would be contained in rock having a copper content greater than 0.5 percent: about one-third of it would be in the 175 million tons having a grade of 0.5 to 0.9 percent and more than one-half of it in the still smaller volume of rock containing more than 0.9 percent copper.

Lasky's analysis is a major contribution to our concepts of grade and tonnage for the type of deposit that he considers. It should be noted, however, that although the curves closely approximate the situation over a range of grade of about 1.5 percent, even for porphyry coppers they do not express the relations either for higher grades of ore or for very lean rocks.

Consider the clarke for copper; in many igneous rocks it is between 0.004 and 0.010 percent. Somewhere between a grade of a few tenths of a percent and a hundredth of a percent, the A/G ratio calls for the tonnage of copper-bearing rocks in porphyry copper deposits to increase astronomically as the grade approaches that of the essentially barren igneous host rocks. There is, however, no geological reason why the curve calculated by Lasky's formula should maintain its slope or change smoothly into one that might express the change in copper content of the various rock units found in the crust of the earth. Geological considerations make it more likely that the cumulative curve would first flatten and then rise precipitously at the abundance-level of the clarke.

Then consider what happens at the end of the A/G curve where grains of the common ore mineral chalcopyrite are concentrated (in mineralized veins, for example). This mineral contains about 35 percent copper. Lasky's formula applied to his cited average porphyry copper deposit shows a "tonnage" of only 1 milligram of ore having a grade of 24.5 percent copper (out of 60 million tons averaging 2 percent copper), or one ton having a grade of 12.9 percent copper. Thus the curve generated by the A/G ratio departs widely from reality between 0.01 percent and 0.3 percent at one end and for any masses of ore containing substantial amounts of the common copper ore minerals at the other.

Even though deposits of the porphyry copper type share many characteristics, each individual deposit is unique. Generalizations based on a half dozen deposits will not apply even to the entire range of porphyry coppers and certainly not to ore deposits of different metals, different origin, and different geologic habitats. The essential point is that the A/G ratio applies only to certain individual deposits and not to ore deposits in general. It should not be used in estimating the unfound reserves of a region or a nation.

Geological Limitations. In his cautious first statement of the principle of the arithmetic-geometric ratio, Lasky says that the curve generated by his equation is meaningful for many types of deposits, but he adds the proviso "the geological evidence permitting." It is this reservation that has been neglected by many users of the equation.

Although there is no geological reason to conclude that the A/G ratio holds for ore deposits in general, it is true that the closer the minable grade of a metal approaches its clarke the more probable is the existence of an A/G ratio reaching well below the grade of currently commercial ore. For iron and aluminum, it seems probable that A/G relations may hold from ore grade down to (or below) the clarke. Even for them, however, it is unsafe to assume A/G relations for all *individual* deposits. And it is naive to postulate that there must be undiscovered low-grade deposits of astronomical tonnage to bridge the gap between known commercial ore and the millions of cubic miles of crustal rocks that have measurable trace amounts of the various less common metals in them, as has been recently suggested (Brooks, 1967). When cumulative curves of metal content are plotted against volume of rock for elements in the earth's crust, the curves generally show abrupt changes in slope, corresponding to changes from one kind of rock to another. A few specifics will illustrate the consequences of such changes.

Most ores are deposited over a geologically appreciable time by complex processes. Beyond the borders of the large mass of mineralized, intensely fractured rock that marks a deposit of the porphyry copper type, the metal content drops off sharply. Most such bodies show a history of repeated fracturing and mineralization. In some, there have been several stages of metallization; in others, only one stage of metallization but several stages of barren alteration may be represented. Where the fractured rock has been enriched by successive waves of metallizing solutions, each wave is apt to be localized in somewhat restricted masses of refractured rock. These localized blocks of richer ore result in stepwise changes in grade for the deposit as a whole. Such changes, however, are not reflected in the product in mining, which represents a mixture of grades determined in advance by economic and metallurgical requirements. Where a very low-grade protore (the lean rock from which the ore is derived) has been enriched by weathering processes, a shallow mass of ore may carry ten times as much metal as the protore. In porphyry copper deposits of this type there is an abrupt transition from ore grade to unminable rock that cannot be described by an A/G curve. Lowering the grade by decrements of 0.1 percent would increase the cumulative tonnage of ore by only small fractions until the grade of the protore was reached. Then an enormous increase might take place in reserves of protore, though not necessarily in total tonnage of contained copper. Some, but far fewer, important molybdenum deposits also have characteristics similar to those of the porphyry coppers.

For lead-zinc replacement deposits in limestone and dolomite, the transition zone from barren rock to ore is commonly but a few feet wide or is lacking entirely. Limestone carrying only 20 or 30 parts per million of metal may be within arm's reach of a huge ore body having a grade 10,000 times that of the country rock (Morris and Lovering, 1952). Lowering the grade mined from that of a typical large high-grade ore shoot containing 20 percent metal down to an ore containing 10 percent metal would not increase the total quantity of reserves greatly; and lowering the grade from 10 percent to 1 percent would increase the reserves only as barren rock was added to the ore to bring its average down to the proposed low cut-off value.

Another instructive example of the limitations of the A/G ratio involves mercury. In the course of intensive exploration by the U.S. Bureau of Mines and the U.S. Geological Survey during World War II, more than 330 mercury occurrences were inspected and 43 deposits were explored in detail. Commercial ore was developed on 38 of the 43, altogether comprising 370,000 tons of ore averaging 0.8 percent mercury (16.2 pounds per ton). These same deposits also included 1,220,000 tons of noncommercial mineralized material averaging 0.125 percent mercury (2.5 pounds per ton) and 285,000 tons averaging 0.08 percent mercury (1.6 pounds per ton). This is equivalent to 2,960 tons of mercury in the 0.8 percent ore and 1,525 tons of mercury in the 0.125 percent "ore," but only 228 tons of mercury in the 0.08 percent "ore." Thus, an arithmetic decrease in grade from 0.8 percent to 0.125 percent, a sixfold change, would result in a threefold geometric increase in tonnage of mercury-bearing rock—*but the total mercury in the larger tonnage would be only one-half that in the smaller high-grade tonnage.* A further decrease of 0.04 percent in grade would add a tonnage less than one-fourth that of the 0.125 percent ore at a grade only one-tenth that of the somewhat larger tonnage of high-grade ore!

The geological processes that operate to give us minable ores include physical, chemical, and biogenic sedimentation, all sources of huge concentrations. Such processes, to be sure, cause dispersal as well as concentration, resulting in far larger volumes of sediments containing metals in amounts measured in parts per million than of ore metals in percent amounts. Yet the A/G ratio in sedimentary rocks may well hold for amounts ranging far down toward the crustal abundance of metals such as iron, aluminum, and magnesium.

Weathering, the precursor of sedimentation, may result in widespread gradational deposits derived from rock protores of huge tonnage. Both residual enrichment through leaching and secondary enrichment through precipitation of elements at depth form important ore bodies having large tonnages. Some of these deposits show abrupt changes from worthless material to valuable ore, as in the upper part of most sulfide deposits; others show a gradual enrichment, as with many lateritic nickel ores.

A special kind of mechanical precipitate would include some magmatic segregations where a desired mineral constituent has been concentrated gravitationally at high temperatures in molten rock below ground (magma)— an igneous "sediment." Many ores of this type show abrupt gradations, and others show gradual changes in concentration, especially when followed along the layers that contain the segregation itself. For some segregation deposits, the A/G ratio will hold through a tenfold change in grade, but for many segregations there is an abrupt change from ore deposit to barren rock.

Both for igneous segregations and for precipitates from aqueous solutions in fractures or in chemically reactive rocks such as limestone and dolomite, there is no geologic reason to expect geometric increase in tonnage with decrease in grade beyond certain well-defined limits that vary not only with the type of deposit but with the individual deposit considered. Nearly all such deposits have an outer margin of mineralization controlled by igneous contacts, by fractures, or by host rock, where the grade decreases sharply.

Fracture-controlled deposits range from those with abrupt transitions between high- and low-grade ores, such as are found in the typical "fissure" veins characteristic of the western United States, to the disseminated ores of the porphyry copper type for which A/G ratios have been established for changes in grade of approximately one order of magnitude.

Ore deposits, the majority of which do not show the A/G ratio, would include not only those of mercury, lead, and zinc (discussed above) but also gold, silver, tungsten, antimony, beryllium, tantalum, niobium, and the rare earth elements. Where submarginal grades of such ores exist, they are likely to take the form of many scattered small deposits whose economic concentration would pose problems comparable to those that would be encountered in the capture of large volumes of rare and small organisms scattered through the forest or the sea. Resources like these, and there are many, threaten real and restrictive shortages in the future.

Few economic geologists see any reason either to expect semi-infinite volumes of metal-bearing rock grading into ore bodies on an A/G curve or to doubt that eventually many metals will be extracted from mineralized rocks that carry only a fraction of the amount now required in commercial ore. Unfortunately, we do not know the location or grade of these future sources of metal. This emphasizes the need for studies of a wide variety of mineralized rocks, guided by geological theory, field mapping, and adequate geochemistry, and undertaken well in advance of impending shortages.

NATURE OF DEMANDS

We live in an epoch of localized affluence such as has recurred throughout historic time following discovery or development of new treasures of metal, mineral, or other resources. In the past, the quest for mineral deposits has led to invasion, conquest, and wealth for a comparative few. Now, more happily, the utilization of mineral resources is contributing to affluence for a larger proportion of the people not only in the industrial countries but also in some of the underdeveloped countries. It is well to realize, however, that mineral deposits are still "quick assets" of the country that possesses them, and that ultimately they become exhausted or decrease to a fraction of their flush production. Both rich and poor countries must be wary of the legacy of resentment that can come when a supplier nation finds that it has literally bartered its industrial potential for a mess of pottage.

Demand for mineral products comes chiefly from the chemical and manufacturing industries and from agriculture. The constant arrival of large quantities of raw materials is essential to maintaining output; and continuing output is vital to a healthy industrial economy. The minerals (apart from fuels) that are currently in greatest demand by industrial civilization are probably iron, copper, aluminum, and the fertilizer minerals. In addition, many metals that are found only in relatively minor quantities in the earth's crust are essential to the alloying and fabrication of others and to the more sophisticated functions of industrial society. Few of the developed countries have adequate internal sources of the principal minerals needed to meet current demands; and none have reserves of marginal grade adequate for the next century under current technology and without recycling. Although it is possible, in times of stress when free access to outside sources is cut off, to work deposits that otherwise are noncommercial, it must be remembered that low-grade deposits require much time and capital to develop. Economic chaos can result if foreign sources of supply are denied to a country that has allowed itself to become dependent on them. And dependent all industrial nations are, entirely or in large part, on foreign sources of supply for some or most of the essential metals demanded by their industries. This dependence increases with the years.

Before considering future supplies of the nonfuel minerals, it is necessary to consider potential future demands. The demand for material things in the modern world is a function of culture and population—of the relation of the real growth rates of the Gross National Product (GNP) to specific populations, as well as to their particular type of culture. The demand for goods, whether in small amounts per capita for a rapidly increasing population or in large amounts per capita for a static population of improving material standards, will strain industrial capacity and mineral productivity over the next century. Per capita consumption in newly industrial nations first shows exponential growth, usually for a few decades; then it flattens to a merely arithmetic increase, usually at a relatively low rate. Even a nearly static population in underdeveloped but aspiring countries would result in a tremendous surge in the demand for the nonrenewable resources of the world.

All over the world, moreover, cultures show a marked convergent trend toward a western way of life which aspires to an increasing material standard of living for all. Where such an increased standard is attained, it is quickly reflected in the per capita income of the population. The average income in the United States in 1965 was a little over $2,500 per capita. In India the average income then was about $80 per capita, and the average income per capita in some underdeveloped countries was even less. For several years the GNP of the United States has grown at a rate of 4 percent or more per year, while the rate of population growth has declined from about 1.5 percent to about 1 percent per year. This results in a minimal growth rate of per capita income of approximately 2.5 percent per year. Projected into the future, this would suggest an increase in per capita income for the United States from $2,500 in 1965 to $5,000 or more in 1993 and to upwards of $10,000 in the year 2021. Meanwhile, if the effective fertility rate of 2.5 percent per year in India were maintained, the population would double every 28 years. The rate of per capita income increase in India, if governed by the present ratio of GNP to population increase, would be far slower. If the GNP were to increase at 4 percent per year, but the population continued to increase at 2.5 percent, the actual increase in per capita income would be at the rate of 1.5 percent per annum. The current per capita income of about $80 would reach $160 in the year 2012 and $320 in the year 2060.

Such figures cannot be dismissed as unrealistic unless we also dismiss the basic (and, in the long term, hazardous) premise of an economy "ever expanding" at a rate of about 4 percent as unrealistic and disregard observed rates of population increase. Even should population growth slow down substantially in an underdeveloped country and its GNP increase greatly, it might be many generations before per capita income could approximate that currently observed in much of the western world. Meanwhile disparity between incomes will not only continue but will increase greatly unless a dramatic change in trends takes place.

During the early years of industrialization, on the other hand, the rate of increase of GNP in underdeveloped countries where outside financial assistance is available may be phenomenal. The investment of excess Japanese capital in South Korea, together with the campaign to control family size, resulted in a steady decline (about 0.1 percent per year) in South Korean birth rates and an increase in GNP of approximately 8 percent per year from 1964 to 1967.

A few demographers (e.g., Bogue, 1967) believe that the present population explosion will soon be regarded as an anachronism and that populations will stabilize themselves. This view is not shared by the majority of demographers, however (see Chapter 3; also Davis, 1967). As Hutchinson (1967, p. 178) points out, *"No amount of dissemination of information on birth-control practice is going to produce a stable population if the members of that population insist on a birthrate that is inconsistent with stability."* The dramatic decline in birth rate and the concommitant increase in GNP in Japan during the 1950's, following a year of intensive propaganda and appropriate legislation, startled the western world—but here the situation was obviously catastrophic, the population literate, the people responsive, and the measures adopted drastic. There is as yet little ground for hope that general worldwide population control will be voluntarily achieved.

For reasons such as those above, it would seem that estimates by Landsberg (1964) of U.S. and world consumption during the rest of the twentieth century are too low. Demand for minerals will probably increase exponentially for at least 50 to 75 years before it begins to level off—as level off it eventually must, if for no other reason than that the accessible crust of the earth is finite.

If events in South Korea and Japan foreshadow those in other Asiatic nations, the demand for minerals and other resources clearly will increase far faster than the rate of 2 percent per year suggested by projection of current fertility rates in the underdeveloped countries and by an assumed 4 percent per year increase in the GNP. The world's production of industrial metals (e.g., demand) has been growing at a rate of more than 6 percent per annum for nearly a decade. Although it is unlikely that all underdeveloped nations will want eventually to have a completely westernized material culture, enough of them have already shown their desire to become industrialized to justify the conclusion that major and exponentially increasing demands will be made on mineral resources far into the twenty-first century.

PAST AND PRESENT TRENDS IN MINERAL PRODUCTION

The amount of metal consumed in about 30 years at the current rate of increase in consumption approximates the total amount of metal used in all previous time. Between 1905 and 1938 more metal was produced than had been mined and consumed in the whole history of the world before 1905. The entire metal production of the globe before the start of World War II was about equal to what has been consumed since. Ore deposits have been sought actively since before the industrial era began, and the major industrial powers have a similar history of mineral exploitation and exhaustion. The Middle East, Greece, Spain, the United Kingdom, Belgium, France, Germany, Sweden, Mexico, Peru, and the United States have all had their day as the world's foremost producer of one or several metals, only to become plagued by either exhaustion or continuing decline.

Meanwhile the world's population has more than doubled, and, like the population, demand for metals is growing exponentially. This growth, moreover, has as yet to feel the expected increase in per capita demands, for the nonmilitary per capita consumption of metals has not grown appreciably in the developed countries, and the rising expectations of the underdeveloped cannot be met without capital.

Geography of Mineral Production

The most accessible high-grade deposits are the first to be mined. Such resources have already been gleaned in the United States as well as in the United Kingdom and other European industrial nations. Future resources will come from countries that are now less industrialized, many of which will be making maximum efforts to become industrialized. The increased vulnerability of industrial nations in both peace and war suggests that the assumption of unlimited access will be affected in the future as it has been in the past by institutional restraints and by the countermeasures that will seem in the best interests of the countries concerned.

As industrial nations use up the cheap supplies in their own countries, they inevitably become more and more dependent on recycled or "scrap" metal and on foreign sources for raw materials (e.g., Figure 6.1). At present all industrial nations except possibly the Soviet Union are net importers of most of the minerals and ores used by them. The dependence of the United States on foreign sources will almost certainly increase greatly during the next generation. Increasing dependence on foreign sources brings increased vulnerability to military, political, or economic action. This is emphasized by the fact that some of the metals most vital to the economic well-being of free-enterprise industrial nations are in areas of political instability or in Communist countries. Most of the known reserves of tungsten and antimony lie in such areas, as well as a large part of the world's manganese, nickel, chromium, and platinum. The present and near-future sources of manganese for North America are mostly in South America, Australia, and Africa, the

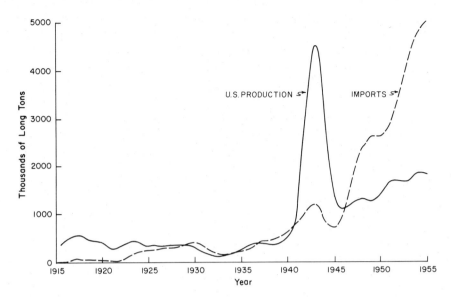

FIGURE 6.1
Bauxite produced in and imported to the United States, 1915–1955.

sources of tin in Southeast Asia, the sources of aluminum ore in various underdeveloped tropical countries.

That sources of supply will inevitably shift is clear, not only from the hard geological facts but also from a review of historical events. Three thousand years ago the Middle East was the center of the iron mining industry of the ancients. For several hundred years ancient Greece was the center of lead and silver mining of the western civilized world. For a long time Germany was the leading producer of lead, zinc, and silver in medieval Europe; but Belgium became the chief producer of zinc at the beginning of the industrial era. In the nineteenth century the United Kingdom was successively the world's foremost producer of lead, of copper, of tin, of iron, and of coal; and during that period she was the wealthiest nation in the world. From 1700 to 1859 the United Kingdom mined 50 percent of the world's lead; from 1820 to 1840 she produced 45 percent of the world's copper; from 1850 to 1890 she increased her iron production from one-third to one-half of the entire world output. At the turn of the century, Russia was the leading producer of petroleum in the world, and during the latter part of the nineteenth century she was the foremost gold producer—until the discovery of the great Transvaal gold deposits in South Africa. Most of the manganese ore mined until World War II came from a comparatively small area in the southern part of the Soviet Union. Large new deposits in Africa, Australia, and Brazil now threaten her dominance and have cut deeply into the manganese market.

Trends Affecting Future Adequacy

The Energy Factor.   Those who are familiar with geological and metal-lurgical limitations on the mineral industry are not impressed with the suggestion that the advent of cheap nuclear energy will transform common rock to "ore" and supply virtually unlimited quantities of all the metals needed by industry (see Figure 6.2). Even the breeder reactor will give us neither free nor unlimited power. The cost of nuclear fuel for the breeder reactor will indeed be negligible; but the cost of the large capital investment, of power transmission, of waste disposal, and of operation combine to bring the likely best price per kilowatt hour to about that of cheap steam-coal electric generating plants. Breeder reactors will be a wonderful asset to industrial nations not because they provide cheaper power but because they may provide desperately needed power when the fossil fuels are depleted and before the fusion reactor can be perfected.

Cheaper energy, in fact, would little reduce the total costs (chiefly capital

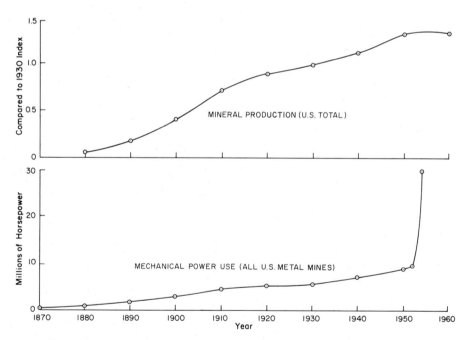

FIGURE 6.2
Increases in energy do not increase metal production. (Data from U.S. Department of Commerce.)

and labor) required for mining and processing rock. The enormous quantities of unusable waste produced for each unit of metal in ordinary granite (in a ratio of at least 2,000 to 1) are more easily disposed of on a blueprint than in the field. After crushing, the rock volume increases by the volume of the intergranular pore space, which ranges from 20 to 40 percent. Nor does leaching in place seem to offer an economical substitute for mining except under very special conditions. To recover materials sought, the rock must be shattered by explosives, drilled for input and recovery wells, and flooded with solutions containing special extractive chemicals. Provision must then be made to avoid the loss of solutions and the consequent contamination of groundwater and surface water. These operations will not be obviated by nuclear power.

Differences in physical and chemical form of the compounds containing the metals in common rock, moreover, require development of a totally new and complex extractive technology, and the unit costs of labor and capital (and even cheap energy) could be orders of magnitude above those of the present. Such considerations imply that, for a very long time to come, metals will come from ores that have metal concentrations well above those in common rock, with only few and quantitatively insignificant exceptions, such as the iron in the magnetic black sands of the Soviet Union.

Technology and Economics. The main escape hatch from scarcity is technical advance along a broad front, as noted by Landsberg (1964, p. 240). This, however, will depend on extensive and effective programs of research and development in the sciences, engineering, economics, and management. Substitutes for many materials having special properties, and for some of the minerals themselves, may be synthesized from cheap chemicals at costs that compete with the natural products. Synthetic diamonds, mica, rubies, and many other acceptable synthetic minerals will ease the demand on natural deposits. Satisfactory substitutes for many other raw materials also exist if the price of the substitute is not a consideration.

Some mineral resources, however, such as helium, mercury, and uranium or thorium, have unique properties, and for them there are no satisfactory substitutes. Metals, moreover, cannot be synthesized from other elements except in minute amounts and through the use of prohibitive quantities of energy.

The relations between economics and mineral resource scarcity are discussed by Barnett and Morse (1963). They look at the net decrease in unit costs for the mineral industry and for certain specific mineral commodities over a period of some 75 years. From this study they concluded that the increased efficiency caused by improved technology has resulted in a continuing net decrease in the cost per unit of mineral extracted. They also assumed that this trend of increasing efficiency would continue into

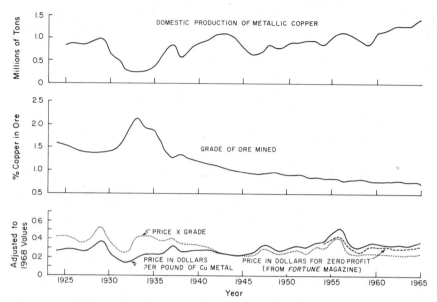

FIGURE 6.3
Economics of copper mining in the United States, 1925–1965. (Data from U.S. Bureau of Mines.)

the indefinite future. And they observed that, within the mineral industry, the mechanization that accompanied the increased production of coal, oil, and natural gas resulted in current costs about one-third to one-fourth of those of 1920. This, then, they interpret as showing the opposite of increased scarcity or the lessening of economic quality. The curves for lead and zinc, however, do not show such a change but rather an increase in unit cost. For copper (Figure 6.3) and for iron, the curves showing the trends toward lower unit cost flatten greatly between 1940 and 1960.

Changing costs in mineral extraction reflect the relative efficiency of operation as opposed to the increasing costs of capital, labor, and energy. Efficiency in operations must approach an irreducible minimum as maximum mechanization is achieved. It would require major innovations not now in sight to start another marked downward slope in the curve representing price times grade. The present trend of the ratio of grade of copper ore to price (in constant dollars) is not encouraging (Figure 6.3), but the discovery rate is.

Unhappily, the widespread belief that technology is continually lowering unit costs while allowing us to work deposits of ever lower grade is contradicted by the trends revealed in the copper industry. Figure 6.3 shows the continuing change in average grade of copper as mined, ranging from a high of 2.12 percent to the current low of about 0.70 percent. The tonnage of copper metal produced yearly shows a general upward trend, as would be expected. Assuming that the price of copper represents the summation of costs plus profit, and that the costs of capital, labor, and energy make up the total costs, it then follows that the product of price times grade (the value of metal in a hundredweight of ore that just pays for its recovery) should give us an index by which to measure the contribution of technology in lowering the cost per unit produced.

The three-year moving average of this "price times grade" is also shown in Figure 6.3. It exhibits the reported downward slope from the middle 1920's to the end of World War II. For the past 20 years, however, this curve was nearly horizontal, with one large upswing in the late 1950's, because improving technology was almost compensating for the ever-decreasing grade of ore mined and the increasing costs of capital and labor. Of special interest in Figure 6.3 is the curve showing price per pound for zero profit, the break-even price at which copper companies might have operated.[1] Beginning in 1958 this line trends upward and then flattens, showing that technology is barely keeping pace with the increased costs of extraction. Contrary to Barnett and Morse (1963), and to Barnett (1967), *unit costs are not declining*, nor have they been for a decade.

To maintain current dividend rates, the major porphyry copper producers will need either a continued price increase or an entirely different and appreciably more efficient way of extracting copper from its ores. A rough approximation for zero profit is that the price (in dollars) times the grade (in percent) must equal 0.20. To maintain present production at the average grade of copper mined in the United States, and to allow net earnings comparable to those currently had by the major copper companies, grade times price (in constant dollars on a 1958–1959 base) would have to be 0.24. To maintain present returns on investment, assuming that the average grade of copper ore mined times the price will be 0.24, would require a price in constant 1958–1959 dollars of 48 cents per pound at an average grade of 0.5 percent copper. The average grade mined in the United States in 1966 was 0.7 percent, calling for a price of 34 cents a pound, and the 1967–1968 price was about 35 cents a pound.

Aluminum, which is relatively abundant, can substitute for copper in many functions and thus help to stretch out reserves and suppress costs; but other critical metals lack such obvious and plentiful understudies [and most aluminum ore used in the United States is now imported (see Figure 6.1)]. The aptly mercurial behavior of mercury illustrates the point.

The relations of price to grade and output of mercury are shown graphically in Figure 6.4, which illustrates trends in price, production, and grade of mercury ore in the United States. The price and production of

---

[1] Figures taken from annual review of 500 major U.S. corporations in *Fortune* magazine.

mercury are increasingly dominated by cartel action. Figures given in the U.S. Bureau of Mines Yearbook for 1965 show that the lowest output of mercury in 25 years for the United States was 5,000 flasks (of 76 pounds each) in 1950 when the price was approximately $90 per flask. This was the average price from 1946 to 1950, during which time the output fell steadily from 25,000 to 5,000 flasks per year. From 1951 to 1953, the price rose rapidly to an average of $200 per flask, and in 1954 the U.S. Government guaranteed a minimum price of $225 a flask for a three-year period—a 250 percent increase in the 1946–1950 price! As a result, United States production climbed to nearly 12,000 flasks by the end of 1953, about half the 1946 production. Although the price after 1956 fluctuated on both sides of $200 per flask, this was not far from the average that obtained until a few years ago. During the 1950's the production from United States mercury

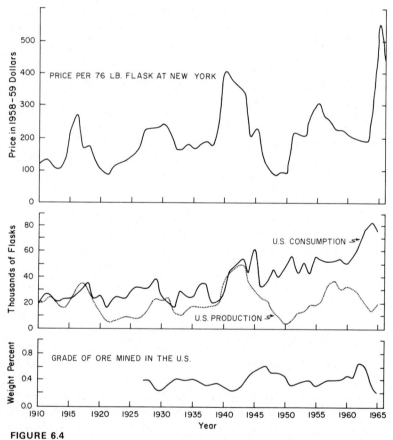

FIGURE 6.4
The mercury industry in the United States, 1910–1965. (Data from U.S. Bureau of Mines.)

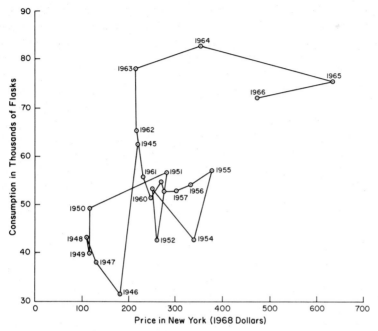

FIGURE 6.5
Consumption of mercury in the United States is not related to price. The
jointed line traces U.S. consumption of mercury and corresponding price
from 1945 to 1966. Figure shows that price and production display the same
lack of correlation. (Data are annual averages from the U.S. Bureau of
Mines *Minerals Yearbooks*.)

mines increased toward a high of 38,000 flasks in 1958; but from then on it
dropped steadily to a low of 14,000 flasks in 1965. In that year, however,
the price of mercury again more than doubled, reaching an all-time high of
about $800 per flask in the latter part of the year, resulting in an average
price of over $500 per flask. The substantial increase in price (sixfold in 21
years) resulted in another increase in domestic production, attaining
22,000 flasks in 1965—somewhat less than was produced in 1947 when the
average price of mercury was only $83 per flask.

The general relations between price and production led mineral economists
of the U.S. Bureau of Mines (1965b) to forecast future production in the
United States at various price levels, on the assumption that a definite
relationship exists between price and quantity produced. In fact this is not a
valid assumption (Figures 6.4 and 6.5). Consider, nevertheless, what happens
if we take it as literally true that both production and reserves are controlled
only by price. At a grade of 0.10 percent, the price of mercury mined in the
United States would have to be $1,000 in constant dollars, while, at a grade

of 0.05 percent (1 pound of mercury per ton), the price would rise to $2,000 per flask. At $1,500 per flask the price of mercury would approximate the legal coinage value of silver at $1.35 per troy ounce.

Mercury, in fact, resembles silver in many of its occurrences, but most silver now produced comes as a by-product from the mining of complex lead ores. The high-grade silver mines are depleted, just as most of the high-grade mercury mines have been depleted. Because very little mercury is recovered as a by-product from complex ores, however, this source will contribute only an insignificant amount of mercury in the future, whereas silver will continue to increase as the production of the complex ores increases. The average consumption of mercury in the United States has increased at a rate of 3 percent per year for 20 years, equivalent to a doubling in consumption every 23 years, but, to meet this demand, in the same period the price of mercury has increased by more than 500 percent.

The U.S. Bureau of Mines (1965b) estimated that the total reserves of mercury in ore in the United States at $200 per flask (in constant dollars) was 140,000 flasks, and that at $1,000 per flask there would be 1,287,000 flasks. The latter is equivalent to current consumption (80,000 flasks) increased at a rate of 3 percent per year for only 15 years! Even the unsubstantiated logic behind the assumption of a price-grade-tonnage relationship, based not on geology but on past production-price relations, does not encourage optimism concerning the resources of mercury for the next generation either in the United States or in other industrial countries.

World reserves of mercury at $200 per flask were estimated by the U.S. Bureau of Mines to be 3,160,000 flasks, but current world production is about 275,000 flasks per year. If the world production were to increase at only half the rate at which the demand is increasing in the United States, far more mercury would have to be mined in the next 20 years than is present in this estimate of world reserves. A price of more than $1,000 per flask might maintain world production of mercury for 50 years or more, but the source of this mercury will be increasingly concentrated in a few large deposits, such as those of Spain and Italy, where cartel action rather than costs per unit output determine market price.

OUTLOOK FOR THE FUTURE

It may well be true that science and technology will continue to provide satisfactory answers to our mineral resource problems far into the future. This can take place, however, only insofar as long-range foresight, lead time, exploration, and research keep pace with diminishing grade, changes in mineralogy, and the need to exploit entirely different types of deposits—it will not happen automatically. Above all, new discovery is required that, together with technological innovation, will develop reserves of mineral resources at an exponential rate until population control and relatively constant or decreasing per capita demand can be achieved—both inevitable requirements on our finite earth.

The lead time between discovery and first production from a major deposit now averages five years or more, and equal or greater time is usually required for exploration resulting in discovery. It is apparent, then, that mineral reserves should be available for a minimum of ten years of future production on the basis of expected trends in demand.

In considering the future, certain factors stand out. Discovery techniques seem to be developing rapidly, and many new deposits have been found and will be found. Future sources of ore will be of two main types:

1. Already known noncommercial deposits will become ore through technical innovations, future availability of cheaper transportation, or rise in price.

2. Deposits that are now unknown will be discovered by exploration. They will be chiefly in remote or underdeveloped areas if they crop out at or near the surface; and, both there and in developed areas, they will be found more and more by a combination of geology, geophysics, and geochemistry. To find such deposits will require well-financed companies or government support because of the high cost of exploration and development. An important type of unknown ore body includes those that do not come to the surface—"blind" ore bodies. To search successfully for them is even more expensive than to find exposed ore bodies in remote areas. Costly preliminary exploration and reconnaissance precedes every drill hole that zeros in on commercial ore, and the cost of discovery and development tends to be proportional to the depth of the ore body below the surface.

Mining costs always increase with depth, and for those deposits that approximate the A/G ratio down to low grades and huge tonnages, technology will inevitably cease to produce larger tonnages at lower unit costs. Such a trend (Figure 6.3), currently evident in open-pit copper mining, manifests itself also in other types of deposits. To maintain supplies would require a steadily rising price for the domestic product or increased dependence on foreign sources and new discoveries (Figure 6.1). For types of deposits other than those characterized by an approximate A/G ratio of grade to tonnage, the increase in price may not be gradual. Instead it may accelerate rapidly to a level at which the metal will price itself out of the market except for the most unusual and essential uses. In other words, a real economic scarcity will develop as measured by the change in price.

General increases in price might well increase the production of many commodities, temporarily hastening producers toward exhaustion and stimulating both marginal and submarginal mines into a flurry of activity. For other commodities, however, even a substantial rise in price does not bring about commensurate production of a new material either at home or abroad—although it may temporarily make available ore from marginal producers and tap secondary or hoarded metal supplies to satisfy demand (stockpiles may be regarded as hoards). This is exemplified by the already discussed supply-price behavior of mercury over the past few decades.

The recycling of mineral resources is another means of increasing mineral supply, with as yet barely tapped potential. With suitable attention to design and disposal of used metals, loss of materials could be reduced toward the point where new resources would be called upon only to meet increased demands and to replace losses from friction, chemical dispersal, and other unavoidable waste.

All postponements allowed for, however, it is clear that exhaustion of deposits of currently commercial grade is inevitable. Yet it is equally true that the increased costs of capital, labor, energy, and transportation for mining deposits of lower grade have in the past been largely offset by improved technology. The question is, can this continue? The answer remains to be given, but there are many signs that technology is not keeping pace with increasing costs of extraction in the United States.

Inventions and innovations in patterns of living, moreover, often bring unexpected changes in the demands on resources. Rarely is forethought shown in anticipating the "what-else-do-you-get" consequences of these changes—such as overproduction or scarcity; the new and different facilities required for related technical support and research; pollution of air, water, or soil; and even profound changes in the biological components of the environment.

To ensure both the ecologically nondestructive procurement of mineral supplies and a more equitable distribution of their beneficial results must surely be among the foremost objectives of a successful economic system. During the next century adequate supplies and equitable distribution will not be achieved merely by recycling scrap metal nor by processing dozens of cubic kilometers of common rock to supply the metal needs of each major industrial nation. When the time comes for living in a society dependent on scrap for high grade metal and on common rocks for commercial ore, the affluent society will be much overworked to maintain a standard of living equal to that of a century ago. Only our best efforts in all phases of resource management and population control can defer that day.

Enhancing our Prospects

Although the general trends covered in the preceding sections of this chapter are inexorable as to direction, their scale and rates can be changed. In this section we discuss some of the things that might be done to postpone or alleviate shortages.

Landsberg (1964, p. 6), in his scholarly survey of natural resources for the United States during the next decades, has proposed projections based on the following assumptions: "continuing gains in technology, improvements in political and social arrangements, and a reasonably free flow of world trade . . . and that there will be neither a large scale war nor a widespread economic depression like that of the early 1930's." If Landsberg's assumptions are to be justified, attention must be given to their alternatives, and the unpleasant consequences of failure of those assumptions must be avoided.

The forseeable exhaustion of ores of some metals, and the continually decreasing grade of most ore deposits now used, warn that ample lead time will be needed for technology to work out such answers as it can and, similarly, to allow the economy and the population density to make the necessary adjustments to changing mineral supplies. To avoid scarcities and the unpleasant results of some of our technical advances will call both for research and for forward-looking institutional action. The more immediate the promise of practical gain, the greater will be the willingness of private industry to finance the necessary research. Much of the required research, however, is of the long-range exploratory kind, the results of which cannot be guaranteed, but from which answers of critical importance will come eventually. Planning and prosecution of such research must be a continuing function of the governments of successful industrial nations. Integrated national and international resource policies are also needed to harmonize or adjudicate the demands of the many special segments of an economy that utilizes natural resources.

Exploration for metals in short supply, or which have diminishing reserves, is an obvious practical safeguard. Because the number of mineral deposits is finite, the lead time necessary for new discoveries increases as undiscovered shallow deposits become fewer. New reserves of metals are likely to be found in blind ore bodies, and the kinds and locale of blind ore bodies can be inferred from study of the metallogenic provinces of the world and their geology. Intensified geochemical and geological mapping of the world to delimit its metallogenic provinces, together with topical studies of the genesis and localizing conditions of blind ore bodies, could enhance the discovery rate—especially where theory is tested by the drill and where the scale of mapping is reasonably large.

National attitude, economic advantages, military advantages, and current leaders will all change with time. Their interplay will require constant vigilance on the part of nations that wish to maintain or develop a healthy industrial economy. To allow sufficient lead time in the decades ahead for economic and technical adjustments, national and international monitoring groups will be needed to warn of impending critical resource shortages and to recommend remedies. Industrial countries would do well to develop geologically oriented continuing national inventories of reserves both at home and abroad, in part to neutralize the all-too-prevalent notions that mineral resources are in effect inexhaustible and that potential mineral shortages can be ignored. As former Bureau of Mines Director Walter Hibbard (1968) has made clear, we are rapidly approaching a time when indifference can be disastrous.

If the present divisiveness of the world persists, moreover, nations will need to buffer their economies against external control of vital resources or else exploit the scarcities of others in those commodities that they have in exportable surplus. It would seem better for all concerned to further policies of coexistence and cooperation.

Broad policy concerning mineral resources will best evolve where appropriate high-level legislators and executives are advised by an active "watchdog" group of qualified commodity specialists, geologists, geo-chemists, and mineral technologists from government, business, and the universities. With such a group monitoring the various complex facets of the mineral industry, and able to assure effective preventive action, stresses caused by utilization of exhaustible foreign and domestic ore sources can be minimized. Without such a group, recurrent or persistent shortages will occur in the supply of some or many metals.

It is appropriate to end this discourse by outlining some steps that might be taken by the staff of such a monitoring group (including behavioral scientists) to improve national and world prospects for the future.

The objective should be to predict from weighted trends of supply and demand which commodities are likely to present serious problems and at what time. Extrapolations from historical data must be coupled with perceptive consideration of population growth and consequent future demands. Attention should be concentrated on critical or near-critical materials and in an ecological context. The energy used and the cost of mining extremely low-grade, currently noncommercial, mineral deposits should be considered in relation to other aspects of the human ecosystem. The loss of options caused by increased numbers of shortages, together with the resulting increase in vulnerability, must be balanced against other potential losses of options accompanying gain in metal supply.

Special attention should be given to the nature of the mineral concentra-tions that might supply various critical metals. Mathematical models of grade-tonnage relations in different kinds of ore deposits should be developed with careful consideration of the geological factors involved. Those deposits that show an A/G ratio should be studied to determine the range of grade through which such a ratio holds. Other types of distribution, such as log-normal and normal distributions, and complex distributions having stepwise curves in the grade-tonnage relation, should all be the subject of intense study. Quantity and position of submarginal grades should be determined and related to known ore deposits and to metallogenic provinces. Do such submarginal grades exist as many small scattered deposits, or do they occur in large individual deposits that could be worked with economies of scale? Elements that show bimodal distribution in their tonnage-grade relation (such as salt, coal, and similar materials) should be considered in terms of the relation between commercial concentration and crustal abundance.

It should be possible to derive for an appreciable number of critical elements of low crustal concentrations a quantitative or semi-quantitative correlation that would relate clarke multipliers for ore to the likelihood of an exponential grade-tonnage relationship reaching well below present ore grades. Such a correlation would furnish a practical basis for separating those elements likely to cause catastrophic shortages at some future date from those that are unlikely to generate such problems. Such studies would go far toward avoiding the mistake of lumping all mineral resources into a single category and would generate a spotlight for those most susceptible to shortages.

References

Barnett, H. J. 1967. The myth of our vanishing resources. *Trans. Social Sciences & Modern Society*, June 1967, pp. 7–10.

Barnett, H. J., and C. Morse. 1963. *Scarcity and growth*. Resources for the Future. Baltimore: Johns Hopkins Press.

Bogue, D. J. 1967. *The prospects for world population control*. Univ. of Chicago, Community and Family Study Center.

Brooks, D. B. 1967. The lead-zinc anomaly. *Trans. Soc. Mining Engrs*. 238: 129–136.

Brown, H., J. Bonner, and J. Weir. 1957. *The next hundred years*. New York: Viking Press.

Davis, K. 1967. Population policy: will current programs succeed? *Science* 158: 730–739.

Evans, B., ed. 1968. *Dictionary of quotations*. New York: Delacorte Press.

Flawn, P. T. 1967. Concepts of resources: Their effects on exploration and United States mineral policy. In *Exploration economics of the petroleum industry*, vol. 5, pp. 5–24. Houston, Tex.: Gulf Publishing Co.

Hibbard, W. 1968. Mineral resources: Challenge or threat? *Science* 160: 143–150.

Hutchinson, G. E. 1967. Ecological biology in relation to maintenance and improvement of the human environment. In *Applied Science and Technological Progress*. Report to the Committee on Science and Astronautics, U.S. House of Representatives, by the National Academy of Sciences, pp. 171–184.

Landsberg, H. H. 1964. *Natural resources for U.S. growth.* Resources for the Future. Baltimore: Johns Hopkins Press.

Lasky, S. G. 1950a. Mineral resources appraisal by the U.S. Geological Survey. *Colorado School of Mines Quarterly* 45(1A): 1–27.

Lasky, S. G. 1950b. How tonnage-grade relations help predict ore reserves. *Eng. Mining J.* 151(4): 81–85.

Lasky, S. G. 1955. Mineral industry futures can be predicted. II. *Eng. Mining J.* 155(9): 94–96.

McMahon, A. D. 1965. *Copper, a material survey.* U.S. Bureau of Mines Info. Circ. 8225. Washington, D.C.

Morris, H. T., and T. S. Lovering. 1952. Supergene and hydrothermal dispersion of heavy metals in wall rocks near ore bodies, East Tintic district, Utah. *Econ. Geol.* 47: 685–716.

Netschert, B. C. 1964. Testimony presented to the Federal Power Commission. Docket Nos. Ar64-2, et al.

Pinchot, G. 1910. *The fight for conservation.* New York: Doubleday Page & Co.

Schurr, S. H., B. C. Netschert, with V. F. Eliasberg, J. Lerner, and H. H. Landsberg. 1960. *Energy in the American economy, 1850–1975.* Resources for the Future. Baltimore: Johns Hopkins Press.

U.S. Bureau of Mines. 1956. *Minerals facts and problems.* Washington, D.C.

U.S. Bureau of Mines, 1965a. Metals and Minerals. *Minerals Yearbook*, vol. 1. Washington, D.C.

U.S. Bureau of Mines, 1965b. *Mercury potential of the United States.* U.S. Bureau of Mines Info. Circ. 8252. Washington, D.C.

U.S. President's Materials Policy Commission. 1952. *Resources for freedom,* 5 vols. William S. Paley, Chairman. Washington, D.C.

7/Mineral Resources from the Sea

Preston Cloud

*"Undersea prospecting for minerals is
plainly a complicated, expensive business where
the risk is great and the rewards are unknown."*
—Willard Bascom, 1967, p. 28

Growing interest in oceanography and marine geology has generated its
share of predictions about a "mineral cornucopia" in and beneath the sea,
waiting only to be harvested (e.g., Borgese, 1968; Mero, 1966; Spilhaus,
1966; Stephens, 1967). Other evaluations of the sea's mineral resources are
less euphoric. Emery (1966a, p. 24) concludes that "the truth probably lies
somewhere between the beliefs of these optimists and the less well represented
pessimists who have found neither gold nor diamonds in their thousands of
ocean-floor samples."

Values of geological resources taken from the sea in 1964 are shown in
Table 7.1, where they are compared with values of the same resources taken
from the land. Figure 7.1 is a graph of related 1964 statistics for world
production of all geological resources. Values, rather than quantities, are
used in these comparisons, because they provide a uniform frame of
reference. It should also be emphasized that, strictly speaking, all the
products here listed as coming from the sea, except those extracted from
seawater, are in truth continental products, even though they were taken
from below water on the submerged continental margins. They are treated

Typescript received October 1967. Final revision, June 1968.

here as marine resources, not because that is geologically reasonable, but because it is conventional to do so.

The data show that, in 1964, offshore production represented about 10 percent of the total known value of the specific mineral products recovered (Table 7.1) and about 5 percent of the entire world mineral output (Figure 7.1). About one-fourth of the production, about a billion dollars in value, was adjacent to the United States. In terms of U.S. and world economies, therefore, significant quantities of oil and gas, sulfur, magnesium, bromine, salt, oyster shells, tin, and sand and gravel are now being produced from the sea. What are the future prospects, both for these and for other substances not now being recovered in quantity? That depends, to be sure, both on what we seek and where we look, but both prophets and pragmatists agree on one thing: before quantities, grades, and recovery costs for most materials can be bracketed within meaningful limits, more extensive studies will be

TABLE 7.1

Approximate values, in millions of dollars, of geological resources taken from offshore in 1964 compared with values of the same resources taken from the land. (Values of land resources include those of resources taken from undersea extensions of land mines.)

Resource	From the sea		From the land	
	United States	Rest of world	United States	Rest of world
From seawater				
Magnesium[a]	50	?	5	?
Bromine	25	?	30	0
Salt (NaCl)	15	25	190	?
From the sea floor				
Diamonds	0	4	0	?
Gold	0	?	50	1,500
Tin	0	>20	negligible	600
Iron	0	1	800	4,500
Manganese	0	0	3	420
Phosphorite	0	0	160	215
Sand and gravel	10±	>15	850	?
Oyster shells	30	?	?	?
From beneath the sea floor				
Oil and gas	800	2,900	10,500	17,000
Sulfur	20	0	150	140
Total	950	2,965+	12,738	24,375

Sources: Emery, 1966a; Gaber and Reynolds, 1965; Weeks, 1965a; Battelle Institute, 1966; U.S. Bureau of Mines. Figures for tin and for world sand and gravel from Lampietti, 1968.

[a]U.S. production of magnesium is about half that of the rest of the world, but information on percentages produced from the sea and from the land outside the United States are not available.

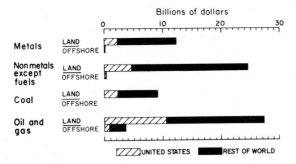

FIGURE 7.1
Value, in billions of dollars, of all geological resources
recovered from the land during 1964 compared with the
value of total production from offshore. (After Emery,
1966a, Figure 2, with slight alterations to include
chemical extraction from seawater.)

needed of sea-floor geology, concentrating processes, and methods of
evaluation and recovery. Legal aspects and tax codes also need to be resolved
(Alexander, 1967; Borgese, 1968).

Pending such developments, however, a review of mineral and chemical
potentialities beyond the coasts can reveal some logical constraints.

Mineral and chemical resources from the sea are to be sought among the
following:

1. *Seawater;*
2. *Placer deposits* within or beneath now-submerged beach or stream
   deposits;
3. *Sediments* other than placers, *and sedimentary rocks* that overlie
   crystalline rocks *(a) on the continental shelves and slopes* (the "continental margins"; about 15 percent of the total sea floor), *and (b)
   beyond the continental margins* (about 85 percent of the total sea floor;
   the truly oceanic realm);
4. *Crystalline rock* exposed at the sea floor or lying beneath sediments
   (a) on the continental margins, and (b) beyond the continental margins.

Let us examine what each of these sources now yields and what it might
yield to innovations in methods of discovery and extraction.

SEAWATER

The sea contains about 1.5×10^{18} metric tons (330 million cubic miles) of
water—an amount so enormous that total quantities of dissolved substances
are large even where their concentrations are small. Yet recovery of such
substances accounts for little more than 2 percent of current production of

TABLE 7.2

**Concentrations of the elements in seawater
and their values in elemental or combined form.**

(The elements are listed in order of abundance; those in italic type have
concentrations valued at $1 or more per million gallons of seawater.)

Element	Concentration ($lb/10^6$ gal)	Value ($/10^6$ gal)	
		as	
Chlorine	166,000	NaCl	924
Sodium	92,000	Na_2CO_3	378
Magnesium	11,800	Mg	4,130
Sulfur	7,750	S	101
Calcium	3,500	$CaCl_2$	150
Potassium	3,300	K_2O (equiv)	91
Bromine	570	Br_2	190
Carbon	250	Graphite	8×10^{-5}
Strontium	70	$SrCO_3$	2
Boron	40	H_3BO_3	3
Silicon	26	—	—
Fluorine	11	CaF_2	0.35
Argon	5	—	—
Nitrogen	4	NH_4NO_3	1
Lithium	1.5	Li_2CO_3	36
Rubidium	1.0	Rb	125
Phosphorus	0.6	$CaHPO_4$	0.08
Iodine	0.5	I_2	1
Barium	0.3	$BaSO_4$	0.01
Indium	0.2	In	4
Zinc	0.09	Zn	0.013
Iron	0.09	Fe_2O_3	0.001
Aluminum	0.09	Al	0.04
Molybdenum	0.09	Mo	0.004
Selenium	0.04	Se	0.2
Tin	0.03	Sn	0.05
Copper	0.03	Cu	0.01
Arsenic	0.03	As_2O_3	0.002
Uranium	0.03	U_3O_8	0.3
Nickel	0.02	Ni	0.02

Element	Concentration (lb/10⁶ gal)	Value ($/10⁶ gal)	
		as	
Vanadium	0.02	V_2O_5	0.04
Manganese	0.02	Mn	0.006
Titanium	0.009	TiO_2	0.003
Antimony	0.004	Sb	0.002
Cobalt	0.004	Co	0.006
Cesium	0.004	Cs	0.4
Cerium	0.004	CeO_2	0.02
Yttrium	0.003	YCl_3	0.3
Silver	0.003	Ag	0.02
Lanthanum	0.003	—	—
Krypton	0.003	—	—
Neon	0.0009	—	—
Cadmium	0.0009	Cd	0.002
Tungsten	0.0009	W	0.002
Xenon	0.0009	—	—
Germanium	0.0006	GeO_2	0.06
Chromium	0.0004	Cr_2O_3	0.00001
Thorium	0.0004	ThO_2	0.0009
Scandium	0.0004	Sc_2O_3	1
Lead	0.0003	Pb	0.00004
Mercury	0.0003	Hg	0.002
Gallium	0.0003	Ga(?)	0.2
Bismuth	0.0002	Bi	0.0008
Niobium	0.00009	Nb_2O_5	0.0001
Thallium	0.00009	Tl	0.00007
Helium	0.00004	—	—
Gold	0.00004	Au	0.02
Protactinum	2×10^{-8}	—	—
Radium	9×10^{-10}	Ra (in salts)	0.002
Radon	5×10^{-15}	—	—

Sources: Concentrations from Goldberg, 1963; values based on 1965 bulk prices for the related industrial form.

minerals and chemicals from the sea. Only magnesium, bromine, and common salt (Table 7.1) are now being extracted in significant quantities, and, for them, the seas do contain reserves that can be considered to be inexhaustible under any forseeable pressures. In 1964 about 90 percent of the magnesium and 45 percent of the bromine produced in the United States came from seawater, and those amounts could easily be increased.

At the other extreme of accessibility is the 10 billion tons of gold in seawater —about 0.005 troy ounce of gold in every million gallons of water. Although capable people and corporations have attempted to recover some, the amount of gold so far reported to have been extracted from seawater is not quite one-tenth of one milligram, with a value considerably less than one mill (Mero, 1965, p. 42).

Table 7.2 shows how the roughly 50 quadrillion (5×10^{16} tons of dissolved substances in the sea are distributed among the elements. Sixty of the 92 naturally occurring elements now known have been detected in seawater with the aid of sensitive modern tests. Of these, however, only the first 15 listed occur in quantities of more than 1.8 kilograms per million liters—or one pound per million gallons on the English scale, which best serves immediate purposes. Another 15, italicized in Table 7.2, include those concentrated at values of $1 or more per million gallons. Only 9, all of them among the first 15 in abundance, represent 1965 values of more than $10 per million gallons. These 9 (or their salts), plus boron, fluorine, and iodine, offer the best promise for direct recovery from seawater through ion exchange, biological concentration, or other processes. Even among this 12, however, most have better sources among the emerged marine sediments.

Omitting these 12, and with the possible further exception of cesium, uranium, yttrium, and remote outside chances for manganese and aluminum, the metal elements we might most like to extract from seawater offer little promise for direct recovery. Take zinc, high among the metals sought by industry. A modest operation aimed at grossing $120,000 per year at 1968 values before costs for salaries, operations, and investment would require the complete stripping of zinc from 9,000 billion gallons (nearly 9 cubic miles) of ordinary seawater annually—a volume equivalent to the combined average annual flows of the Hudson and Delaware rivers. The production from this operation, however, would be only about 400 tons of zinc; a trickle compared with the 122,400 tons used industrially in the United States in the same year. The practicality of such an operation is not impressive.

Direct extraction from ordinary seawater, however, is not the only alternative. Some natural waters contain higher than usual concentrations of all or particular dissolved substances. The Dead Sea, for instance, is roughly 10 times as concentrated as normal seawater, and the Red Sea shows a cadmium concentration about 10,000 times greater than that of the oceans. There are also places in the Red Sea, and conceivably along parts of the rifted oceanic rises, where waters containing relatively high concentrations of economically interesting dissolved ions are issuing from fracture zones beneath the sea floor (Miller et al., 1966). This may be true especially where such rises emerge beneath or have been overridden by continental types of rocks. A different type of concentration takes place in relatively deep basins that are isolated by barriers from the general oceanic circulation and thus from mixing. Such basins characteristically are near the coast or are inland seas. In these basins, oxygen is commonly depleted at depth, affecting the amounts and concentration ratios of dissolved ions as well as the substances that accumulate at the sea floor. The most concentrated such anoxic waters may occur at great depths, but engineering problems associated with tapping them are small compared with the problems involved in mining the sea bottom for solid materials. Some constraints pertinent to mining in only 200 meters of water are not significant in tapping a liquid resource at 2,000 or even 5,000 meters. Liquids are easily pumped, the effective head is small (even if chemical processing is to be done at the surface), and precise positioning of pumping platforms is not crucial. The troublesome difficulties are those of inventing and applying satisfactory concentrating processes and of handling economic volumes of water.

Research is needed to establish what will be profitable, marginal, or unlikely in the realm of extraction from seawater. Although eventual industrial recovery seems feasible for such elements as sodium, sulfur, potassium, iodine (in addition to magnesium and bromine), and perhaps for fluorine, strontium, and boron, it seems highly improbable for such elements as silver, gold, platinum, tin, molybdenum, nickel, tungsten, mercury, and most of the others below the first 15 listed in Table 7.2. In developing a plan to test the potential of seawater as a source of metals, therefore, it would be wise to begin with those occasional areas where biological, chemical, or subcrustal processes may have concentrated elements of interest. The ability of some organisms to concentrate selectively a limited number of metals should also be studied to see if it could be utilized directly or replicated synthetically.

SUBMERGED PLACER DEPOSITS

Placer deposits now offshore were formed by gravitational segregation during transport in and beneath former beach and stream deposits when the sea stood at lower levels or the land at higher ones. The general outer limit of depth at which such deposits can be expected is about 100 to 130 meters, the probable position of the beach at times of maximal volume of continental ice during Pleistocene glaciation. Where the land itself has undergone movement, this depth may be greater or less. It is not impossible

TABLE 7.3
Production values of some dry-land placer deposits.

Metal or Mineral	Place	Approximate Value Produced in Millions of 1967 U.S. Dollars	Average Value per Cubic Yard in 1967 U.S. Dollars
Platinum (at $100 per troy oz)	Goodnews Bay, Alaska	70	2.00
	Choco, Columbia	90	0.65
Gold (at $35 per troy oz)	Nome, Alaska[a]	125	0.50
	Calif. placers	1,000	?
	Pato, Colombia	100	0.25
	Bulolo, New Guinea	75	0.30
Tin	Bangka, Indonesia[b]	1,500	0.75
	Kinta Valley, Malaysia	2,800	0.50
Rutile and ilmenite	Trailridge, Florida[a]	75	0.35
	Queensland, Australia[a]	40	0.50

Source: Supplied by F. J. Lampietti, 1968, with permission of Ocean Mining, A.G.
[a] Originally concentrated in the littoral zone, although now emerged.
[b] About 10 percent of Bangka tin has come from offshore areas.

that a different kind of placer might be found beneath the moving sedimentary carpet in the upper parts of submarine canyons, but nothing of this sort has as yet been reported.

Diamonds, gold, and tin are currently being recovered from nearshore submarine placers (the diamonds, up to 1967 at least, at a cost in excess of their value). Approximate 1964 global values, omitting cost of recovery, were: diamonds, $4 million; tin, "at least $21 million" (Lampietti, 1968); gold, unknown. None of this was produced adjacent to North America. Although geological knowledge of source areas and shore zone displacements indicate good prospects for gold off Alaska, detailed investigations of this region will be needed to establish reserves and grades.

It should be emphasized that submarine placers offer the best current prospects of obtaining metals other than magnesium from the sea at a profit. Table 7.3, indicating the values of some placer deposits on land, suggests the possible magnitude of target areas—although comparable deposits offshore will be much harder to locate, delimit, and exploit than similar deposits on land. In planning for the optimal use of such potential resources, a future-minded world and nation might give careful thought to the kind of development program that would produce the most over the longest term with the least injury to the natural environment and its bio-logical resources. In seeking to develop such a plan it would be well to begin with a much more comprehensive knowledge than we now possess of the geology and biology of the continental shelf and the areas directly inland and seaward from it. Development of such knowledge should not exclude a modest exploitative program, useful in developing methods, skills, and legislation; but it should precede large-scale operations, which, if un-controlled, might result in greater losses to other resources than gains from those exploited.

SEDIMENTS AND SEDIMENTARY ROCKS

On the Continental Margins

Continental-shelf sediments of post-Paleozoic age, and salt-dome structures within them, account for nearly 98 percent of all the mineral and chemical wealth currently produced from within and beneath the sea—by far the greater part of this being oil and gas (Table 7.1, Figure 7.1). About 17 percent of the world's petroleum and natural gas now comes from offshore fields, nearly half the fields and about one-fourth the production being contiguous to the United States.

Exploration for oil and gas on the continental shelves is far more advanced than for other minerals, some 60 or more countries now being actively involved in the search. From data available in 1965, Weeks (1965a, p. 1680, 1688; 1965b, p. 32) has estimated that 700 billion barrels of petroleum liquids can be produced by primary recovery methods from beneath the continental shelves of the world—perhaps one-third to one-fourth of the total ultimately recoverable petroleum reserves of the world at large. By including 300 billion barrels each for petroleum-gas and hoped-for secondary recovery, and a further 1,200 billion barrels for liquid fuels to be recovered from as yet unknown offshore "tar sands," "oil shales," and other bitu-minous rocks except coal, Weeks gets a grand total of 2,500 billion barrels of liquid fuels considered to be potentially recoverable from offshore areas world wide.

The data, however, are interpreted differently by different people, and the figures most generally accepted are 700–1,000 billion barrels. The postulated 200 billion barrels enclosed in "tar sands" and 1,000 billion barrels in "oil shales" and other bituminous rocks are hypothetical, and, if present, would involve enormous recovery problems. To handle the neces-sarily large volumes of target rock and overburden is difficult enough on dry land. Beneath the sea the difficulties escalate.

As for the petroleum itself, it is shown in Chapter 8 that even the largest

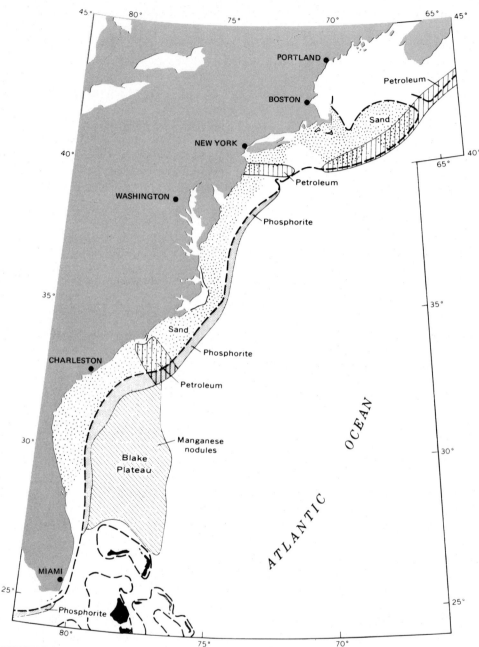

FIGURE 7.2
Distribution of the most favorable areas for some potential mineral resources off the Atlantic coast
of the United States. The dashed line denotes the position of the edge of the continental shelf, about
80 meters deep in the south and about 140 meters deep in the north. The area indicated for
manganese nodules corresponds to the surface of the Blake Plateau. (After Emery, 1965, Figure 1.)

quantities likely to be found offshore (including petroleum that may now be forming) will not greatly prolong the exhaustion of estimated reserves at current rates of consumption. Energy requirements eventually will have to be met by nuclear sources. Such sources, indeed, will probably dominate the energy market before the end of the century. Meanwhile the continental shelves are an attractive and large (but temporary) target for new oil production.

Some of the offshore features that produce oil in the Gulf of Mexico (the vertically cross-cutting structures called salt domes) also yield sulfur. More than 5 percent of the world's sulfur now comes from such sources. Current reserves, however, will have been depleted by about 1990 (Flawn, 1966, p. 350), and new discoveries or other sources (e.g., gypsum) will have to take up the slack.

Sand, gravel, and shells for construction and other purposes are a major potential continental-shelf resource, especially nearshore deposits in coastal regions; although there are problems about rates of replenishment and destruction of the shell resource. Values of such products recovered off the coast of the United States in 1964 include about $30 million for oyster shells, but good figures for sand, gravel, and other nonmetal industrial materials are not available. The figures listed for sand and gravel in Table 7.1 are only educated guesses. Nevertheless, quantities available are large and recovery could easily be increased, given both economic conditions that make it worthwhile and more detailed information on distribution and thickness.

Phosphate deposits have been found on the continental shelves, the continental slopes, or on offshore banks off both coasts of the United States, off the west coasts of Central and South America, and off Argentina, Japan, and South Africa. They may be widespread in regions of upwelling water. They occur as blanketing deposits of nodules, crusts, and fine sediments on the sea floor. Although their areal extent is often reported to be large, it is not well established, and their thicknesses, where known, appear to be small. Some of these submarine phosphorites, however, are comparable in grade to those mined on land, occur at depths that are probably workable by known techniques, and may one day become a competitive resource. As it is, they could well be a source of local fertilizer phosphate near areas remote from current sources. Over the long term, in combination with large onshore reserves (McKelvey, 1967) and the possibility of recycling, they permit the hope, though not the assurance, that man is not likely to want for the fertilizer phosphate essential to agriculture (Chapter 4) as long as he has land to put it on and is willing to pay the price. Phosphate is one nonplacer submarine mineral that offers relatively good prospects both for respectable volume in known deposits and for future additions as a result of new discovery—in part because there is a good theory of origin to direct the search for it (McKelvey, 1967). One locality that calls for further investigation if off the Pacific Coast of Central America, about 1,000 kilometers south of

San Diego, where Mero (1966, p. 77) estimates a fine-grained unconsolidated deposit to be very large and easily recoverable.

Glauconite, once considered a potential source of potash, occurs under conditions comparable to those in which phosphorite is found—as lag-deposits on the continental shelves in areas of little or no recent sediment accumulation. Other sources of potash render glauconite unimportant for that purpose, however, and, if it were needed for potash, there are large quantities of easily accessible glauconite in elevated marine deposits on the continents. The supplies on land are also sufficient to meet other likely uses of glauconite, unless the land under which it lies is pre-empted for other purposes.

The potential resources of the continental-shelf sediments should not be passed over without mention of freshwater. Coastal regions with wide continental shelves whose blanketing sediments are continuous with deposits on land and are inclined offshore may contain large quantities of pure artesian water in aquifers below impervious beds. The Atlantic continental shelf of the United States displays such conditions on a grand scale. Although this particular source may not compete with surface waters and wells on land (because of good adjacent onshore water supply and problems of withdrawal and transport in the sea), it could be locally useful in supplying long-term installations at sea or in providing emergency sources of un-contaminated water. In other parts of the world, freshwater from the seabed is in greater demand. It has long been a source of water supply for some islands, and an intensive search for freshwater has been in progress off the coasts of Greece and Lebanon, under United Nations auspices, since 1963.

Recent reconnaissance studies have made the Atlantic continental shelf of the United States one of the best known large offshore regions in the world —at least insofar as features at the surface of the seafloor are concerned (Emery, 1965, 1966b). Figure 7.2 delimits the areas within which prospects of finding particular mineral deposits are considered to be favorable. It will be obvious from this coarse-grained map, however, that a great deal remains to be done even here, let alone in less explored parts of the world, before any really useful assessment of practicability or economic potential can be made. Studies needed include detailed sea-bottom mapping and subsurface exploration in areas judged to be promising.

Beyond the Continental Margins

Seaward from the continental slopes, the blanketing sediments are of three main genetic types. Most extensive by far are the pelagic sediments,[1] con-

---

[1] Including sedimentary rocks, such as the Eocene chert reported from the deep Atlantic Ocean by the Deep Sea Drilling Project Staff in *Geotimes*, March 1969, and by M. N. A. Peterson in *Ocean Industry*, May 1969.

sisting of particles of biologic, windborne, and chemical origin that settle through the overlying water column throughout the ocean basins but which are conspicuous only in the absence of other sediments. Of lesser but still significant areal extent are the deposits of the abyssal plains that were carried out by sediment-laden density currents from the continental margins. Third, and least extensive of the oceanic sediments, are those of the continental rises, sediments that have slumped or slid away from the continental slopes to form relatively thick but areally not very extensive wedges of sediments (about 5 percent of the total sea floor) that extend from the outer edge of the continetal slope out over the deep sea floor, at places for hundreds of miles.

The tops of the continental rises have characteristics that could make them promising targets for petroleum exploration when it becomes practicable to operate beneath water depths of 2 to 2.5 kilometers (Emery, 1963).

The detrital abyssal-plain deposits are of little interest from the viewpoint of mineral resources. Consisting mainly of poorly sorted siliceous detritus, they occur at depths generally greater than 4,000 meters, and the existence of ample more convenient sources of sand, rule out their use as construction materials. Heavy metals that might once have been contained in them as placers would most likely have been left behind far up the slope or would have become dispersed. They might conceivably serve as reservoir rocks for petroleum, should they be found within a sufficiently thick column of possible source sediments and beneath an impervious seal. The limited thicknesses of underlying sedimentary columns indicated by seismic refraction data, however, and the probable geologic history of the sea floor beneath them, make it very unlikely that the abyssal plain sediments of the open ocean (as distinct from inland seas and gulfs) will be found to contain substantial quantities of recoverable petroleum.[2]

Pelagic sediments at both bathyal (200–4,000 meters) and abyssal (greater than 4,000 meters) depths, to be sure, do represent an enormous volume of material having peculiarities that would be of interest as source sediments for certain metal elements *were they to be found on land in areas susceptible to enrichment processes*. Figure 7.3 shows that, compared with igneous rocks, pelagic sediments are enriched by 5 to 10 times in manganese, nickel, copper, cobalt, lead, molybdenum, ytterbium, yttrium, lanthanum, scandium, barium, and boron. This suggests, however, not that we should consider such marine deposits as potential ores, but that we might seek former pelagic sediments in now emerged parts of mobile regions where they are both accessible and may have locally been affected by postdepositional enrichment

---

[2] The discovery of oil and gas in a Jurassic salt dome at a depth of more than 3,600 meters in the geosynclinal Gulf of Mexico, reported by D. M. Taylor in *Ocean Industry*, Oct. 1968, is not really an exception to this conclusion. See also notes by M. N. A. Peterson, and by A. H. Bouma and R. Rezak, in *Ocean Industry*, May 1969, and an intervening anonymous article in the same issue.

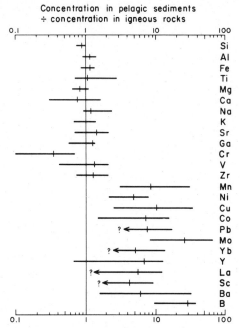

FIGURE 7.3
Abundances of metal elements in Pacific
pelagic sediments compared with those in
igneous rocks. Ranges are shown by the
horizontal lines and the position of averages by
the short vertical lines. (After Goldberg and
Arrhenius, 1958, Figure 3, p. 172, with the
permission of the authors and the Pergamon
Press.)

processes. As James (1968) points out, the danger in evaluating things like
the metal potential of currently forming pelagic sediments is to fall into an
arithmetic trap in which impressive *sums* of leanly dispersed (and remote)
metals are falsely equated with recoverable ores.

The manganese nodules and crusts of the deep sea have been widely
publicized as a potential major metal reserve. They are discussed at length by
Mero (1965, pp. 127–241), who considers them to constitute a vast potential
source, not only of manganese, but of various other metals in which they are
enriched—especially iron, nickel, copper, and cobalt, and possibly molybdenum, vanadium, lead, zinc, titanium, aluminum, and zirconium. Industrial interest to date has focused on the nickel, cobalt, and copper in
the nodules. Deposits of manganese nodules generally occur within a range
of depths from 3,000 to 6,000 meters, with a mean depth between 4,000 and
5,000 meters. They appear to be most abundant in the Pacific Ocean but
are found in all oceans. They reach their shallowest known depths of only

200 to 1,000 meters in the Atlantic Ocean—on the Blake Plateau off the Carolina coast (Figure 7.2). Thickness of accumulation is unknown, but available data suggests that known deposits are but a thin veneer at the sea floor. Suggested methods of recovery, therefore, involve devices to sweep or suck up this veneer from over large areas.

Based on a few hundred widely scattered data points, Mero estimates that there are between 90 billion and 1,660 billion metric tons of manganese nodules averaging 32 percent MnO_2 on the floor of the Pacific Ocean alone. The silica content of the nodules, however, is often as great as or greater than the content of manganese. This would render the latter unavailable under current metallurgical techniques—even were the nodules concentrated at a convenient place on land. Data are fewer for waters other than the Pacific Ocean, and distribution is apparently much less extensive.

Until information adequate for reliable estimates of volume has been accumulated, until there has been a revolution in techniques for recovering dispersed materials from great depths in the sea, and until a metallurgical process has been developed for treating silica-rich host rocks, the deep-sea nodules and crusts cannot be regarded as manganese ores. If the desired metallurgical advance is eventually achieved, moreover, it would make available large reserves of low-grade siliceous manganese deposits on land. Finally, the concept of the bathyal and abyssal manganese nodules as a rapidly self-renewing resource seems to be invalidated by recent data indicating accretion at the rate of only about 1 millimeter per 1000,000 years (Manheim, Pratt, and McFarlin, 1967).

Nevertheless, commercial interest continues with respect to other base metals in these nodules, and the technical risks involved are partially offset by the freedom from political and physical risks and taxation losses involved in many foreign operations on dry land. Evidently the last word is yet to be said on the potentialities of the manganese nodules. The ever-changing technological, cultural, and ecological aspects of the world's mineral resource needs and capabilities will have a crucial bearing on what that final word will be.

CRYSTALLINE ROCK

On the Continental Margins

Finding and exploiting mineralized crystalline rock on the sea floor—even on the continental shelves—involves the same problems as on land, plus many more. Although it is generally agreed by geologists that the substructure of the shelf and slope is of a continental rather than an oceanic type, and that comparable mineral deposits are to be expected, problems peculiar to the region are involved. Bedrock is more likely to be blanketed by postsubmergence sediments on the continental shelf than on the eroding elevated lands. Because of this, not to mention the overlying water, we cannot expect to find as high a proportion of the mineral deposits at the seabed of the continental shelf and slope as we find on the land.

The problem of sampling deposits found is beset by the same difficulties as their discovery, with extra complications because of weather and sea-surface conditions. Nevertheless, it seems a statistical certainty that even though *none* are as yet known, ore deposits will be found to occur in crystalline rocks somewhere on or beneath the continental shelves. How many of them will eventually be discovered and worked is another questior

Beyond the Continental Margins

Beyond the continental margins difficulties increase and prospects become even dimmer. With rare exceptions, perhaps, such crystalline rock at or beneath this part of the sea floor has never been exposed to atmospheric weathering or to the effects of percolating meteoric waters. Hence it cannot include the zones of surface enrichment produced by such processes, which both facilitate discovery and upgrade whatever mineralized parent rocks may be present.

Seismic velocities, moreover, and the little geological data available, imply that truly oceanic rocks beneath, within, and beyond the pelagic and abyssal-plain sediments are not similar to the more richly mineralized siliceous (sialic) rocks of the continental regions, including their submerged parts. The crystalline rocks of the ocean basins appear to be mainly basalts, probably limited both in the variety' of included minerals and in the degree of enrichment to be found. Nickel, chromium, copper, and platinum may be present, but (excluding the slim prospects of the already discussed manganese nodules) the first submarine ore of any of these is yet to be found. Iron and magnesium are probably the most abundant metal elements in the oceanic rocks, but these rocks could not compete with sources from dry land and from seawater.

Outcrops are to be sought in seamounts and along the mid-ocean rises, which comprise by far the most extensive and geologically most promising area to search (as well as that within easiest reach of current technology). Other geologic considerations, however, suggest that, if mineral deposits are found in truly oceanic rocks, they will either be unimportant or of kinds hitherto unknown on land—extensive continental outcrops of similar rock are generally characterized by a restricted content of ore minerals. One possibility is that base metals such as nickel and cobalt may be found in ultrabasic rocks or in mineralized fluids that may occur along the crests of mid-ocean rises. Another is that metallic-sulfide deposits may be formed at or close to the sea floor within and adjacent to active submarine volcanic piles (Kinkel, 1966). However, the now seemingly well documented modern theory of sea-floor spreading implies that, beneath a thin veneer of later sediments, the ocean basins are generally floored with relatively young and sparsely mineralized basaltic rocks. On the continents it is above all in the ancient sialic Precambrian shields, the most "continental" part of the continents, and in the thin platform sediments and intrusives that mantle and penetrate them, that we find our largest and richest metalliferous deposits. So far as we know, neither Precambrian shields nor platform sediments extend into the truly oceanic realm.

ANTICIPATING THE FUTURE

Man observes the floor of the sea in various ways. He measures depths by means of weighted lines or wires and by sonic sounding devices. He scans it with cameras, television, or from manned submersibles. He samples it with a battery of coring, dredging, and grabbing devices. And he uses geophysical techniques to estimate its magnetic, electrical, gravitational, acoustical, and elastic properties. A dazzling array of devices has recently become available, and others are being made ready, to extend his capability for direct observation. An industry tabulation ("Oceanography—an industry darling," 1967) lists 20 different manned submersibles built or being built by at least 10 different companies to operate at depths from 60 to 6,000 meters. An evaluation of the potential use of this equipment is given by Arnold (1967).

With such a battery of equipment, and with the scientists and engineers to man it, we might hope in a few more decades of exploration to come up with a more realistic idea than is now available about what is down there. Contrary to some suggestions, however, it will be difficult to get the information on thicknesses of deposits, as well as the samples, that will be needed to make useful estimates of volumes and grades. This will require boreholes into the sea floor from floating, anchored, or submerged platforms. Costs for such exploration, of course, are large, and accurate positioning is essential. Estimates for operations currently or recently in progress in relatively shallow water indicate that even these costs may exceed by 10 to 100 times the costs of land-based operations seeking similar information.

The maximum depth from which substances other than oil and gas were being recovered from the seabed in 1967 was about 40 meters, where placer tin was being taken from sea-floor sediments off Indonesia. Sampling with a view to eventual placer mining was being done in 1967 at a depth of 110 meters, however, and it would probably be feasible in the near future to extend the depth of surface mining to 200 meters if values were sufficiently large. It is a far cry from this to the manganese nodules that are so widely distributed at depths of 3,000 to 6,000 meters (Mero, 1965), but a depth of operation of 200 meters would put much of the now unworked resources of the continental shelves potentially within reach. Some of the problems to be expected in evaluating and mining these resources are discussed by Bascom (1967) and by Howard and Padan (1966). The problems of mining metals from crystalline rock beneath the floor of the sea will, of course, be much more difficult. It is unlikely that conventional explosives or mining methods will work there. Should valuable resources be found in such rock, completely new mining techniques will be required to extract them.

Finally, rising sea level, from melting ice caps or from movements of the land itself, should not be underrated as a long-range factor that could inundate present coastal cities and cause some resources now above sea level to become submerged resources of the future. Because melting of all present ice would raise sea level about 60 meters, and since the main trend of sea level over the past 20,000 years or so has been upward, eventual flooding is a real prospect for coastal cities that last as long as Rome or Marseilles. Informed foresight suggests that we should avoid overconcentrating urban development along present low coasts, that it would be prudent to know the location and value of resources now emerged to elevations of less than 60 meters, and that we should bear in mind that schemes for generating ice-free, high-latitude coasts imply accelerated rates of inundation throughout the world.

CONCLUSIONS

The mineral and chemical resources of the sea that will be of practical interest to man over the next half century are those that can be extracted from seawater or recovered from the seabed of the continental shelf and oceanic rises. About 5 percent of the world's known production of geological wealth came from the shelves and seawater in 1964 (Figure 7.1), and the trend is upward. In terms of current values, oil and gas are by far the most important products, although their duration at prevailing and expected rates of consumption will be limited. Seawater can supply all the magnesium and bromine that we need, as well as common salt and some other substances. Such a source, however, appears practicable for few important metal elements other than magnesium, sodium, potassium, iodine, and perhaps strontium and boron. Oyster shells (which are by no means an inexhaustible resource) are being taken from the shallower parts of the shelves in relatively large quantities, and the use of nearshore submarine sand and gravel will probably increase.

The sediments of the continental shelves and the crystalline rocks beneath them can be expected to produce mineral commodities similar to those of the immediately adjacent land. One way of guessing the magnitude of such resources has been tried by the U.S. Bureau of Mines (Hibbard, 1968). When points along the hundred-fathom depthline are reflected across the shoreline, they define an onshore area equivalent to the continental shelf and having roughly similar geologic properties. For the equivalent onshore area in the United States, in terms of 1966 dollars, the total cumulative value of minerals extracted since the beginning of the U.S. mineral industry was found to be $160 billion, excluding oil and gas ($240 billion including oil and gas). Because of geological differences, and other obstacles that beset discovery and recovery in the subsea environment, however, this figure is probably larger than the yield we can reasonably expect from the continental shelves. It should also be emphasized that most of the minerals in the onshore equivalent of the continental shelves are in the sediments and sedimentary rocks, not in the crystalline rocks beneath them; the same is likely to be true within the continental shelves. This exercise, nevertheless, supports the expectation that the submerged continental margin will prove to be a favorable target for further mineral exploration, not only for oil and gas but for metal, chemical, and construction resources as well.

In finding such deposits, geophysical methods will play an even more important part than they do on land. This is partly because direct observation cannot be made at the same scale of detail and with the same speed as on land and partly because many of the geophysical measurements are made more cheaply and effectively at sea than on land.

The ocean basins beyond the continental margin are not promising places to seek mineral resources. It is not by accident, but for good geological and geochemical reasons, that so many of the world's large and rich metalliferous deposits are found in the sialic Precambrian basement rocks at the cores of the continents, around younger continental intrusions of siliceous igneous rocks, and in the overlapping platform sediments. Nevertheless, being curious and experimental, man would like to see what can be obtained from the ocean depths. It is, moreover, by no means out of the question that materials of substantial value will be won there. What we must avoid is to succumb to the misleading notion that a great variety of resources are available in large volumes, such that when we run out of terrestrial resources we can simply turn to the sea. There are other and better reasons for studying the ocean basins than for their supposed endemic mineral wealth.

A "mineral cornucopia" beneath the sea thus exists only in hyperbole. What is actually won from it will be the result of persistent, imaginative research, inspired invention, bold and skillful experiment, and intelligent application and management—and resources found will come mostly from the submerged continental shelves, slopes, and rises. Whether they will be large or small is not known. It is a fair guess that they will be respectably large; but if present conceptions of earth structure and of sea-floor composition and history are even approximately correct, minerals from the seabed are not likely to compare in volume or in value with those yet to be taken from the emerged lands. As for seawater itself, despite its large volume and the huge quantities of dissolved salts it contains, it can supply few of the substances considered essential to modern industry.

References

Alexander, L. M., ed. 1967. *The law of the sea.* Columbus: Ohio State Univ. Press.

Arnold, H. A. 1967. Manned submersibles for research. *Science* 158: 84–95.

Bascom, W. 1967. Mining the ocean depths. *Geosci. News* 1(1): 10–11, 26–28.

Battelle Institute. 1966. *Development potential of U.S. continental shelves.* U.S. Dept. of Commerce, Coast and Geodetic Survey. Washington, D.C.

Borgese, E. M. 1968. The republic of the deep seas. *The Center Magazine* 1(4): 18–27.

Emery, K. O. 1963. *Oceanographic factors in accumulation of petroleum.* Sixth World Petroleum Congress, 19–26 June 1963, Frankfort am Main, Sec. 1, Paper 42.

Emery, K. O. 1965. *Some potential mineral resources of the Atlantic continental margin.* U.S. Geol. Survey Prof. Paper 525-C.

Emery, K. O. 1966a. Geological methods for locating mineral deposits on the ocean floor. In *Marine Technology Society*, *Trans.* 2nd Marine Technology Society Conference, pp. 24–43.

Emery, K. O. 1966b. *Atlantic continental shelf and slope of the United States— Geologic background.* U.S. Geol. Survey Prof. Paper 525-A.

Flawn, P. T. 1966. *Mineral resources.* Chicago: Rand McNally.

Gaber, N. H., and D. F. Reynolds, Jr. 1965. Economic opportunities in the oceans. *Battelle Technical Review* 14(12): 5–11.

Goldberg, E. D. 1963. The oceans as a chemical system. In *The Sea*, M. N. Hill, ed., vol. 2, pp. 3–25. New York: Wiley.

Goldberg, E. D., and G. Arrhenius. 1958. Chemistry of Pacific pelagic sediments. *Geochimica et Cosmochimica Acta* 13: 153–212.

Hibbard, W. R., Jr. 1968. Mineral resources: challenge or threat? *Science* 160: 143–150.

Howard, T. E., and J. W. Padan. 1966. Problems in evaluating marine mineral resources. *Mining Eng.*, June 1966, pp. 57–61.

James, H. L. 1968. *Mineral resource potential of the deep ocean.* U.S. Dept. of the Interior, release of a paper presented at a "Symposium on Mineral Resources of the World Ocean," Newport, Rhode Island, 11 July 1968.

Kinkel, A. R., Jr. 1966. Massive pyritic deposits related to volcanism, and possible methods of emplacement. *Econ. Geol.* 61: 633–694.

Lampietti, F. J. 1968. Letter of 17 January to Preston Cloud.

Manheim, F. T., R. M. Pratt, and P. F. McFarlin. 1967. *Geochemistry of manganese and phosphate deposits on the Blake Plateau.* Geol. Soc. America, Program 1967 Ann. Mtg., New Orleans, p. 139.

McKelvey, V. E. 1967. *Phosphate deposits.* U.S. Geol. Survey Bull. 1252-D.

Mero, J. L. 1965. *The mineral resources of the sea.* New York: Elsevier.

Mero, J. L. 1966. The future of mining the sea. *Oceanology Internat.*, Oct. 1966, pp. 73–78.

Miller, A. R., C. D. Densmore, E. T. Degens, J. C. Hathaway, F. T. Mannheim, P. F. McFarlin, R. Pocklington, and A. Jokela. 1966. Hot brines and recent iron deposits in deeps of the Red Sea. *Geochimica et Cosmochimica Acta* 30: 341–359.

Oceanography—an industry darling. 1967. *Investor's Reader* 49(2): 2–10. New York: Merrill Lynch, Pierce, Fenner and Smith, Inc.

Spilhaus, A. 1966. Exploiting the sea. *Industrial Research, Special Report on The Sea*, p. 62–68.

Stephens, W. M. 1967. Ocean harvest. *Sea Frontiers* 13(3): 158–168.

Weeks, L. G. 1965a. World offshore petroleum resources. *Am. Assoc. Petrol. Geol. Bull.* 49: 1680–1693.

Weeks, L. G. 1965b. Offshore oil. *Oil and Gas J.* 63(25): 127–148.

8/Energy Resources

M. King Hubbert

"The optimist proclaims that we live in the best of all possible worlds; and the pessimist fears this is true."
—James Branch Cabell, 1926, p. 129

Into and out of the earth's surface environment there occurs a continuous flux of energy, in consequence of which the material constituents of the earth's surface undergo continuous or intermittent circulation. By far the largest source of this energy flux is solar radiation, a small fraction of which is captured by the leaves of plants and stored as chemical energy. This chemically stored solar energy becomes the essential biological energy source for the entire animal kingdom. In particular, it supplies the energy required as food for the human population at an average rate of about 2,000 kilocalories per capita per day, or at a per-capita consumption rate of about 100 thermal watts.

During geologic history, a minute fraction of the organic matter of former plants and animals became buried in sedimentary sands, muds, and limes, under conditions of incomplete oxidation. This has become the source of our present supply of fossil fuels—coal, petroleum, and natural gas.

During the last hundred thousand years or so, the human species has slowly learned to manipulate the energy supply of its biologic and inorganic environment in such a manner as to produce a continuous increase in its total energy supply, and a resulting increase in its population. However,

Typescript received 28 October 1968. Final revision, 21 March 1969. Further revision of "Geothermal Energy," 3 July 1969.

until recent centuries the increase in the rate of total energy consumption was very much less than the increase in the rate of population growth. Consequently, the population has tended to remain in balance with the increase in energy supply, while the biologic and inorganic energy consumed per capita remained at a low, nearly constant level—only slightly more than that of the food supply.

Release from this constraint was not possible until an energy supply capable of exploitation faster than the human population could grow should become available. Such an energy supply is that represented by the fossil fuels. Continuous mining of coal began about eight centuries ago and production of petroleum just over one century ago. From small beginnings, the use of energy from these sources has grown until, during most of the last century, world consumption of energy from the fossil fuels has increased at about 4 percent per year. The world's human population has also responded to this stimulus and is now growing at a rate of just under 2 percent per year. Hence, at present, the world's average nonnutrient energy consumption per capita is increasing at about 2 percent per year.

Since the earth's deposits of fossil fuels are finite in amount and non-renewable during time periods of less than millions of years, it follows that energy from this source can be obtained for only a limited period of time. In the present study, it is estimated that the earth's coal supplies are sufficient to serve as a major source of industrial energy for two or three centuries. The corresponding period for petroleum, both because of its smaller initial supply and because of its more rapid rate of consumption, is only about 70–80 years.

In particular, it is estimated that the United States (exclusive of Alaska) will reach its culmination in crude-oil production near the end of the 1960-decade and its culmination in the production of natural gas about a decade later. The date at which world production of petroleum will reach its maximum is estimated to be about the year 2000, or about 30 years hence.

In view of the fact that 60 percent of the world's present production of energy for industrial purposes, and 67 percent of the United States', is obtained from petroleum and natural gas, the imminent culmination and decline in the annual supplies of these fuels poses problems of immediate concern. In the United States, in particular, there is a need for immediate formulation of policies concerned with making up the deficit in the supply of liquid and gaseous fuels soon to result from the decline in the production rate of oil and natural gas.

Looking farther into the future, the energy needs of the United States and the world could be met for another century or two by coal alone. After that, dependence upon other sources of energy would become unavoidable. Of these, large-scale power production directly from solar energy appears technologically unpromising. The world's potential supply of water power is comparable in magnitude to the present rate of energy consumption from the fossil fuels. However, most of this occurs in the industrially undeveloped areas of Africa, South America, and southeast Asia, and could only be utilized by a parallel industrialization of these areas. In addition, although water power is capable of continuing for periods of geologic time, a practical limit in the case of large dams and reservoirs is set by the period of a few centuries required for the reservoirs to fill with sediments.

Geothermal and tidal energy is now being exploited in a few suitable sites around the world, but the ultimate amount of power from these sources does not promise to be larger than a small fraction of the world's present power requirements.

This leaves us with nuclear energy as the only remaining energy source of sufficient magnitude and practicability of exploitation to meet the world's future energy needs at either present or increased rates of consumption. Of the possible sources of nuclear energy, that from fusion has not yet been achieved and may never be. Power from the fission of uranium-235 is an accomplished fact, and reactors in the 500 to 1,000 megawatt-capacity range, fueled principally by this isotope, are rapidly being constructed. However, the supply of uranium-235 is such that serious shortages in the United States are already anticipated within the next two decades.

In the light of present technology, we are left then with the development of full-breeding nuclear reactors capable of consuming all of natural uranium or of thorium as our only adequate source of long-range industrial power. In view of the impending shortage of uranium-235, which is essential as an initial fuel for breeder reactors, it is urgent that the present generation of light-water reactors using uranium-235 be replaced by full breeders at as early a date as possible. Once this has been done, power production from low-concentration deposits of uranium and thorium becomes economically practicable. The amount of energy represented by these sources is many times larger than that of the fossil fuels.

With the nation's and the world's principal industrial energy requirements supplied by nuclear energy, it would be desirable to conserve the remaining fossil-fuel resources for chemical purposes. More important, with an adequate energy supply, and with a stabilization of the world's human population at some near optimum magnitude, it should be possible to extend the high energy-per-capita standard of living now characteristic of its more industralized areas to all of the world's peoples.

ENERGY IN HUMAN AFFAIRS

When *Homo sapiens* evolved from his immediate hominid ancestors a hundred thousand years or so ago, he existed in some sort of ecological adjustment with the rest of the ecological complex, and competed with other members of that complex for a share of the contemporary flux of solar energy essential for his existence. At its earliest stage, the sole capacity of the human species for the utilization of energy must have been limited to the food which it ate—then, as now, about 2,000 kilocalories, or 8 million thermal joules, per capita per day.

Between this earliest stage and the dawn of recorded history, this species distinguished itself from all others in its inventiveness of means for the conquest of a larger and larger fraction of the available energy. The invention of clothing, the use of weapons, the control of fire, the domestication of animals and plants, all had this in common: each increased the fraction of solar energy available for use by the human species, thereby upsetting the ecologic balance in favor of an increased population of the human species, forcing adjustments of all other populations of the complex of which the human species was a member.

From that early beginning until the present this progression has continued at an accelerating rate. It has involved the employment of beasts of burden, the smelting of metals, using first wood and later coal as fuel, and the development of power from water and wind. However, throughout this period until within the last few centuries the rate at which these changes were accomplished was slow enough that the growth of population was more than able to keep pace. The rate of consumption of energy per capita, therefore, increased but slightly.

Emancipation from this dependence on contemporary solar energy was not possible until some other and hitherto unknown source of energy should become available. This had its beginning about the twelfth or thirteenth century when the inhabitants of the northeast coast of England discovered that certain black rocks found along the shore, and thereafter known as "sea coales," would burn. From this discovery, there followed in almost inevitable succession, the mining of coal and its use for domestic heating and for the smelting of metals, the development of the steam engine, the locomotive, steamships, and steam-electric power.

This progression was further augmented when, a little more than a century ago, a second large source of fossil energy from petroleum and natural gas was tapped, leading to the internal combustion engine, the automobile, the aeroplane, and diesel-electric power.

A third source of energy, that from the atomic nucleus, was first brought under control as recently as 1942, but already it is rapidly becoming the world's largest source of power.

INDUSTRIAL ENERGY

Our principal concern in the present chapter is with the large quantities of energy required for industrial purposes, as contrasted with biological requirements. This had its principal development as the result of the exploitation of the fossil fuels. Although this began some eight centuries ago, the magnitudes reached before the nineteenth century were almost negligible compared with those reached subsequently. Our present analysis, accordingly, need not extend earlier than about the year 1800. Furthermore, earlier than 1860, statistical data become increasingly unreliable and difficult to assemble.

Since 1800, the principal sources of the world's industrial energy have been the fossil fuels and water power. The rise in the world's annual production of coal and lignite since 1860 is shown graphically in Figure 8.1, that of the world's crude-oil production since 1880 in Figure 8.2, and the annual production of energy from coal and crude oil in Figure 8.3. From Figure 8.3, it is seen that the energy from oil, as compared with that from coal, was almost negligible until after 1900. Since then, the contribution of oil to the total energy supply has steadily increased until now it is approximately equal to that of coal, and increasing more rapidly. Not included in Figure 8.3 is the energy from natural gas and natural-gas liquids. Were this added to that of crude oil, the energy represented by the petroleum group of fuels would by now (1968) be about 60 percent of the total from coal, petroleum, and water power. Water power alone contributes only about 2 percent.

The corresponding growth in the rates of production of coal, of crude oil,

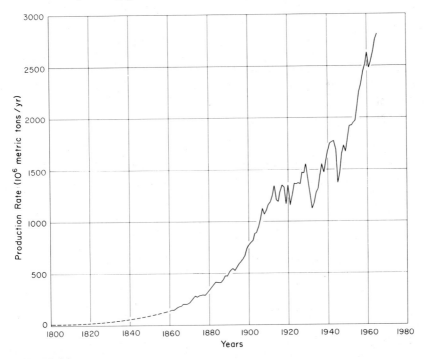

FIGURE 8.1
World production of coal and lignite.

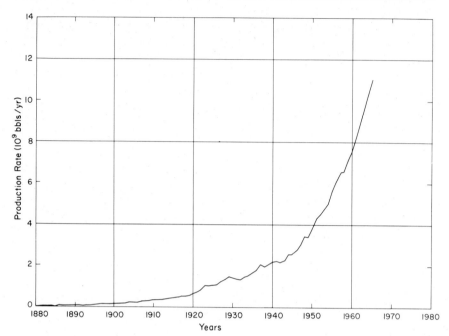

FIGURE 8.2
World production of crude oil.

and of natural gas in the United States are shown in Figures 8.4, 8.5, and 8.6, respectively. The growth in annual production of energy in the United States from coal, oil, natural gas, and water and nuclear power is shown in Figure 8.7. In the United States, as in the case of the world, since 1900 there has been a progressive increase in the fraction of the total industrial energy contributed by oil and natural gas. This fraction increased from 7.9 percent in 1900 to 67.9 percent by 1965. The contribution of coal, during the same period, decreased from 89.0 percent to 27.9. Water power, although continually increasing in magnitude, maintained a nearly constant percentage of the total energy produced. It increased only from 3.2 percent in 1900 to 4.1 percent in 1965. Nuclear power, by 1965, represented only 0.1 percent of the total.

These several growth curves have many properties in common. When replotted on semilogarithmic paper, each plots as a straight line for a period of a half-century or longer, indicating a constant exponential rate of growth. Following this period of constant growth rate, the rate of production falls steadily below its initial linear projection.

In the case of world coal production shown in Figure 8.1, the production rate falls into three distinct phases. During the first, extending from before 1860 to 1913 (the beginning of World War I), the production rate increased exponentially at an average rate of 4.4 percent per year, with the annual production doubling every 16 years. During the second period, including the two world wars and the intervening depression, the growth rate slowed to 0.75 percent per year with a doubling period of 93 years. Finally, during the third period from World War II to the present, a growth rate of 3.6 percent with a doubling period of 20 years has been resumed.

The world production of crude oil, except for a slight retardation during the depression of the 1930's and during World War II, has increased from 1890 to the present at a nearly constant exponential rate of 6.9 percent per year with a doubling period of 10 years. The second phase of retarded growth rate has not yet been reached.

From 1850 to 1907, the curve of the U.S. production of coal and lignite followed a constant exponential growth rate of 6.6 percent per year with a doubling period of 10.5 years. Before 1850, the growth rate was somewhat higher, but the production rate was so small that this period is not significant. From about 1910 to the present, production has oscillated about an average rate of about 550 million short tons per year.

U.S. crude-oil production, from 1875 to 1929, increased at a rate of 8.3

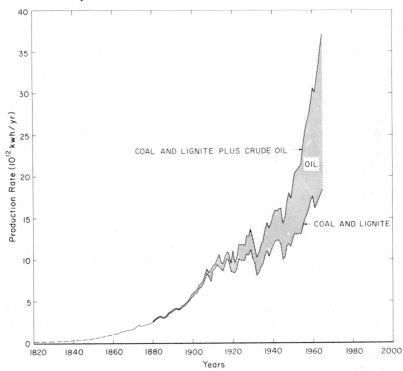

FIGURE 8.3
World production of thermal energy from coal and lignite plus crude oil.

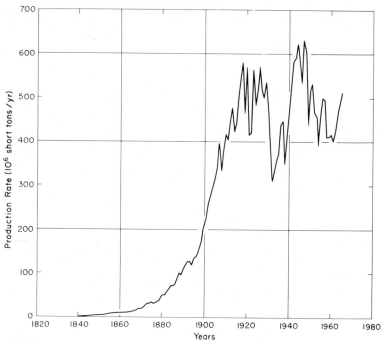

FIGURE 8.4
United States production of coal and lignite.

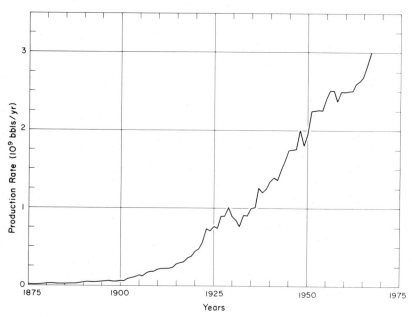

FIGURE 8.5
Production of crude oil in the United States, exclusive of Alaska.

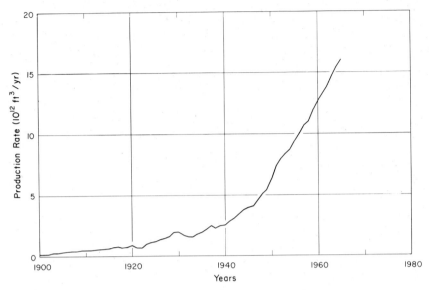

FIGURE 8.6
Production of marketed natural gas in the United States, exclusive of Alaska.

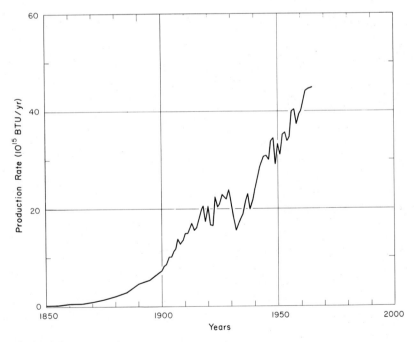

FIGURE 8.7
Production of thermal energy from coal, oil, gas, and water power in the United States, exclusive of Alaska.

percent per year with a doubling period of 8.4 years. Since 1929, the curve has gradually leveled off as the rate of production approaches its maximum. In parallel with crude oil, the U.S. production of marketed natural gas, from 1905 to the present, has increased at an almost constant exponential rate of 6.6 percent per year with a doubling period of 10.5 years.

Finally, U.S. production of total energy from coal, oil, natural gas, and water power, divides into two distinct growth periods. From before 1850 to 1907, energy was produced at a growth rate of 6.9 percent per year with a doubling period of 10.0 years. Then, from 1907 to the present, the growth rate dropped to 1.77 percent per year with a doubling period of 39 years.

Future Outlook for the Production
of the Fossil Fuels

When consideration is given to the factual data pertaining to both the world and the U.S. rates of production of coal and oil, as shown in the preceding figures, two results of outstanding significance become obvious. The first of these is the extreme brevity of the time during which most of these developments have occurred. For example, although coal has been mined for about 800 years, one-half of the coal produced during that period has been mined during the last 31 years. Half of the world's cumulative production of petroleum has occurred during the 12-year period since 1956. Similarly, for the United States, half of the cumulative coal production has occurred during the 38-year period since 1930, and half of the oil production during the 16-year period since 1952. In brief, most of the world's consumption of energy from the fossil fuels during its entire history has occurred during the last 25 years.

The second obvious conclusion from these data is that the steady rates of growth sustained during a period of several decades in each instance cannot be maintained for much longer periods of time. The reason for this is that a steady exponential rate of growth implies a doubling of the production rate at equal intervals of time. This also involves the doubling of the cumulative production during the same time interval. Take, for example, the production of crude oil in the United States prior to 1930. During this period, the cumulative production was doubling every 8.4 years, and by 1930 it had reached 12.3 billion barrels. Were this rate of growth to be maintained for another century, about 12 more doublings would occur and the cumulative production would reach 48,000 billion barrels, which is about 74 times the highest estimates on record of the possible amount of oil that may ever be produced in the United States. Similar results are obtained for each of the other fuels shown in the preceding figures.

From such considerations we are led to the conclusion that the time span for the exhaustion of the bulk of the various fossil fuels, under modern industrial rates of consumption, is measurable in centuries, whereas the time required for the formation of these fuels by geological processes was about 600 million years. Hence, the rates of formation of these deposits are negligible as compared with their rates of consumption. Consequently, during the period of human exploitation, the resources of the fossil fuels may be considered to consist of fixed initial supplies which are continually diminished by human consumption. The quantity remaining in the ground at any given time must be equal to the difference between this initial supply and the cumulative production up to that time. Therefore, the complete history of the production of any fossil fuel must display the following characteristics. The curve of the rate of production, plotted against time on an arithmetic scale, must begin at zero, rise until it passes over one or more maxima, and finally decline gradually to zero.

If Q be a quantity of a given fuel, and t the time, then

$$P = dQ/dt \tag{1}$$

will be the production rate, where d signifies the amount of change. Then, if the production rate P be plotted on an arithmetic scale as a function of time, as we have done in Figures 8.1 to 8.6, the element of area under the curve with a base of dt and an altitude P, will be

$$dA = Pdt = (dQ/dt)\, dt = dQ. \tag{2}$$

Hence, on such a graph, the cumulative production Q up to any given time t will be proportional to the area between the curve of production rate and the time-axis from the beginning of production until the time t.

For the entire cycle of production, where the production rate begins at zero, and eventually returns to zero, the total area under the curve is a measure of the ultimate amount, Q_∞, of the given fuel produced during the cycle, as is illustrated in Figure 8.8. This fact provides a powerful means of keeping within reasonable limits in our estimations of the future course of the production of a given fuel. If an estimate can be made from geological data of the amount Q_i of the given resource which was initially present in the geographical area considered, then any extrapolation of the production curve for that area must be such that the ultimate area under the curve satisfies the condition

$$Q_\infty \lessgtr Q_i. \tag{3}$$

Mathematically, such a curve may assume an indefinite number of shapes, but the technology of production essentially requires that the early phase be one of a positive exponential rate of increase, and the declining phase an exponential rate of decrease, so between these two requirements, and that of

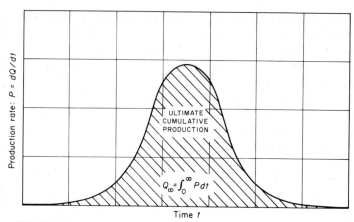

FIGURE 8.8
Full cycle of production of an exhaustible resource. (By permission of
the American Petroleum Institute, from *Drilling and Production Practice*,
1956, Figure 11, p. 12.)

the limitation of the area circumscribed, the amount of latitude in such a
curve is greatly reduced.

THE PETROLEUM GROUP OF FOSSIL FUELS

Let us first consider the petroleum group of fossil fuels. We have already
seen that in just over a century this group of fuels has risen to dominance as
the nation's and the world's leading source of industrial energy. Because of
this fact, major policy questions resulting from scarcity of resources are
likely to arise sooner for petroleum than for coal.

For statistical purposes, the petroleum group of fossil fuels is divided into
gaseous, liquid, and solid components. The principal gaseous component is
methane of chemical composition CH_4, which is the natural gas of commerce.
The principal liquid component is crude oil, which is the stock-tank oil
obtained by flow from the underground reservoir rocks by means of oil
wells. It ranges all of the way from natural gasolines to very heavy and
viscous oils which flow only with difficulty. The principal solid or pseudo-
solid components are tars, found in tar sands, and the solid hydrocarbon,
kerogen, found in oil shales. Actually, so-called tars are not solids, but
viscous liquids whose principal distinction from crude oil is that they cannot
be extracted from the ground by means of wells. Kerogen, on the other hand,
is a true solid.

A product intermediate between natural gas and crude oil is natural-gas
liquid (NGL). Natural-gas liquids, originally known collectively as "casing-
head gasoline," constitute a family of hydrocarbons extracted as liquids

during the production of natural gas. In addition to its principal component methane, natural gas also frequently contains diminishing fractions of heavier hydrocarbons of the series of compositions C_nH_{2n+2}, the first five members of which are methane, ethane, propane, butane, and pentane, for which n has the values 1 to 5, respectively. Natural-gas liquids consist of mixtures of propane and heavier components. A subclass of natural-gas liquids is liquified petroleum gases (LPG), consisting principally of mixtures of propane and butane, which are gaseous at atmospheric pressure but liquid at slightly higher pressures. These are familiar as "bottled gas" used for cooking and heating.

Until recent decades, only small amounts of natural-gas liquids were produced in the United States, and prior to 1945 the statistics of this production were lumped with those for crude oil. Since 1945, the annual production of natural-gas liquids and of crude oil have been reported separately. In the meantime, the production rate of natural-gas liquids has increased progressively until by the end of 1967 it amounted to 17.5 percent of the United States production of total liquid hydrocarbons.

As yet, only minor production of solid hydrocarbons has been achieved. Experimental work on the oil shales of Colorado has been under way for about two decades, but large-scale production has not yet begun. The mining of veins of the solid hydrocarbon, gilsonite, in the Uinta Basin of Utah has been in operation for more than a decade, but the reserves are not large. However, successful large-scale exploitation of the large Athabasca tar sands of northeastern Alberta, Canada, was begun in late 1967 by Great Canadian Oil Sands Limited, with a plant having a design capacity of 45,000 barrels of oil per day; other companies are only awaiting approval by the Canadian government to install additional productive capacity.

The production history of crude oil for the world has already been given in Figure 8.2, and of crude oil and natural gas for the United States in Figures 8.5 and 8.6. Were it possible to make reasonably accurate estimates from geological data of the amounts of oil and gas initially present underground, then, by use of the technique described heretofore and illustrated in Figure 8.8, reasonably good approximations of the future of the respective production curves could be made.

Unfortunately, because of the erratic manner in which accumulations of oil and gas occur underground, the problem of estimating the quantities of these fluids still undiscovered by drilling in any given region is difficult. For a preliminary appraisal of the petroleum-producing potentialities of a given region, the only available procedure is geological. Most of the geologists in the world are engaged in exploration for petroleum; and the knowledge of the geology of petroleum, and of the sedimentary basins of the world, that has been accumulated during the last half century is extensive.

In essence, the geological procedure is the following. It is generally agreed that petroleum is derived from plant and animal debris that was buried in sediments under conditions of incomplete decay during the geologic past. Consequently petroleum is now found only in or immediately adjacent to basins filled with sedimentary rocks. The geographical location and extent of the sedimentary basins in the land areas of the world are now reasonably well known. Sedimentary rocks are porous with an average porosity (ratio of pore volume to total volume) of about 15 to 20 percent. The pores are normally filled with water except where the water has been displaced by oil or gas. Oil and gas, being fluids, are driven by physical forces in this underground rock-water environment into limited regions of space where they are in stable equilibrium. These equilibrium positions are to some degree determinable by detailed studies of the subsurface structure of the rocks, and the associated state of rest or of motion of the water, by geological and geophysical procedures. Oil or gas wells are then drilled in what appears to be the most favorable locations for oil or gas entrapment.

Unfortunately, there is nothing in this procedure that permits better than a crude estimate of the quantity of oil or gas that a given basin may produce. The geological appraisal of the petroleum-producing potentialities of a new territory is carried out largely by analogy with known territories. For example, the geology of the coastal region of Nigeria was found to be similar to that of the coastal region of Texas and Louisiana. By analogy, it was assumed that the Nigerian sediments would probably contain a quantity of oil per unit of volume comparable to that which had already been discovered in the Texas-Louisiana gulf coastal region. Subsequent drilling in Nigeria has confirmed this assumption.

U.S. Crude-Oil Resources

Since the petroleum industry in the United States is the most advanced of that of any major region in the world, the United States experience is commonly used as one of the principal yardsticks in appraisals of the petroleum-producing potentialities of the rest of the world. The difficulty in this procedure, however, lies in the question of how good is the yardstick? How accurately are the undiscovered resources of oil and gas in the United States known? In this regard, it may be mentioned that estimates published within the last 12 years of the ultimate production of crude oil in the United States, exclusive of Alaska, have a fourfold range from about 145 to 590 billion barrels. Corresponding estimates for natural gas have a threefold range from 850 to 2,650 trillion cubic feet.

Estimates of the ultimate amount of crude oil which the world will produce have tended to be roughly proportional to the estimates made by the same authors for the United States.

In view of these circumstances, it is clear that the problem of estimating petroleum resources of the world is closely linked with the primary problem of estimating those of the United States. For the latter, geological analogy is no longer appropriate. We are left with the problem of a direct estimation, and this can only be based on the cumulative experience which is condensed into the statistics of exploration, drilling, discovery, and production of the petroleum industry in the United States. A problem of comparable or even greater importance is that of estimating the degree of advancement that the U.S. petroleum industry has reached in its evolutionary cycle. For these purposes two procedures have been evolved which yield reasonably un-ambiguous results (Hubbert, 1962, p. 50–65; 1967).

The first of these concerns the relationship between cumulative production, Q_p, cumulative proved discoveries, Q_d, and proved reserves, Q_r. Statistics on annual production of crude oil in the United States are available since 1860, and, from these, cumulative production up to any given year can be computed. Estimates of proved reserves of crude oil at the end of each year have been made annually by the reserves committee of the American Petroleum Institute (API) since 1937, and the series of proved reserves, based on older estimates, has been extended by the API statistical staff back to 1900. Cumulative proved discoveries up to any given time may be defined to be the sum of all of the oil produced up to that time plus the proved reserves. Hence, if we know the cumulative production and the proved reserves for any given time, the cumulative discoveries may be given by the equation

$$Q_d = Q_p + Q_r. \tag{4}$$

The corresponding rates of discovery are given by

$$dQ_d/dt = dQ_p/dt + dQ_r/dt, \tag{5}$$

in which the three terms represent the rates of discovery, of production, and of the increase of proved reserves, respectively.

From the principles previously set forth, we already know the general properties of each of the quantities in equations (4) and (5), when plotted graphically as a function of time. The production rate dQ_p/dt must begin at zero, increase to one or more maxima, and ultimately return to zero. The integral of this curve, the cumulative production Q_p, must begin at zero and then increase at an exponential rate as long as the production rate so increases. Then, when the production rate reaches its maximum value, the curve of Q_p will have its maximum slope. Finally, as the production rate declines, the Q_p-curve will gradually approach an ultimate quantity Q_∞, which represents the ultimate amount of oil produced during the entire cycle. The cumulative curve will accordingly exhibit the familiar S-shape common to growth phenomena. It can only increase with time, and it is asymptotic to zero at the beginning and to Q_∞ at the end.

The curve of proved reserves plotted against time has a different shape. At the beginning of production proved reserves are zero, and again at the end. The proved-reserves curve over the entire cycle must accordingly begin at zero, increase to a maximum, and then decline to zero.

From equation (4) it follows that the cumulative-discovery curve must resemble that for cumulative production except that discoveries must precede production by some time interval, Δt. At the end of the cycle, when $Q_r = 0$, the value of Q_d must be the same as Q_p. Hence both the Q_d- and the Q_p-curves must approach the same ultimate value Q_∞.

Strictly, the foregoing relations apply for a single-cycle growth curve. For oil production in a small area—the State of Illinois for example—there may be multiple cycles of production. For the whole United States, small local variations superpose and cancel one another out. Accordingly, all present evidence indicates that in this case we are dealing with but a single major cycle of discovery and production.

The general forms of the three curves of Q_d, Q_p, and Q_r, for a single growth cycle, are those shown in Figure 8.9. Corresponding curves of the rate of discovery, of production, and of increase of proved reserves, are shown in Figure 8.10. On these curves, one point is worthy of note. When the proved-reserves curve in Figure 8.9 reaches its maximum value, its slope, dQ_r/dt, which is the rate of increase of proved reserves, becomes zero. Then at this time equation (5) becomes

$$dQ_d/dt = dQ_p/dt. \tag{6}$$

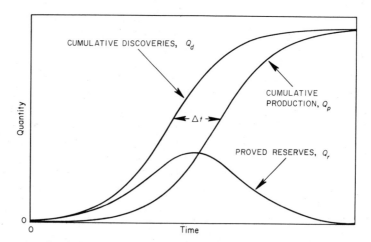

FIGURE 8.9
Generalized form of curves of cumulative discoveries, cumulative production, and proved reserves for a petroleum component during a full cycle of production. Δt indicates the time lapse between discovery and production. (From Hubbert, 1962, Figure 22, p. 55.)

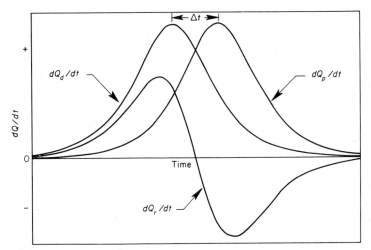

FIGURE 8.10
Relations between rate of production (dQ_p/dt), rate of proved discovery (dQ_d/dt) and rate of increase of proved reserves (dQ_r/dt) during a full cycle of petroleum production (From Hubbert, 1962, Figure 24, p. 56.)

This indicates that at the peak of proved reserves the curves of the *rate* of production and the *rate* of discovery cross one another, with the production rate still rising but the discovery rate already on its decline. The time at which this occurs is roughly halfway between the peaks in the discovery rate and the production rate. The study of the actual data of the U.S. petroleum industry in the light of these relationships can be very informative.

The data of U.S. cumulative discoveries, cumulative production, and proved reserves of crude oil, exclusive of Alaska, are shown graphically in Figure 8.11. The discontinuity at 1945 is caused by the separation, starting at that time, of natural-gas liquids data from crude oil data. The time delay, Δt, between cumulative discovery and cumulative production is shown in Figure 8.12. This is obtained by tracing the Q_d-curve and sliding it parallel to the time axis until it most nearly matches the Q_p-curve. For the last decade, as seen in the figure, this time-delay, Δt, has been about 12 years. Earlier, it would have been somewhat less, about 10–11 years. What is most significant is that for the last 40 years the curve of cumulative production has faithfully followed that of cumulative discoveries with a time delay rarely outside the range of 10–12 years. In consequence of this relationship, the Q_d-curve acts as about a 12-year preview of the behavior of the Q_p-curve In other words, the state of crude-oil production 12 years from now will probably not differ greatly from the state of discovery at present.

The proved-resources curve in Figure 8.11 is plotted on too small a scale to show all of its significant detail. It is accordingly replotted on a magnified scale in Figure 8.13. From this it may be seen that a smooth curve

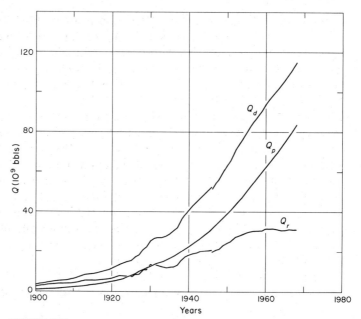

FIGURE 8.11
Data for the United States, exclusive of Alaska, on cumulative production (Q_p), cumulative proved discoveries (Q_d), and proved reserves (Q_r)
of crude oil.

approximating the actual curve would have its maximum value at about
1961. This becomes even more clear in Figure 8.14, representing the rate of
increase of proved reserves. The dashed-line curve represents the computed
value of dQ_r/dt from an analytical curve approximating the actual proved-
resources curve. The solid-line zig-zag curve represents the actual year-to-
year data of increase of proved reserves. From the general form of the
proved-resources curve, its slope, or rate of increase, must have a positive
loop while reserves are increasing, and a negative loop while decreasing, and
the curve must cross the zero line from the positive to the negative loop at
the time when reserves reach their maximum value. From Figure 8.14 it can
be seen that this cross-over also occurred about 1961. As evidence that this is
not merely a temporary aberration, it may be noted that the rate-of-increase
curve reached the maximum of its positive loop about 1942 and the actual
year-to-year data, with only minor oscillations, have declined steadily since
1951.

Data of the rates of discovery and of production of crude oil in the United
States are shown in Figure 8.15. As in the case of Figure 8.14, the dashed-line
curves are analytical derivatives of smooth curves fitting the cumulative
discovery and cumulative production curves of Figure 8.11. The solid line
zig-zag curves are the actual yearly data. The maximum rate of discovery,

according to the analytical curve, would have been about 1957. In the
figure, a time-delay, Δt, of 10.5 years is shown between discovery and production. However, during the last decade the delay averaged about 12 years.
Accordingly, the peak in the rate of production, which should lag behind that
of discovery by about the same time interval, should be expected to occur
about 1969 plus or minus a year or two.

Strictly speaking, this peak in the rate of production refers to the smooth
analytical curve rather than to that of the actual year-to-year production
oscillations. Since the actual production rate is somewhat less than the
productive capacity of the country, it is possible that an all-time peak in the
oil produced during a single year might occur during any given year within a
time interval of five years or more. The data of Figures 8.11 to 8.15 are
consistent in indicating that the U.S. petroleum industry, exclusive of
Alaska, is now (1969) in the region of its all-time maximum rate of production, but it will probably not be possible to assign an accurate date to this
event until about five years after it has happened.

Another result obtainable from the data in Figures 8.11 to 8.15 is an
estimate of the magnitude of Q_∞, the ultimate amount of oil to be produced.

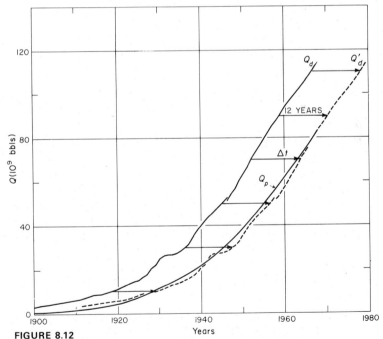

FIGURE 8.12
Time delay, Δt, between United States cumulative proved discoveries
(Q_d) and cumulative production (Q_p) of crude oil. The dashed line Q'_d
reflects the form of the curve Q_d when it is slid to the right, parallel to
the time axis, until it most nearly matches the curve Q_p.

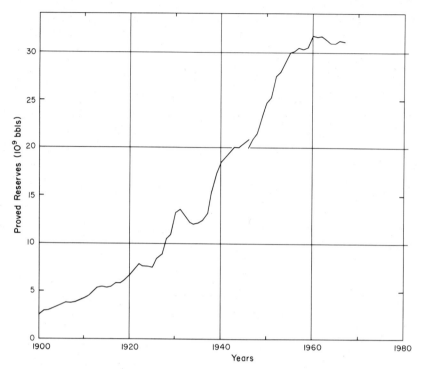

FIGURE 8.13
Proved reserves of crude oil in the United States, exclusive of Alaska

If we assume that peak rates in discovery and in production occur at about the halfway points of cumulative discoveries and production, then each of these curves will give an estimate for the value of Q_∞. At the beginning of 1957, the approximate date of the peak in the proved-discovery rate, cumulative discoveries amounted to 85.3 billion barrels. Twice this would give a figure of 170.6 billion barrels as an estimate for Q_∞. During the last decade, the time delay Δt of production with respect to discovery has averaged about 12 years. If we take the beginning of 1969 (12 years after the peak in the discovery rate) as the approximate date of the peak in the production rate, the cumulative production will be about 86.5 billion barrels. Twice this amount would give a value of 173.0 billion barrels for Q_∞.

It is to be emphasized that these figures are only approximate, since in either case it is possible that the peak rates of discovery or of production could occur somewhat earlier or somewhat later than the halfway points.

While the foregoing procedures are especially well suited for the determination of such critical dates as the peaks in the rates of discovery and production, and of that of proved reserves, they are somewhat less reliable as a means of estimating the ultimate amount of oil Q_∞ that will be produced.

For the latter purpose, a much better procedure has been developed; it was suggested by the studies of A. D. Zapp (now deceased) of the United States Geological Survey (Zapp, 1962, pp. H-22–H-33). The procedure is to express the rate of discovery in terms of barrels of oil discovered per foot of exploratory drilling, and then determine how this rate varies as a function of the cumulative footage of exploratory drilling. In this system of coordinates, if Q is the quantity of oil discovered, and h the cumulative footage drilled, then the rate of discovery dQ/dh would be plotted as the vertical coordinate in bbls/ft against cumulative footage, h, as the horizontal coordinate.

This system is mathematically analogous to that which we have used heretofore where the time-discovery rate dQ/dt has been plotted against cumulative time t. In both systems of coordinates, the area under the curve represents cumulative discoveries up to the cumulative depth h, or the cumulative time t, respectively. The former has several advantages over the latter, however. In the first place, the rate of discovery per foot depends principally on technological factors and is relatively insensitive to economic

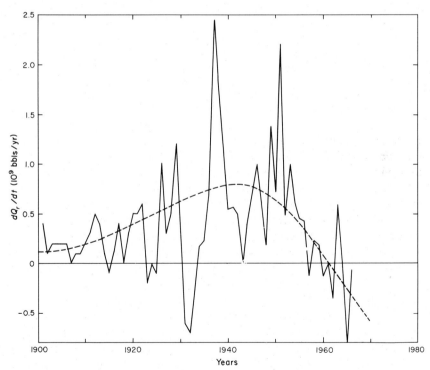

FIGURE 8.14
Rate of increase of proved reserves of crude oil in the United States, exclusive of Alaska. Solid line shows actual year-to-year increase in proved reserves, dashed line the computed rate of increase dQ_r/dt.

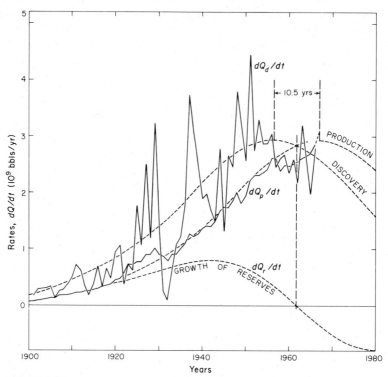

FIGURE 8.15
Rates of proved discovery (dQ_d/dt), production (dQ_p/dt), and increase
(dQ_r/dt) of reserves of crude oil in the United States, exclusive of Alaska.
Dashed line curves are analytical derivatives, solid lines are actual yearly data.

conditions. The rate of discovery per year, on the contrary, can swing widely
from one year to the next in response to economic and political conditions.
In the second place, a practical limit can be set to the ultimate amount of
cumulative exploratory drilling in a given area, whereas no such limit can
be assigned to cumulative time.

Although Zapp did not develop this method, its main features were
implied in his important paper, "Future Petroleum Producing Capacity of
the United States" (Zapp, 1962), whose principal results can only be presented
graphically in this system of coordinates. This method thus permits not only
a graphical presentation of the Zapp estimates, and of others based on the
same premises, but it also permits an easy verification of those premises by
means of petroleum-industry statistical data. And, more important, it
permits a direct evaluation of the discovery history of the U.S. petroleum
industry up to the present, and a more reliable appraisal of its future than
has been obtainable previously.

Therefore, instead of reviewing initially the estimates of the ultimate amounts of crude oil which the United States may produce (estimates that have been made by Zapp and others) and the premises on which they have been based, it will be more economical for us to proceed directly with our own analysis of the data. What we seek is the curve of oil discovered per foot of exploratory drilling as a function of cumulative footage from the beginning of the industry to the present. Then, on the basis of this information—whether the curve is still rising, remaining stationary, or declining— we can make some prognostications on ultimate crude-oil production. This study has in fact already been made and published (Hubbert, 1967) and only its principal results will be summarized here.

To obtain the desired result, we must first work with the statistical data published by years. We thus require estimates of the oil discovered each year and of the footage of exploratory drilling each year. The ratio of these quantities then gives the oil discovered per foot *as a function of time.* By adding cumulatively the drilling footage, as a function of time, we are then able to determine the quantity of oil, ΔQ, discovered for each successive equal increment, Δh, of cumulative footage, and this ratio, $\Delta Q/\Delta h$, versus h will be a finite approximation to the desired curve.

For discoveries assignable to a given year, we require a different definition of discoveries from that of *proved discoveries* used heretofore. For this purpose, we adopt a procedure initiated by the Petroleum Administration for War (PAW) (Frey and Ide, 1946) in a study as of 1945, and continued in successive similar studies by the National Petroleum Council (NPC, 1961, 1965) and, finally, jointly by the American Gas Association (AGA), American Petroleum Institute (API), and Canadian Petroleum Association (CPA) (AGA, API, and CPA, 1967), in which all of the oil contained in any given field is credited to the year of discovery of the field. Studies have been made on this basis and estimates published as of January 1 for the years 1945, 1960, 1964, and 1967.

In these studies, the oil credited to a given year, as of a later date, consists of the sum of the cumulative production up to the date of the study plus the estimated proved reserves, of all of the fields discovered in the given year. However, by the rules of the API reserves committee, proved reserves at any given time are not intended to represent all of the oil that will eventually be produced by the fields already discovered at that time. Rather, they represent a working inventory of oil that is present and producible by wells and equipment already in operation. Additional reserves are added as the fields are developed.

For this reason, the oil discoveries ascribed to any given year, based in part on the API reserves estimates, gradually increase with time. This effect was studied (Hubbert, 1967), and on the basis of the successive published estimates, the *ultimate* amount of oil that the fields discovered each year since 1860 would produce was estimated. This involved negligible additions over the recent NPC estimates for fields discovered more than 50 years ago, but required progressively larger additions (up to 5.8-fold) as the year of discovery approached the present.

In this manner, the cumulative proved discoveries, computed on the basis of the NPC studies and brought up to 1 January 1967, amounted to 111.7×10^9 bbls for the United States exclusive of Alaska. The estimated ultimate production of the fields already discovered amounted to 136.2×10^9 bbls, an increase of 24.5×10^9 bbls.

For the feet of exploratory drilling per year, and cumulative exploratory footage, drilling statistics are available intermittently from 1927 to 1944 and annually since 1945. For the earlier periods, statistics exist on the total number of wells drilled per year, classified as oil wells, gas wells, and dry holes. During the period since exploratory well statistics have become available, the number of exploratory wells drilled has averaged about 0.67 of the total number of dry holes. Assuming that about the same ratio prevailed during earlier drilling, the approximate number of exploratory wells could be estimated from the dry-hole data. Then, to obtain the footage per year, the number of exploratory wells was multiplied by the estimated average depth. The latter is known approximately from the known depths of the fields discovered at successive times.

The net result of this study was that by 1 January 1967, the estimated cumulative footage of exploratory drilling amounted to 15.2×10^8 feet. This divides conveniently into 15 units of 10^8 feet for each of which the oil discovered, ΔQ, can be evaluated from previous discovery data, and the average discoveries per foot, $\Delta Q/\Delta h$, determined.

The results are shown in Figure 8.16. During the first 10^8-ft interval of drilling, which extended from 1859 to 1920, the average oil discovery rate was 194 bbls/ft. During the second interval, from 1920 to 1928, the rate dropped to 167 bbls/ft. Then, during the third interval, extending from 1928 to 1937 and including the discovery of the East Texas oil field, the discovery rate reached an all-time peak of 276 bbls/ft. Following this, the rate has fallen precipitately to a present level of about 35 bbls/ft.

This decline during the 30-year period since 1937 is particularly significant in view of the fact that the oil credited with having been discovered during this period represents the cumulative results of all of the advances in the techniques of exploration and production of the petroleum industry during its entire history up to 1967. This also was the period of the most intensive research and development in exploratory and production techniques in the history of the industry. The observed decline in the rate of discovery during this period is, accordingly, difficult to account for on any other basis than that undiscovered oil is becoming scarce.

The tops of the columns in Figure 8.16 represent approximately the curve of dQ/dh versus h, and the area under this curve represents cumulative

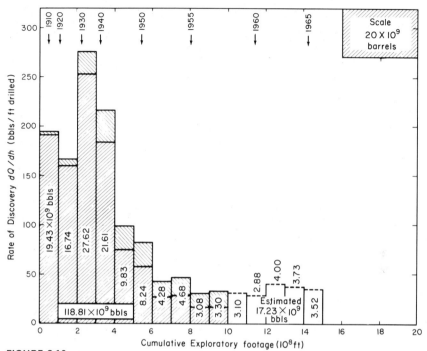

FIGURE 8.16
Crude-oil discoveries per foot of exploratory drilling versus cumulative exploratory footage in the United States, exclusive of Alaska, 1860–1967. (By permission from *Bulletin of American Association of Petroleum Geologists*, 1967, vol. 51, Figure 15, p. 2223.)

discoveries. Future discoveries can accordingly be estimated by extrapolating the decline curve of Figure 8.16, and computing the additional oil corresponding to the added area. In the study cited (Hubbert, 1967), this was done using two different negative-exponential rates of decline, the first an approximate average for the whole period, and a second slower rate from 194 bbls/ft for the first column to 35 bbls/ft for the last. The faster rate of decline gave 153 × 10^9 bbls as an estimate of Q_∞, and the slower rate, 164 × 10^9 bbls.

It will be noted, however, that during the last seven 10^8-ft units of drilling, the discoveries per foot have remained nearly constant. The reason for this is twofold. The time required for these last seven units of drilling was only the 12-year period from 1955 to 1967. This was the period during which the rate of exploratory drilling decreased sharply from an all-time peak of 16,207 wells in 1956 to 10,275 (excluding Alaska) in 1966. Since the highest-grade prospects are customarily drilled in preference to those of lower grade, a reduction in the number of wells drilled in a given year tends to increase the average grade of the prospects drilled, and hence to improve the rate of discovery per foot. The second, and principal reason for the slowdown in the decline of the discovery rate per foot, however, is that this was also the period during which most of the large discoveries were made, with a minimum of exploratory drilling, in offshore Louisiana.

Because these two effects are both intrinsically temporary, the slowdown in the decline rate of discoveries per foot during the last 12 years must be regarded as only a temporary episode in a long-term trend of decline. However, even in the improbable event that the discovery rate could be held constant at the present rate of 35 bbls/ft and the drilling rate also maintained at the 1967 level of 49×10^6 ft/yr, until the year 2000, the new oil discoveries would amount to but 57 billion barrels. When this is added to the 136 billion barrels already discovered by the beginning of 1967, the total by the year 2000 would still amount only to 193 billion barrels.

Independent confirmation of this long-term decline in the rate of discovery with cumulative drilling is afforded by the statistics published annually by the Committee on Statistics of Drilling of the American Association of Petroleum Geologists. Each year this committee reports on the number of new-field wildcat wells that were required 6 years previously to make one profitable discovery of either oil or gas. A profitable discovery is defined as 1 million barrels of oil or an equivalent amount of oil plus gas. In 1945, the first year of the series, 26 new-field wildcat wells were required per profitable discovery; by 1961, the last year of the series, this number had increased to 70 wells per discovery. (Dillon and Van Dyke, 1967, p. 994, Fig. 9; Van Dyke, 1968, p. 918, Fig. 9).

Hence, on the basis of the results shown in Figure 8.16, the highest figure that at present can be justified for Q_∞, the ultimate amount of oil to be produced by the conterminous part of the United States and its adjacent continental-shelf areas, is about 165×10^9 bbls. Of this, the amount of 136×19^9 bbls, or 83 percent, is accounted for by fields already discovered, leaving but 17 percent for fields still to be discovered.

The absolute value of Q_∞, for these same fields, could be increased above the figure of 165×10^9 bbls, should a drastic improvement in the efficiency of recovery from the oil in place be effected. Even in this case, however, the improvement would involve the fields already discovered to the same degree as those still to be discovered so that the ratio of oil already discovered to that still to be discovered would remain essentially unchanged.

Offsetting any expectancy of a drastic improvement of the present recovery efficiency of somewhere near 40 percent are the following facts: (1) Every technique of improved recovery efficiency so far devised by petroleum-industry research is already in operation to about its economic limit. (2) More expensive procedures could be justified only by a corresponding increase in the price of oil. The latter, however, is precluded by the fact that should domestically-produced oil become more expensive, the public has access to alternate sources of less expensive liquid fuels, obtainable both from imports and from oil shales and coal.

The figure of 165×10^9 bbls is accordingly the best present estimate of the value of Q_∞ for the conterminous United States, although it is admitted that a somewhat higher figure resulting from further improvement in recovery efficiency is a physical possibility.

Having obtained the estimate of $Q_\infty = 165 \times 10^9$ barrels for the crude-oil production in the conterminous United States, we are now in a position to plot the complete cycle of production, utilizing the principle illustrated in Figure 8.8. This is shown in Figure 8.17 of which one grid square has the dimensions

$$10^9 \text{ bbls/yr} \times 20 \text{ yrs} = 20 \times 10^9 \text{ bbls.}$$

Hence, if the figure of 165×10^9 barrels is approximately correct as a value for Q_∞, the total area under the curve can contain only $8\frac{1}{4}$ of the grid squares of the figure. The area to the left of the vertical line at the year 1934 represents a cumulative production of 16.5×10^9 barrels, or the first 10 percent of Q_∞; the area to the right of the vertical curve at the year 1999 represents the last 10 percent. The area under the curve between these two dates represents the middle 80 percent of Q_∞. Hence, the time that will be required to produce and consume the middle 80 percent of the ultimate amount of crude oil to be produced in the conterminous United States is only about 65 years, or less than a single lifetime.

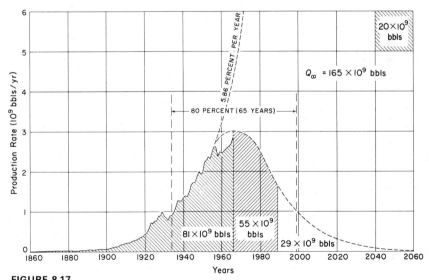

FIGURE 8.17
Complete cycle of crude-oil production in the United States and adjacent continental shelves, exclusive of Alaska.

The dashed-line curve in Figure 8.17 shows what the production rate would have been after 1955 had the rate of growth that prevailed from 1935 to 1955 continued.

In this estimate, Alaska has been excluded because it represents a large, almost virgin territory which has not yet developed far enough to contribute to the statistics on which the foregoing analysis has been based. Significant Alaskan oil production was begun in the Kenai-Cook Inlet area only as recently as 1958, with cumulative proved discoveries by 1 January 1968, amounting to 0.474 billion barrels, with an estimate of about 1 billion barrels of ultimate production.

Also, a very large oil discovery has been announced (*Oil and Gas Journal*, 22 July 1968, p. 34–35), near Prudhoe Bay on the Alaskan North Slope, which, according to a report by the consulting firm of DeGolyer and McNaughton, promises to be in the 5 to 10 billion-barrel class. This would make it equal to or larger than the East Texas field—the largest in the United States thus far—and comparable to the world's largest fields in the Middle East.

Aside from these developments, the Alaskan potentialities for petroleum production can at present be based only on comparisons by means of geological analogy. According to Hendricks (1965, p. 7) the total potential oil-producing area of the United States, including Alaska, and adjacent continental-shelf areas, is just over 2 million square miles; and for the United States minus Alaska, 1.86 million square miles. This would give for Alaska a potentially productive area of about 0.14 million square miles, or an area equal to 7.5 percent of that of the rest of the United States. If we use the crudest type of comparison (which could easily be wrong by a factor of 2 or more), we may assume that Alaska will produce as much oil per square mile of potentially productive area as the rest of the United States. This would give for Alaska a potential production of about 12 billion barrels.

As a consequence of the new Prudhoe Bay discovery, this figure appears to be too low. Even so, a provisional allowance of 25 billion barrels for the ultimate crude-oil production of Alaska is about as large a figure as can be justified from present evidence. This figure, when added to the 165 billion barrels for the remainder of the United States, gives 190 billion barrels as our present estimate of the approximate amount of crude oil ultimately to be produced by the whole United States and its adjacent continental shelf areas.

Estimates by Others

As we have remarked earlier, estimates published within the last 12 years of the ultimate amount of crude oil to be produced within the United States and its adjacent continental shelves, exclusive of Alaska, have had a fourfold range from 145 to 590 billion barrels. Estimates in the higher range fall into two principal groups: (1) estimates based on the Zapp hypothesis, or its modification, and (2) estimates based on geological analogy.

Production estimates based on the Zapp hypothesis (p. 177), or its modification, include: 590 billion barrels of crude oil for the United States, exclusive of Alaska (Zapp, 1961); 650 billion barrels, presumably including Alaska (McKelvey and Duncan, 1965); and 400 billion barrels, including Alaska (Hendricks, 1965). Since these have already been analyzed in detail in a recent paper (Hubbert, 1967), only brief comment regarding them will be made here.

The Zapp hypothesis, in the form that produced the above estimates, is based on the assumption that the oil to be discovered per foot of exploratory drilling in any given petroliferous region will remain essentially constant until an areal density of about one exploratory well per two square miles has been achieved. The nature of this hypothesis, as formulated by Zapp (1962, pp. H-22–H-23) for the conterminous United States as of the year 1959, is shown graphically in Figure 8.18.

In this, only percentages of ultimate exploration were given, Later (after the foregoing report was written, but before its publication), Zapp (1961) estimated that by 1961, about 130 billion barrels of crude oil had already been discovered in the United States by about 1.1 billion feet of exploratory drilling. This would have been at a rate of 118 bbls/ft. He also estimated that the cumulative footage required by a density of one well per two square miles, drilled either to the basement or to 20,000 feet, in the United States would amount to 5 billion feet, and that by such drilling 590 billion barrels of producible crude oil would be discovered. This corresponds to the maintenance of an average discovery rate of 118 bbls/ft for the entire 5 billion feet of drilling.

A simple test of the validity of this hypothesis can be made by determining whether or not the discoveries per foot made by past exploratory drilling have remained approximately constant. This we have done, and the results, which are given in Figure 8.16, show unequivocally that the Zapp hypothesis

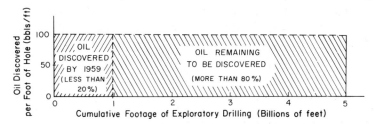

FIGURE 8.18
The Zapp hypothesis of the rate of oil discoveries per foot of exploratory drilling versus cumulative footage.

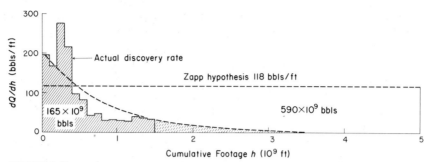

FIGURE 8.19
Comparison of Zapp hypothesis with actual United States discovery data
from Figure 8.16.

in this simple form is untenable. Instead of remaining constant, discoveries per foot have fallen drastically during the last 35 years from a maximum value of 276 bbs/ft during the period 1928–1937 to a present figure of about 35 bbls/ft. In Figure 8.19 the data of Figure 8.16 are shown superposed on the rectangle generated by the Zapp hypothesis of a constant discovery rate of 118 bbls/ft. From this, it is evident why the estimate derived deductively from the Zapp hypothesis is about 3.5 times the highest figure of about 165 billion barrels that can be justified by the discovery data—an over-estimate of about 425 billion barrels.

Consequently, since the Zapp hypothesis is not compatible with petroleum-industry data and leads consistently to figures that are much too high, estimates obtained by the use of that hypothesis in the form applied must be discounted.

Of the higher range of estimates based on geological premises and analogy, among the most notable are those by L. G. Weeks (1948; 1950; 1958; 1959), formerly a geologist of Standard Oil Company of New Jersey, and now a consultant. In 1948, Weeks gave a summary estimate, based on the technology and economics of that date, of 110 billion barrels as the ultimate amount of crude oil to be produced on the land areas of the United States. In 1958, he increased this to 240 billion barrels of "liquid petroleum" for both the land area and the adjacent continental shelves. When corrected for natural-gas liquids, this would reduce to about 200 billion barrels of crude oil. Then, in the following year (1959), he increased this estimate to 460 billion barrels of liquid petroleum, which would correspond to about 380 billion barrels of crude oil.

As to how these estimates were made, Weeks has remained consistently unclear. The figures apparently are to be accepted on the authority of the author's extensive knowledge of petroleum geology. Moreover, for the 11-year period from 1948 to 1959, for which Weeks more than tripled his estimate, there was no commensurate increase in the knowledge of the petroleum geology of the United States. It is, therefore, not possible to appraise the reliability of Weeks' estimates in terms of the methods used; they can only be checked against other sources of information. By this criterion, it appears that Weeks' earlier estimate of 110 billion barrels for the land area is more reliable than his later estimates. For, if to the figure of 110 billion barrels for the land area, we add a liberal additional 20–30 billion barrels for the adjacent continental shelves and another 25 billion barrels for improvements in exploratory and production techniques, we obtain an estimate in the range of 155 to 175 billion barrels, which is consistent with other present information. No justification, geological or otherwise, has yet been found for Weeks' more recent, much higher estimates.

Natural-Gas Resources of the United States

The rate of production of natural gas in the United States has been shown in Figure 8.6. As in the case of crude oil, we require an estimate of the ultimate quantity, Q_∞, of natural gas that the United States and adjacent continental shelf areas, exclusive of Alaska, may be expected to produce before we can construct a curve of the complete cycle of production.

The problem of estimating Q_∞ for natural gas is essentially the same as that for crude oil. However, because of the close genetic relationship between natural gas and crude oil, a good approximation of Q_∞ for gas can be obtained from the results of the analysis for crude oil which has already been given. We have seen that by 1 January 1967, the ultimate amount of crude oil that the fields already discovered in the conterminous United States are estimated to produce is taken to be 136 billion barrels, leaving 29 billion barrels for future crude-oil discoveries.

During the last 20 years, the ratio of natural-gas discoveries in the United States to those of crude oil have averaged about 6,000 ft^3/bbl.

Making a liberal assumption of 7,500 ft^3/bbl for the gas-oil ratio of future gas discoveries, we would then obtain an estimate of 218 trillion cubic feet for the gas to be discovered while the 29 billion barrels of future crude-oil discoveries are being made.

By 1 January 1967, the cumulative proved discoveries (cumulative production plus proved reserves) of natural gas in the conterminous United States amounted to 604 trillion cubic feet and the proved reserves alone to 286 (AGA, API, and CPA, 1967). In our previous study of crude oil, we found an estimated 24.1 billion barrels of producible crude oil in fields already discovered in excess of the 31.1 billion barrels of proved reserves. Assuming that about the same ratio prevails for natural gas, we obtain a figure of 222 trillion cubic feet for the fields already discovered beyond the 286 trillion cubic feet of proved reserves.

Then, adding these three figures, we obtain a rough estimate for the ultimate amount of gas Q_∞:

	(10^{12}ft^3)
Proved discoveries, as of 1-1-67	604
Additional gas in already discovered fields	222
Future discoveries	218
Total Q_∞	1,044

This figure is in close agreement with the estimate of 1,000 trillion cubic feet obtained from different data in the National Academy of Sciences report on *Energy Resources* (Hubbert, 1962, pp. 75–80) of 1962. It is much less than the Zapp (1961) estimate of 2,650 trillion cubic feet, and the Hendricks (1965) estimate of about 2,000 trillion cubic feet, including Alaska, or about 1,800 trillion cubic feet, excluding Alaska.

An estimate of a totally different character has recently become available as the result of the work of an industry committee, the Potential Gas Committee, under the chairmanship of B. Warren Beebe. At its meeting in Vancouver on 15–17 September 1967, the Committee on Resources and Man received from Beebe a confidential preview of a forthcoming report of the Potential Gas Committee.

This committee is made up of about 200 members from the oil and gas industry. It consists of a central committee, and 15 separate regional committees whose members are chosen on the basis of their extensive knowledge of the region concerned. The committee is a continuing committee and plans to revise its estimates at two-year intervals. Beginning at the local level, and using confidential information from the petroleum-industry files, local estimates are made, which are then assembled into regional estimates and these, finally, into an estimate for the whole conterminous United States.

The report of the Potential Gas Committee, released in October 1967, presents the following estimate of the natural-gas situation of the United States, exclusive of Alaska and Hawaii, as of 31 December 1966:

	(10^{12}ft^3)
Cumulative past production	314
Proved reserves	286
Total proved discoveries	600
Potential supply	690
Ultimate supply	1,290

The total potential supply of 690 trillion cubic feet is the sum of the following amounts of gas classified according to decreasing probability of discovery:

	(6^{12}ft^3)
Probable	300
Possible	210
Speculative	180
Total Potential Supply	690

A minor discrepancy exists between the Potential Gas Committee's figure of 600 trillion cubic feet for cumulative proved discoveries up to the beginning of 1967, and the figure of 604 trillion cubic feet used herein. The latter agrees with that given in the AGA, API, and CPA report of 1967 (p. 161). However, the principal difference lies in the amounts of gas estimated to be obtained from new fields still to be discovered, over and above the 825 trillion cubic feet estimated to be ultimately producible from fields already discovered. In the Potential Gas Committee's estimate, this would amount to 465 trillion cubic feet, which is just over twice the amount of our estimate of 218 trillion cubic feet, based on future oil discoveries.

At a gas-oil ratio of 7,500 ft^3/bbl, the new discoveries of crude oil that would have to accompany the future discovery of 465 trillion cubic feet of gas would amount to 62 billion barrels. The data in Figure 8.16 definitely do not support any such quantity but, rather, a figure of about half that amount.

Hence, although the estimate of the Potential Gas Committee of 1290 trillion cubic feet and that of 1044 trillion cubic feet based on a crude-oil analysis in conjunction with the gas-oil ratio are in substantial agreement, there still exists an excess of about 250 trillion cubic feet in the Potential Gas Committee's report which is difficult to reconcile with any likely amount of crude oil still to be discovered. If the 180 trillion cubic feet of gas classed as "speculative" by the Potential Gas Committee should be withdrawn, then a satisfactory agreement would be obtained.

Using the Potential Gas Committee's figure, $Q_\infty = 1290$ trillion cubic feet, the complete cycle of U.S. gas production is shown in Figure 8.20. According to this, a peak production rate of about 25 trillion cubic feet per year will occur about the year 1980. The time required to produce the middle 80 percent of the ultimate cumulative production will be the approximately 65-year period from about the years 1950 to 2015. Also shown is a curve of what the production would be until about 1985 if it were to continue the growth rate of 6.34 percent per year which has prevailed during recent decades.

A curve analogous to that in Figure 8.20 has also been computed for

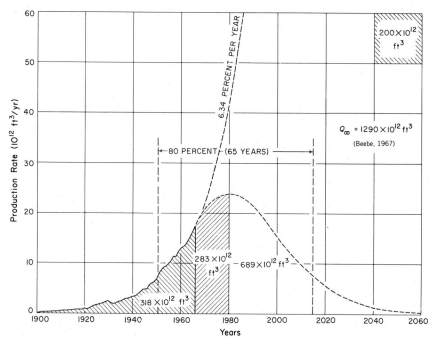

FIGURE 8.20
Complete cycle of natural-gas production in the United States and adjacent continental shelves, exclusive of Alaska.

$Q_\infty = 1040$ trillion cubic feet; it closely resembles the curve in Figure 8.20 except that the peak production rate is reduced to about 21 trillion cubic feet per year, and occurs at about the year 1978.

Estimates of Natural-Gas Liquids

The foregoing discrepancy in the estimates of future discoveries of natural gas carries over into estimates of natural-gas liquids. By 31 December 1966, the cumulative discoveries and proved reserves of natural-gas liquids for the conterminous United States were the following (API, AGA, and CPA, 1967, p. 116, 118, 207):

Cumulative production	9.86×10^9 bbls
Proved reserves	8.33×10^9 bbls
Cumulative discoveries	18.19×10^9 bbls

Since natural-gas liquids are produced along with natural gas, the significant ratio for these two fluids is that of gas/NGL. If we take the cumulative discoveries of these two fluids from 1860 to 1967, this ratio is

$$\text{gas/NGL} = \frac{604 \times 10^{12} \text{ ft}^3}{18.2 \times 10^9 \text{ bbls}}$$

$$= 33{,}200 \text{ ft}^3/\text{bbl}.$$

If, on the other hand, we take the corresponding ratio for the decades 1947 to 1957 and 1957 to 1967, we obtain:

For 1947-1957,

$$\text{gas/NGL} = 27{,}000 \text{ ft}^3/\text{bbl};$$

For 1957-1967,

$$\text{gas/NGL} = 26{,}000 \text{ ft}^3/\text{bbl}.$$

From these figures, it appears that the gas-NGL ratio is progressively decreasing with cumulative gas production. In view of this progressive decline in the gas-NGL ratio, it is difficult to justify a figure larger than 25,000 ft^3/bbl for future U.S. discoveries. Using this figure, in conjunction with cumulative proved discoveries of 604 trillion cubic feet by the beginning of 1967, and the two estimates of Q_∞ for natural gas, of 1044 trillion and 1290 trillion cubic feet, we obtain for the estimates of future discoveries of natural-gas liquids:

For $Q_\infty = 1044 \times 10^{12} \text{ ft}^3$,

$$\text{NGL} = \frac{(1044 - 604) \times 10^{12} \text{ ft}^3}{2.5 \times 10^4 \text{ ft}^3/\text{bbls}} = 17.6 \times 10^9 \text{ bbls};$$

For $Q_\infty = 1290 \times 10^{12} \text{ ft}^3$,

$$\text{NGL} = \frac{(1290 - 604) \times 10^{12} \text{ ft}^3}{2.5 \times 10^4 \text{ ft}^3/\text{bbl}} = 27.4 \times 10^9 \text{ bbls}.$$

When these figures are added to the 18.2 $\times$ 10^9 bbls of cumulative proved discoveries, we obtain 35.8 billion and 45.6 billion barrels for the estimated ultimate quantity of natural-gas liquids to be produced in the conterminous United States. On the basis of our previous comments concerning the natural-gas estimates, only the lesser of these two figures is compatible with our earlier analysis of crude oil, and is accordingly favored here. Using the smaller figure, rounded off to 36 billion barrels, the full cycle of U.S. production of natural-gas liquids is shown in Figure 8.21. According to the calculations on which this figure is based, a peak production

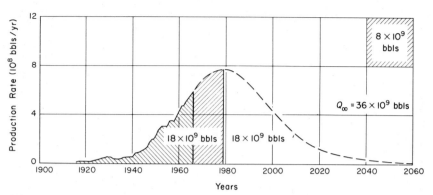

FIGURE 8.21
Complete cycle of production of natural-gas liquids in the United States and adjacent continental shelves, exclusive of Alaska.

rate of about 775 million barrels of natural-gas liquids per year will be reached at about 1980.

Total Petroleum Liquids

The sum of the production rate of crude oil and that of natural-gas liquids gives the production rate for petroleum liquids. Likewise, the sum of the ultimate amount of crude oil and of natural-gas liquids gives the ultimate amount of petroleum liquids to be produced. For the United States, exclusive of Alaska, this amounts to 165 billion barrels of crude oil plus 36 billion barrels for natural-gas liquids, or to 201 billion, rounded to 200 billion, barrels as the estimated magnitude of Q_∞ for petroleum liquids.

Using this value for Q_∞, the complete cycle of production of petroleum liquids is shown in Figure 8.22. A peak rate of production of about 3.5 billion barrels per year is estimated to occur during the first half of the 1970-decade, and production of the middle 80 percent of Q_∞ is expected to occur during the 64-year period from about the year 1937 to 2001. Also shown in Figure 8.22 is the course that the annual production would follow were it to continue at the constant rate of growth of 5.13 percent per year which prevailed from 1934 to 1952.

Estimates for Alaska. As stated above, the exploration for petroleum in Alaska is just in its beginning stages, and significant production of crude oil began only in 1958. Consequently, about the only guide for estimates at present is geological analogy coupled with the exploratory successes achieved thus far. On this basis a tentative allowance has already been made for an ultimate production of 25 billion barrels of crude oil. If we assume an average gas-oil ratio of 6,000 ft³/bbl, which is about that for the rest of the

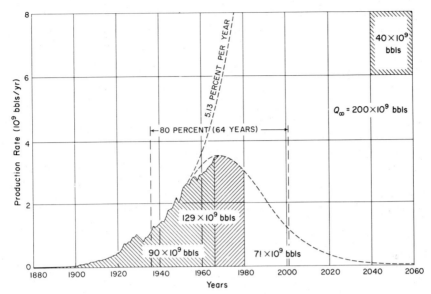

FIGURE 8.22
Complete cycle of production of petroleum liquids in the United States and adjacent continental shelves, exclusive of Alaska.

United States, this would give about 150 trillion cubic feet for the ultimate production of natural gas. And, at an average rate of 30,000 ft^3/bbl for the natural-gas—natural-gas liquids ratio, the estimated ultimate amount of natural-gas liquids would be about 5 billion barrels.

Total Petroleum for the Whole United States.   These figures added to those already obtained for the rest of the United States give our present estimates for the ultimate amounts of petroleum fluids that the whole United States and its adjacent continental-shelf areas may reasonably be expected to produce. These estimates are given in Table 8.1.

TABLE 8.1
Estimated ultimate amounts of petroleum fluids to be produced by the United States (including contiguous continental shelves).

Region	Crude Oil (10^9 bbls)	Natural-gas Liquids (10^9 bbls)	Petroleum Liquids (10^9 bbls)	Natural Gas (10^{12} ft^3)
Conterminous United States	165	36	201	1,050
Alaska	25	5	30	150
Total	190	41	231	1,200

WORLD RESOURCES OF PETROLEUM

The Committee on Resources and Man is indebted to W. P. Ryman, Deputy
Exploration Manager of Standard Oil Company of New Jersey, for several
different world estimates of ultimate crude oil recovery, by major geographical areas (Table 8.2). Column one of Table 8.2 contains estimates made
in January 1967 by *World Oil* of "proved" ultimately recoverable crude oil.
Column two presents estimates of December 1966 made by *World Petroleum*
of "proved and probable" ultimately recoverable crude oil. Finally, column
three presents a 1962 estimate of L. G. Weeks, and column four a tentative
estimate as of 1967 by W. P. Ryman of ultimately recoverable crude oil
under normal expected recovery practices. The estimates of the last two
columns each represent the sum of cumulative production plus proved
reserves plus probable reserves plus future discoveries.

Our concern here is only with the estimates of Weeks and Ryman given
in columns three and four, for these are the only ones that include future
discoveries.

TABLE 8.2

**Estimated ultimate recovery (EUR) of world crude oil, by geographical area (in
billions of U.S. barrels).**

	World Oil, Jan. 1967 Proved Reserves	World Petr., Dec. 1966 Proved & Probable Reserves	L. G. Weeks, 1962 EUR[a]	W. P. Ryman, 1967 EUR[a]
Free World outside United States				
Europe	3.6	4.0	19	20
Africa	31.9	49.0	100	250
Middle East	273.7	304.1	780	600
Far East	15.1	17.1	85	200[b]
Latin America	56.9	64.4	221	225[b]
Canada	10.9	11.4	85	95
Total	392.1	450.0	1,290	1,390
United States	113.4	128.6	270	200
Total Free World	505.5	578.6	1,560	1,590
U.S.S.R., China, and satellites	65.5	86.7	440	500
Total World	571.0	665.3	2,000	2,090

Source: W. P. Ryman, Deputy Exploration Manager, Standard Oil Company of New Jersey.
[a] Based on normal expected recovery. Estimate includes: Produced + Proved + Probable + Future
Discoveries.
[b] Includes offshore areas.

The Ryman estimates follow closely the earlier estimates of Weeks, but with some minor adjustments of the Weeks estimates for separate areas. With the exception of three cases, these adjustments to the Weeks estimates have been less than 11 percent. In the three exceptional cases, the Weeks estimate for Africa was increased from 100 billion to 250 billion barrels, that for the Far East from 85 billion to 200 billion barrels, and that for the United States was *decreased* from 270 billion to 200 billion barrels. For the world total, the Weeks estimate of 2,000 billion barrels was increased to 2,090 billion.

It is here considered that the Ryman estimates given in column four of Table 8.2 are about as accurate *relative* estimates of crude-oil resources of the various major regions of the world as can be made at the present time. The word "relative" is stressed, because the Ryman estimates follow closely those of Weeks. However, the Weeks estimates include a figure of 270 billion barrels for the United States, which is about 50 percent more than the highest figure that can be justified by the petroleum-industry data reviewed herein. Hence, if the Weeks method gives for the United States—the most completely explored region in the world (and its standard yardstick)—an estimate that is about 50 percent too large, it is a fair presumption that the same may be true of his estimate for the rest of the world also. In view of this possibility, two separate figures are here taken as the value of Q_∞ for the ultimate world production of crude oil: Ryman's estimate rounded off to 2,100 billion barrels, and a smaller figure of 1,350 billion barrels, which is about two-thirds of the Weeks estimate. It appears that the uncertainty of the world estimates at present is roughly within these limits.

The estimated full cycles of world crude-oil production, based on the two values, $Q_\infty = 2,100$ and $Q_\infty = 1,350$ billion barrels, are shown in Figure 8.23. For the smaller figure, a peak production rate of about 25 billion barrels per year is estimated to occur at about the year 1990, with the middle 80 percent of the cumulative production requiring only the 58-year period from 1961 to 2019. For the higher figure, the peak of the production rate of about 37 billion barrels per year would be delayed by only 10 years to about the year 2000. In this case, the time required to produce the middle 80 percent of the ultimate cumulative production would be increased to the 64-year period from about 1968 to 2032.

Mention should also be made of the recent world crude-oil estimates by Hendricks (1965). In these estimates, Hendricks used the same modification of the Zapp hypothesis that he used to obtain his estimate for the United States. Hendricks' estimate for the world crude oil eventually to be discovered is 6,200 billion barrels. This includes his estimate of 1,000 billion barrels for the United States. With an assumed 40-percent recovery factor, these two figures reduce to 2,480 billion and 400 billion barrels of recoverable crude oil for the world and the United States, respectively. Since his figure

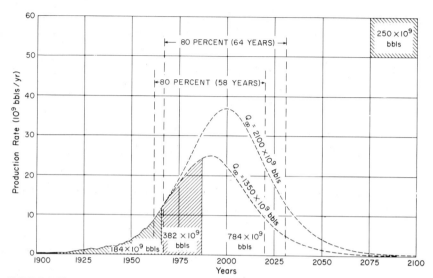

FIGURE 8.23
Complete cycles of world crude-oil production for two values of Q_∞.

of 400 billion barrels for the United States includes Alaska, it is to be compared with our present estimate of 190 billion barrels for the whole United States. Then, if a proportionate reduction is applied to the Hendricks world estimate, his figure of 2,480 billion barrels is reduced to 1,180, which is of the approximate magnitude of our lower figure of 1,350 billion barrels.

Another recent review of world petroleum resources was that given by D. C. Ion (1967) before the Seventh World Petroleum Congress in Mexico City, April 1967. This, however, was based so heavily upon the Hendricks estimate of 1965 that it can hardly be regarded as an independent estimate.

WORLD RESOURCES OF NATURAL GAS AND NATURAL-GAS LIQUIDS

As was true for U.S. production of natural gas during the earlier phases of the petroleum industry in the United States, the world production of natural gas has been handicapped in many areas by the absence of an accessible market. Consequently, much of the gas produced has been flared and wasted. However, recent advances in technology are eliminating much of this waste, so that eventually it is probable that most of the natural gas and natural-gas liquids produced will be conserved for industrial uses. Three main factors make this possible. One is an increase in gas-consuming industries, such as power production and the manufacture of Portland cement near centers of gas production. The second is the building of large-diameter pipelines for the transmission of gas from remote production areas to main industrial centers of consumption. The third is the development of cryogenic tankers for transoceanic transportation of natural gas in a liquefied form.

To make a rough estimate of the world resources of natural gas and natural-gas liquids, about the best that can be done at present is to assume that the ratios of natural gas and of natural-gas liquids to crude oil for the whole world will be about the same as those for the United States, and that shortly most of these fluids will be utilized rather than wasted.

For the United States, the ratio of the estimated ultimate amount of natural gas to be produced to that of crude oil is about 6,400 ft³/bbl; the corresponding ratio of natural-gas liquids to crude oil is about 0.22 bbls/bbl. For a rough estimate, these figures may be rounded off to 6,000 ft³/bbl for the natural gas—crude-oil ratio and to 0.2 bbls/bbl for the natural-gas liquids—crude-oil ratio. Applying these ratios to our two previous estimates for the ultimate world crude-oil production gives corresponding estimates for the ultimate world production of natural gas and natural-gas liquids. These are given in Table 8.3. The estimates given by W. P. Ryman at the Vancouver conference for the ultimate world production of natural-gas liquids and natural gas were 375×10^9 bbls and $12,000 \times 10^{12}$ ft³, respectively. Both of these figures are within the ranges indicated in Table 8.3.

TAR OR HEAVY-OIL SANDS

So-called tar, or heavy oil sands are impregnated with what is essentially a heavy crude oil that is too viscous to permit recovery by natural flowage into wells. Since such sands are as yet almost unexploited, no convenient world inventory of their occurrence is available. However, the best known of such deposits, and possibly the world's largest, are in the Province of Alberta, Canada. Pow, Fairbanks, and Zamora (1963) report on the large Athabasca deposit near Fort McMurray in northeastern Alberta and two

TABLE 8.3
Estimates of ultimate world production of natural-gas liquids, total petroleum liquids, and natural gas, based on two estimates of the ultimate production of crude oil.

Ultimate world crude-oil production (10^9 bbls)	Ultimate natural-gas liquids production (10^9 bbls)	Ultimate total petroleum liquids production (10^9 bbls)	Ultimate natural-gas production (10^{12} ft³)
1,350	250	1,620	8,000
2,100	420	2,520	12,000

TABLE 8.4
Tar-sand deposits of Alberta, Canada.

Area	Evaluated Reserves (10^9 bbls)
Athabasca	266.9
Bluesky-Gething	20.6
Grand Rapids	13.3
Total	300.8

Source: Pow, Fairbanks, and Zamora (1963).

smaller groups: the Bluesky-Gething deposits in northwestern Alberta, and the Grand Rapids deposits in north-central Alberta.

Of these, the Athabasca deposit has an area of about 9,000 square miles and contains about 88 percent of the total evaluated tar-sand reserves of the Province. The Bluesky-Gething deposits have an area of about 1,800 square miles and contain about 7 percent of the evaluated reserves. The remaining deposits have an aggregate area of about 1,600 square miles and contain about 5 percent of the evaluated reserves. The thickness of overburden in the various deposits ranges from 0 at surface outcrops to about 2,000 feet.

The evaluated reserves of recoverable upgraded synthetic crude oil from the three groups of deposits are given in Table 8.4.

During the last half century, small-scale efforts to exploit these sands have repeatedly failed. Since 1966, however, the first large-scale mining and extraction plant, developed by a combination of major oil companies, has gone into successful operation. Development work has also been under way since 1958 by a number of other oil companies, who only await the approval of the provincial government to begin further exploitation.

If we compare the magnitude of the reserves of these deposits with that of the crude-oil resources of the United States, their potential importance in the comparatively near future, when domestic crude-oil production begins its decline, is immediately apparent. The oil from these sands has the additional advantage that, being in the same chemical family as crude oil, it can be processed by existing oil refineries without major modifications.

OIL SHALES

As remarked previously, oil shales differ from tar or heavy-oil sands in that their hydrocarbon contents are in a solid rather than a viscous-liquid form. Also shale oil differs considerably from crude oil in chemical content; it includes objectionable nitrogen and other impurities. Consequently, the oils from oil shales pose special problems in refining.

In the United States, the principal and best known oil-shale deposits are those of the Green River Formation in the Piceance Basin of northwestern Colorado, the Uinta Basin of eastern Utah, and the Green River Basin of southwestern Wyoming. Because the oil contents of these shales range from about 65 U.S. gallons per ton (1.5 barrels/ton) for the richest shales to near zero, some confusion exists in where to place the cutoff limit of oil content in estimating the magnitude of the resources. According to a study by Duncan and Swanson (1965, p. 13):

> Known oil-shale deposits that yield 10-25 gallons of oil per ton contain about 800 billion barrels oil equivalent in the Piceance Basin, Colo.; about 230 billion barrels in the Uinta Basin, Utah; and about 400 billion barrels in the combined Green River Basin and Washakie Basin, Wyoming.

These figures tend to be misleading unless tempered with the same authors' discussion elsewhere of "recoverable resources." These are said to be (ibid., p. 6):

> . . . (1) deposits yielding 25-100 gallons of oil per ton, in beds a few feet thick or more, extending to depths of 1,000 feet below surface and (2) some lower grade deposits yielding 10-25 gallons of oil per ton, in units 25 feet thick or more, which are minable by open-pit methods. About 50 percent of the oil shale in place is assumed to be minable under present conditions, although larger percentages could be recovered from parts of deposits minable by open-pit methods.

In view of these restrictions, the same authors list (their Table 2, p. 9) only 80 billion barrels as being "recoverable under present conditions" from the Green River Formation in Colorado, Utah, and Wyoming. Duncan and Swanson also list the carbonaceous Devonian and Mississippian shales of east-central United States, and other shale deposits, whose aggregate chemical energy contents are enormous, but the oil-equivalent content per ton is so small that they are classed as "marginal and submarginal."

The same authors have compiled a comprehensive summary of the known major deposits of carbonaceous shales throughout the world, and have given estimates of their oil contents in their Table 3 on page 18 (our Table 8.5). Again, it is significant that although the table gives a figure of about 2×10^{15} barrels as the order of magnitude of the total oil-equivalent content of these shales, only 190×10^9, or 190 billion barrels (including 80 billion for the U.S. Green River Shale), is listed as recoverable under present conditions.

Hence, the organic contents of the carbonaceous shales appear to be more promising as a resource of raw materials for the chemical industry than as a major source of industrial energy.

TABLE 8.5
Estimates of shale oil resources of world land areas (in billions of barrels).

Continents	Known Resources				Possible Extensions of Known Resources			Undiscovered and Unappraised Resources			Order of Magnitude of Total Resources[b]		
	Recoverable under Present Conditions	Marginal and Submarginal (oil equivalent in deposits)									Oil Equivalent in Deposits		
	Range in grade (oil yield, in gallons per ton of shale)												
	10–100	25–100	10–25	5–10	25–100	10–25	5–10	25–100	10–25	5–10	25–100	10–25	5–10
Africa	10	90	Small	Small	ne[a]	ne	ne	4,000	80,000	450,000	4,000	80,000	450,000
Asia	20	70	14	ne	2	3,700	ne	5,400	106,000	586,000	5,500	110,000	590,000
Australia and New Zealand	Small	Small	1	ne	ne	ne	ne	1,000	20,000	100,000	1,000	20,000	100,000
Europe	30	40	6	ne	100	200	ne	1,200	26,000	150,000	1,400	26,000	140,000
North America	80	520	1,600	2,200	900	2,500	4,000	1,500	45,000	254,000	3,000	50,000	260,000
South America	50	Small	750	ne	ne	3,200	4,000	2,000	36,000	206,000	2,000	40,000	210,000
Total	190	720	2,400	2,200	1,000	9,600	8,000	15,000	313,000	1,740,000	17,000	325,000	1,750,000

Source: Duncan and Swanson, 1965, Table 3, p. 18.
[a] ne = no estimate.
[b] Of the approximately 2×10^{15} bbls here indicated, 190×10^9 were considered recoverable under 1965 conditions.

RESOURCES OF COAL

World production of coal from 1860 to 1965 has already been shown in
Figure 8.1, and that for the United States in Figure 8.4.

Unlike petroleum, coal occurs as stratified deposits in sedimentary basins.
These commonly are continuous over wide areas and also frequently crop
out at the surface of the ground. Consequently, by means of surface geological
mapping, and a few widely spaced drill holes, it is possible to make reasonably
accurate estimates of the coal resources of a given sedimentary basin in
advance of mining, and to estimate the coal resources of the various sedimentary basins of the world. Then, with this knowledge, by means of the
technique illustrated in Figure 8.8, it is possible to anticipate the period of
time during which coal may be depended upon to supply a major part of
the world's requirements for industrial energy.

The first world-wide inventory of coal, based on such considerations, was
that reported to the Twelfth International Geological Congress at Toronto
in the year 1913. Although many of the estimates at that time were very
provisional, the estimate of minable coal resources for the entire world
amounted to about 8×10^{12} metric tons. Since that time, geological
mapping has been extended to all the land areas of the world. The result has
been that large coal deposits in Siberia and China, which were little known
in 1913, have been added to the estimates of that time, and estimates for
other areas have been adjusted upward or downward as geological knowledge
has increased.

During the last two decades, the U.S. Geological Survey has been engaged
in a detailed study of the country's coal resources, and in connection with
this study Paul Averitt has also made a succession of estimates of the coal
resources of the world, using published national estimates of various
countries, interpreted in conjunction with accruing geological information.
In a report submitted to the Natural Resources Subcommittee of the
Federal Council of Science and Technology, Averitt (1961) gave a table
(Hubbert, 1962, p. 37) of the estimated remaining producible coal reserves
of the world by principal regions and countries. Minable coal was taken to
be 50 percent of the coal in the ground in seams 14 inches (0.36 meters) or
more thick and less than 3,000 feet (900 meters) deep. Averitt's figure for the
world was 2.3×10^{12} metric tons.

The foregoing figures pertain to coal deposits whose extent and magnitude
are fairly accurately known from geological mapping and other data.
Subsequently, Averitt has extended his studies to include not only the coal
resources determined by mapping but also additional coal resources which,
from geological information on the various coal-bearing areas, may

TABLE 8.6

Estimates of total original coal resources of the world by continents[a] (in billions of short tons).

Continent	Resources determined by mapping and exploration	Probable additional resources in unmapped and unexplored areas	Estimated total resources
Asia and European U.S.S.R.	7,000[b]	4,000	11,000[c]
North America	1,720	2,880	4,600
Europe	620	210	830
Africa	80	160	240
Oceania	60	70	130
South and Central Americas	20	10	30
Total	9,500[b]	7,330	16,830[c]

Source: Paul Averitt, 1969, Table 8, p. 82.

[a] Original resources in the ground in beds 12 inches thick or more and generally less than 4,000 feet below the surface, but includes small amounts between 4,000 and 6,000 feet.

[b] Includes about 6,500 billion short tons in the U.S.S.R.

[c] Includes about 9,500 billion short tons in the U.S.S.R. (Hodgkins, 1961, p. 6).

reasonably be inferred to exist. The results of these studies were presented to the Committee on Resources and Man during its meeting in Vancouver, 15–17 September 1967, and have since been published (Averitt, 1969) by the U.S. Geological Survey.

Averitt's current estimates, by continents, of the original coal in place are given in Table 8.6. In this case, the depth has been extended to 4,000 feet (1,200 meters), and in some cases to 6,000 feet (1,800 meters). Also the minimum thickness of seams considered has been reduced to 12 inches (0.3 meters). He pointed out, however, that the amount of coal added for the additional depth of 4,000–6,000 feet is small compared with that between 0 and 4,000 feet. In the United States, the coal in the 4,000–6,000-foot interval amounts only to about 10 percent of the total.

The data in Table 8.6 are expressed in short tons, and no breakdown by countries is given. However, in the footnote the Soviet Union is credited with $9,500 \times 10^9$ short tons, or $8,600 \times 10^9$ metric tons. In a separate detailed table, the original coal resources of the United States were given as $3,275 \times 10^9$ short tons, or $2,971 \times 10^9$ metric tons. From these data, the initial quantities of minable coal, taken as 50 percent of the coal present, have been computed by continents, and expressed in metric units, with separate estimates for the United States and the Soviet Union included. The results are shown graphically in Figure 8.24.

According to these estimates, about 65 percent of the world's initial coal resources were in Asia (including the European part of the Soviet

Union), about 27 percent in North America, less than 5 percent in Western Europe, and less than 3 percent in Africa, South and Central Americas, and Oceania (which includes Australia) combined. From these data, it is evident that the world's coal resources are not uniformly distributed.

World and United States production of coal and lignite have already been shown (Figures 8.1 and 8.4). Now, using Averitt's estimates of the ultimate amounts of minable coal for both the world and the United States, in conjunction with the principle that the area under the curves must not exceed those corresponding to the amounts of coal initially present, we can gain a reasonably reliable impression of the future possibilities in coal production. For world production, this is shown in Figure 8.25, using for the ultimate cumulative production Q_∞, Averitt's estimate of 7.6×10^{12} metric tons, and also a smaller figure of 4.3×10^{12}, which is approximately the amount of coal established by mapping.

For the larger value for Q_∞ of 7.6×10^{12} metric tons, should the annual production rate double only three more times to a maximum rate of eight times that of the present, the date of this peak rate would occur about 170 to 200 years hence. Should the maximum rate be higher than this, the peak date would occur sooner; should it be lower, later. For the smaller value for Q_∞ of 4.3×10^{12} metric tons, the curve is drawn for a sixfold increase in the production rate over that of the present. In this case, the peak rate would occur somewhat earlier, or about 140 years hence.

Corresponding graphs of future coal production in the United States are shown in Figure 8.26 for two values of Q_∞. The larger figure of $1,486 \times 10^9$

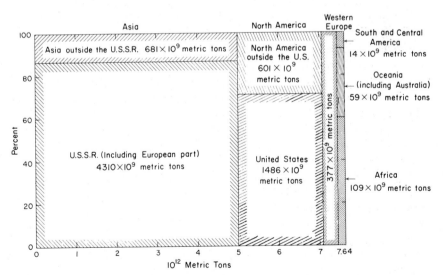

FIGURE 8.24
Estimates of world resources of minable coal and lignite. (Data from Averitt, 1969.)

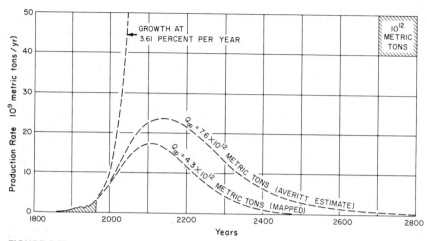

FIGURE 8.25
Complete cycles of world coal production for two values of Q_∞.

metric tons represents minable coal based on Averitt's recent estimate of the initial U.S. coal resources. The smaller figure of 740×10^9 metric tons is approximately the amount of coal determined by mapping. For the higher-rate curve, the assumed maximum production rate represents an eightfold increase over the present rate, or three future doublings. The smaller-rate curve assumes a fivefold increase in the rate of production. The peak production rates for these two curves would occur at about the years 2220 and 2170, respectively.

As was true for petroleum, the significant question about coal is not how

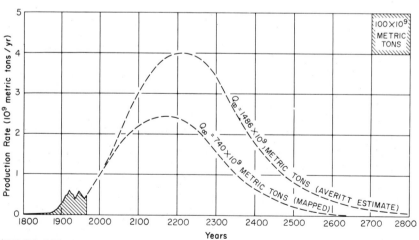

FIGURE 8.26
Complete cycles of United States coal production for two values of Q_∞.

long it will last, but rather, over what period of time can it serve as a major source of industrial energy? In answer to this, we may eliminate the long periods of time at relatively low rates of production required to produce the first and last 10-percentiles of the ultimate cumulative production Q_∞, and consider only the time span required to consume the middle 80 percent. For the world, using the higher value for Q_∞ of 7.6 × 10^{12} metric tons, the time required for the middle 80 percent, as determined from Figure 8.25, would be approximately the 340-year period from the year 2040 to 2380. For the United States, using the larger figure for Q_∞ of about 1.49 × 10^{12} metric tons, the time required to consume the middle 80 percent, as determined from Figure 8.26, would be approximately the 400-year period from about the year 2040 to 2440.

These figures, of course, are only approximate, but they do indicate the expectable order of magnitude of the length of time during which coal could serve as a major source of energy for the nation and the world. In both cases, should the smaller values of Q_∞ shown by the lower curves in Figures 8.25 and 8.26 be used, or should the peak rates of production be higher than those shown, the time would be correspondingly shortened.

CONCLUSIONS CONCERNING THE FOSSIL FUELS

For the purpose of the present study, the principal result of the foregoing estimates of the approximate magnitudes of both the United States' and the world's supply of the fossil fuels are the following:

If these substances continue to be used principally for their energy contents, and if they continue to supply the bulk of the world's energy requirements, the time required to exhaust the middle 80 percent of the ultimate resources of the members of the petroleum family—crude oil, natural gas, and natural-gas liquids, tar-sand oil, and shale oil—will probably be only about a century.

Under similar conditions, the time required to exhaust the middle 80 percent of the world's coal resources would be about 300 to 400 years (but only 100 to 200 years if coal is used as the main energy source).

To appreciate the bearing of these conclusions on the long-range outlook for human institutions, the historical epoch of the exploitation of the world's supply of fossil fuels is shown graphically in Figure 8.27, where the rate of production of the fossil fuels as a function of time is plotted on a time scale extending from 5,000 years ago to 5,000 years in the future—a period well within the prospective span of human history. On such a time scale, it is seen that the epoch of the fossil fuels can only be a transitory and ephemeral event—an event, nonetheless, which has exercised the most drastic influence experienced by the human species during its entire biological history.

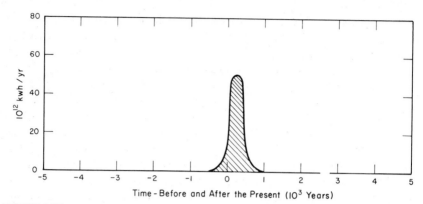

FIGURE 8.27
Epoch of exploitation of fossil fuels in historical perspective from minus to plus 5,000 years from present. (From Hubbert, 1962, Figure 54, p. 91.)

OTHER SOURCES OF ENERGY

In view of the exhaustibility and comparatively short time span for the duration of the fossil fuels, if the world's state of industrialization is to survive the decline of fossil fuels, other sources of energy and power of comparable magnitude must be found. Possible sources will now be reviewed with this requirement in mind.

Solar Energy

The first and most obvious of possible large energy sources is solar radiation, which is extensively discussed by Farrington Daniels (1964) in his excellent book, *Direct Use of the Sun's Energy*. In magnitude, the thermal solar power per square centimeter at the mean distance of the earth from the sun amounts, outside the earth's atmosphere, to 0.139 watts/cm^2, and the thermal power intercepted by the earth's diametral plane is 17.7×10^{16} watts, which is about a hundred-thousand times larger than the world's present installed electric-power capacity. Hence, solar power is of adequate magnitude. It also has the virtue of remaining nearly constant over time periods of millions of years—much longer than the probable duration of the human species. Solar radiation is also the energy source, through the mechanism of photo-synthesis, for the entire biological system.

As Daniels discusses in detail, many practical nonbiological uses can be made of solar energy on a small scale. These include such uses as water and house heating, air conditioning, distillation, solar furnaces, solar cookery, and numerous thermoelectric, photoelectric, and other means of electrical conversion or storage of solar energy. However, our principal concern at present is with the question of whether it is likely that our requirements for large-scale electrical power, now supplied by the fossil fuels and water power, could be met by means of solar power. In particular, since modern power stations fall largely in the range of 100 to 1,000 megawatts each, what is the likelihood of building solar power plants of such magnitudes?

Consider, in particular, a solar-electric power plant of 1,000 electric megawatts capacity. With a conversion factor from solar power to electrical power of 10 percent, such a plant would require a solar power input of 10,000 megawatts, or 10^{10} thermal watts. According to Daniels (1964, Table 1, p. 22), the average solar power at the earth's surface amounts to about 500 cal/cm^2/day. This, when averaged over a full day, gives an average solar power input of about 2.4×10^{-2} watts/cm^2. Then, the area of the earth's surface required to collect 10^{10} watts of solar power would be

$$10^{10} \text{ watts}/(2.4 \times 10^{-2} \text{ watts/cm}^2) = 42 \times 10^{10} \text{ cm}^2,$$

which would be 42 km^2, or a square area of 6.5 km per side.

There is no question that it is physically possible to cover such an area with energy-collecting devices, and to transmit, store, and ultimately transform the energy so collected into conventional electric power. However, the complexity of such a process, and its cost in terms of the metals and physical, chemical, and electrical equipment required, in comparison with the requirements for present thermoelectric or hydroelectric equipment of the same capacity, renders such an undertaking to be of questionable practicability.

At present, therefore, the principal uses of solar energy, in addition to the natural processes of photosynthesis and the maintenance of the atmospheric, hydrologic, and oceanic circulations, appear to be small-scale, special-purpose uses.

Water Power

Water power represents the largest concentration of solar power that is produced by any natural process, and five hydroelectric plants already exist in the United States with power capacities exceeding 1,000 megawatts each. The history of the use of water power dates from Roman times, and, in the United States, water power has been extensively employed for the driving of grist mills, saw mills, textile mills, and other manufacturing establishments during the eighteenth and nineteenth centuries. However, because of the difficulties inherent in power transmission by mechanical devices, such plants rarely exceeded a few hundred kilowatts in power capacity.

It was not until the development of electrical-power transmission at about the beginning of the present century that large-scale generation and trans-

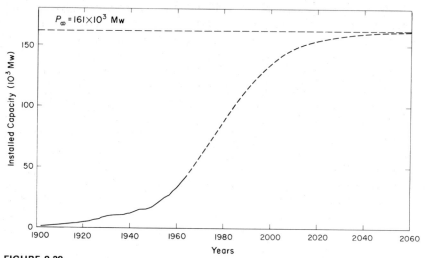

FIGURE 8.28
United States installed and potential water-power capacity.

mission of water power became possible. Since that time, the installation of hydroelectric power capacity in the United States has followed the customary growth curve shown in Figure 8.28. Installed capacity at present amounts to about 45,000 megawatts. As to the future, there is a fairly definitely determined ultimate maximum power capacity, P_∞, which for the United States is given by the Federal Power Commission to be about 161,000 megawatts. This is determined from the stream-flow records for the whole country which have been recorded for many years by the U.S. Geological Survey.

The Geological Survey has also made estimates from time to time of the potential water-power capacities of the various continents for the world as a whole.

Table 8.7, prepared from a summary by Francis L. Adams (Hubbert, 1962, p. 99), of the Federal Power Commission, utilizing basic U.S. Geological Survey data, gives the potential water-power capacities of the world by principal regions. The total world capacity is given as 2,857,000 megawatts. Of this, it is significant that the continents of Africa and South America, both of which are deficient in coal, have the highest potential water-power capacities of all the continents—780,000 megawatts for Africa and 577,000 for South America.

By 1964, the installed water-power capacity of the world amounted to 210,000 megawatts (U.S. Federal Power Commission, 1966, Table 5, p. 7), which is only about 7.5 percent of its potential capacity. The total installed electrical-power capacity of the world amounted at the same time to 734,000 megawatts. Hence, the total potential water-power capacity of the world is still about four times as large as total installed electric-power capacity.

It thus appears that if the world's potential conventional water-power capacity were fully developed it would be of a magnitude comparable to the world's total present rate of energy consumption. From this, it might be inferred that without the present supply of fossil fuels, the world could continue at an industrial level comparable to that of the present on water-power alone. Offsetting such an expectation are two contrary considerations. The first is the aesthetic one of whether the people of the world wish to sacrifice some of their most beautiful natural scenery in order to develop fully the associated water power. The second concerns the fact that in all reservoirs formed by dammed streams, the streams are continuously depositing their loads of sediments, so that in periods of a century or two most man-made reservoirs are due to become completely filled by such sediments. This problem has not been satisfactorily solved, and may never be. Hence, although the stream rates of discharge may remain relatively stable for millenia, most water-power sites may have periods of maximum usefulness measured by a century or two. It is accordingly questionable to what extent the world may be able to depend upon water power as a substitute for the depleted fossil fuels.

Tidal Power

Another source of power having a longevity measurable in geologic time is tidal power. Tidal power is similar in all essential respects to hydroelectric power except that, whereas hydroelectric power is obtained from the energy of unidirectional streamflow, tidal-electric power is obtained from

TABLE 8.7
World water-power capacity.

Region	Potential (10^3 Mw)	Percent of total	Development (10^3 Mw)	Percent developed
North America	313	11	59	19
South America	577	20	5	
Western Europe	158	6	47	30
Africa	780	27	2	
Middle East	21	1	—	
Southeast Asia	455	16	2	
Far East	42	1	19	
Australasia	45	2	2	
U.S.S.R., China and satellites	466	16	16	3
Total	2,857	100	152	

Source: M. King Hubbert, 1962, Table 8, p. 99, computed from data summarized by Francis L Adams, 1961.

the oscillatory flow of water in the filling and emptying of partially enclosed coastal basins during the semi-diurnal rise and fall of the oceanic tides. This energy may be partially converted into tidal-electric power by enclosing such basins with dams to create a difference in water level between the ocean and the basin, and then using the waterflow while the basin is filling or emptying to drive hydraulic turbines propelling electric generators.

In order to obtain a quantitative evaluation of the amount of tidal energy potentially obtainable from a given basin, it is useful to determine the maximum amount of energy that can be dissipated into heat during one complete tidal cycle. This is the amount of energy that would be dissipated if the dam gates were closed at low tide when the water in the basin is at its lowest level, and then opened wide allowing the basin to fill at the crest of the tide; and, in a similar manner, by closing the gates when the basin is filled at high tide, and then allowing the basin to empty at low tide.

This maximum possible amount of energy dissipated during one tidal cycle is given by

$$E_{max} = \rho g R^2 S, \tag{7}$$

where ρ is the density of sea water, g the acceleration of gravity, R the tidal range, and S the surface area of the basin. When all of the quantities to the right in equation (7) are in meter-kilogram-second units, the energy will be in joules.

The maximum possible average power obtainable from such a basin would be obtained if all of the energy E_{max} in equation (7) were converted into electrical energy. This maximum average power would then be given by

$$\bar{P} = \frac{E_{max}}{T} = \frac{\rho g R^2 S}{T}, \tag{8}$$

where T is the half period of the synodical lunar day. This is 12 hours and 24.4 minutes, or 4.46×10^4 seconds. When T is in seconds, $\bar{P}$ will be expressed in joules/second, or watts.

The actual energy and power obtainable by means of turbines and electrical generators from such a basin can be only a fraction of the quantities given in equations (7) and (8). In engineering design computations for various tidal-power projects, the amounts of energy and power producible are commonly within the range of 8–20 percent of these maximum amounts, although in one instance, that of la Rance in France, the realizable power approaches 25 percent.

The source of tidal energy is the combined kinetic and potential energy of the earth-moon-sun system. Hence, as this energy is dissipated on the earth, equivalent changes must occur in the rotational energy of the earth, and in the orbital motions of the moon about the earth and of the earth about the sun. These motional changes, which have been observed astronomically over a period of about three centuries, indicate that the day is lengthening by about 0.001 second per century with a corresponding decrease in the earth's rotational velocity. From such astronomical data, Munk and MacDonald (1960, p. 219) have recently estimated that the rate of tidal dissipation of energy on the earth is about 3×10^{12} watts.

A considerable fraction of this dissipation occurs in the oceans, especially in the shallow seas, bays, and estuaries, where the tidal ranges and tidal currents, because of inertial effects, become much greater than those in the open oceans. The oceanic tides, as measured on islands in the open oceans, have ranges commonly of less than a meter, whereas those in bays and estuaries have ranges, as shown in Table 8.8, from 1 to more than 10 meters.

A method of estimating the amount of energy dissipated by tides in shallow seas was developed in 1919 by G. I. Taylor and applied to the Irish Sea. The following year, this method was extended by Harold Jeffreys (1920; 1959, p. 241–245) to most of the shallow seas of the earth for which he estimated a rate of energy dissipation at spring tides of about 22×10^{11} watts, of which 15×10^{11} watts, or two-thirds of the total was accounted for by the Bering Sea alone.

Recently, using oceanographic data subsequently acquired, Munk and MacDonald (1960, p. 209–221) have re-estimated the energy dissipation in shallow seas. They obtained an average rate of, at most, 10^{12} watts, which is slightly less than the 1.1×10^{12} watts obtained when Jeffrey's rate for spring tides is reduced by a factor of 0.5 to give an average rate. Munk and MacDonald obtained a drastic reduction of Jeffrey's estimate for the Bering Sea from 75×10^{10} ($\frac{1}{2}$ of 15×10^{11}) to only 2.4×10^{10} watts.

The significance of these estimates is that they establish a limit to the maximum amount of power that could possibly be developed from tidal sources. In Table 8.8, which is based on data compiled by Trenholm (1961) and by Bernshtein (1965), a summary is given of the average tidal ranges and basin areas for most of the more promising tidal-energy localities of the world. In addition, the average potential power, and maximum energy dissipation per year, as computed from equations (7) and (8), are given for each locality. The total maximum rate of energy dissipation for these localities amounts to 6.4×10^{10} watts, or 64,000 megawatts. This is about 6 percent of the Munk and MacDonald estimate of a dissipation rate of 10^{12} watts for all of the shallow seas. If we make a liberal allowance of 20 percent for the actual average power recoverable at each of these sites, we obtain a result of about 13×10^9 watts, or 13,000 megawatts as the approximate magnitude of the average value of the world's potential tidal-electric power. Comparing this with the estimate of the world's potential water power of about 2,900,000 megawatts given in Table 8.7, it will be seen that the world's potential tidal power amounts to less than 1 percent of its potential water power.

TABLE 8.8
Tidal power sites and maximum potential power.

Location	Average range R (meters)	R^2 (m²)	Basin area S (km²)	R^2S (m²)(km²)	Average potential power P (10³ kw)	Potential annual energy E (10⁶ kwh)
North America						
Bay of Fundy						
Passamaquoddy	5.52	30.5	262	7,990	1,800	15,800
Cobscook	5.5	30.3	106	3,210	722	6,330
Annapolis	6.4	41.0	83	3,440	765	6,710
Minas-Cobequid	10.7	114	777	88,600	19,900	175,000
Amherst Point	10.7	114	10	1,140	256	2,250
Shepody	9.8	96	117	11,200	2,520	22,100
Cumberland	10.1	102	73	7,450	1,680	14,700
Petitcodiac	10.7	114	31	3,530	794	6,960
Memramcook	10.7	114	23	2,620	590	5,170
Subtotal					29,027	255,020
South America						
Argentina						
San José	5.9	34.8	750	26,100	5,870	51,500
Europe						
England						
Severn	9.8	96.0	70	7,460	1,680	14,700

France						
Aber-Benoît	5.2	27.0	2.9	78	18	158
Aber-Wrac'h	5.0	25.0	1.1	28	6	53
Arguenon & Lancieux	8.4	70.6	28.0	1,980	446	3,910
Frênaye	7.4	54.8	12.0	658	148	1,300
La Rance	8.4	70.6	22.0	1,550	349	3,060
Rothéneuf	8.0	64.0	1.1	70	16	140
Mont Saint-Michel	8.4	70.6	610	43,100	9,700	85,100
Somme	6.5	42.3	49	2,070	466	4,090
Subtotal				11,149	97,811	
U.S.S.R.						
Kislaya Inlet	2.37	5.62	2.0	11	2	22
Lumbovskii Bay	4.20	17.6	70	1,230	277	2,430
White Sea	5.65	31.9	2,000	63,800	14,400	126,000
Mezen Estuary	6.60	43.6	140	6,100	1,370	12,000
Subtotal				16,049	140,452	
Grand Total				63,775	559,483	

Sources: N. W. Trenholm, 1961; L. B. Bernshtein, 1965 (1961), Table 5-5, p. 173.

Although small tidal mills for the grinding of grain and similar purposes have been used since about the twelfth century, it is only within recent decades that tidal-electric installations have been given serious engineering consideration, and only within the last three years actually brought into operation.

One of the best known of such projects has been that of Passamaquoddy Bay on the United States-Canadian boundary off the Bay of Fundy. This bay has an area of 262 km^2 and an average tidal range of 5.52 meters, with a maximum potential average power (Table 8.8) of 1,800 megawatts. Plans were drafted for such a project during the early 1930's and construction was actually started before the project was finally killed by lack of Congressional appropriation. In 1948, interest in a Passamaquoddy Tidal Power Project was revived and a new engineering study was authorized by the United States and Canadian governments. This involved the establishment of an International Joint Commission and The International Passamaquoddy Engineering Board to study and draw engineering plans for such a project.

The Engineering Board, in its report of 1959, recommended a two-pool project involving both Passamaquoddy and Cobscook Bays, but with the power obtained solely from Passamaquoddy Bay during its emptying phase. This would have a power plant consisting of 30 unidirectional turbogenerator units of 10,000 kw capacity each, or a total installed capacity of 300,000 kw, with an annual energy production of 1,843 × 10^6 kwh. Comparing the latter figure with that of 15,800 × 10^6 kwh given in Table 8.8 as the maximum energy obtainable annually indicates that the proposed system would utilize but 11.8 percent of the energy potentially available.

After studying this report, the International Joint Commission concluded that the project would be economically infeasible. In response, President John F. Kennedy, by letter of 20 May, 1961, requested the Department of the Interior to restudy the project and propose modifications. This resulted in a recommendation (Udall, 1963) that the power capacity be increased from 300,000 to 1 million kw in order to deliver most of the power during the brief period of peak demand. It also involved a slight reduction from 1,843 × 10^6 to 1,318 × 10^6 kwh in the annual energy production.

This was recommended to the President for authorization, but as yet no authorization has been obtained.

For the installation of the world's first major tidal-electric plant, that of la Rance estuary which began operation in 1966 (*Engineering*, July 1966, pp. 17–24), honor is due to France. Here, the average tidal range is 8.4 meters, and the power plant is in a dam enclosing an area of 22 km^2. The power plant comprises 24 units of 10,000 kw capacity each, and the annual production of energy was estimated to be 544 × 10^6 kwh, which amounts to about 18 percent of the total energy available (Table 8.8). If the capacity is increased, as planned, to 320,000 kw, this would increase the power utilization to about 24 percent of that potentially obtainable. This high figure has been made possible by the use of turbines of an advanced design. These are horizontal, axial-flow turbines with adjustable blades permitting operation during both the filling and the emptying of the basin, and also their use as pumps.

The most recent tidal-electric project to go into operation, as reported by *The New York Times* on 30 December 1968, is a small Russian experimental station in the Kislaya Inlet on the Coast of the Barents Sea, 80 kilometers northwest of Murmansk. This consists of a single unit driven by a 400-kilowatt turbine of French manufacture. A second unit is to be installed later, bringing the total power capacity to 800 kw.

According to the same article, a much larger 320,000-kilowatt plant is planned for the Lombovska River (Lumbovskii Bay, Table 8.8) on the northeast coast of the Kola Peninsula, and a 14-million-kilowatt plant for the Mezen Bay on the east side of the mouth of the White Sea. Since the stated capacities of these two plants are both larger than the maximum potential average power obtained from the Bernshtein data in Table 8.8, either the figures are exaggerated, or else it is now planned to enclose larger basins than those given by Bernshtein (1965, Table 5-5, p. 173).

In summary, it may be said that although the world's potential tidal power, if fully developed, would amount only to the order of 1 percent of its potential water power, and to an even smaller fraction of the world's power needs, it nevertheless is capable in favorable localities of being developed in very large units. It has the additional advantage of producing no noxious wastes, of consuming no exhaustible energy resources, and of producing a minimum disturbance to the ecologic and scenic environment. There are accordingly many social advantages and few disadvantages to the utilization of tidal power wherever tidal and topographical factors combine to make this practicable.

Geothermal Energy

One of the energy inputs into the earth's surface environment consists of the heat conducted from the earth's interior as a result of the increasing temperature with depth; another consists of the heat convected to the surface by volcanoes and hot springs. In special geological situations in volcanic areas, underground water is trapped in porous or fractured rocks and becomes superheated from volcanic heat. Wells drilled into such reservoirs of superheated water or steam permit the steam to be conducted to the surface where it can be used as an energy source for a conventional steam-electric power plant.

It is only within recent decades that large geothermal-electric power plants have been built (Table 8.9). The earliest utilization of geothermal

TABLE 8.9
Developed and planned geothermal-electric power installations.

Country and locality	Installed capacity 1969 (megawatts)	Planned additional capacity (megawatts)	Total capacity by early 1970's (megawatts)	Date of earliest installation
Italy[a]				
Larderello	370		370	1904
Monte Amiata	19		19	ca 1962
Total	389		389	
United States[b]				
The Geysers, California	82	100	182	1960
New Zealand[b]				
Wairakei	290		290	Nov. 1958
Mexico[b]				
Pathé	3.5		3.5	ca 1958
Cerro Prieto (Mexicali)		75	75	ca 1971
Total	3.5	75	78.5	
Japan[b, c]				
Matsukawa	20	40	60	Oct. 1966
Otake	13	47	60	Aug. 1967
Goshogate		10	10	
Total	33	97	130	
Iceland[d] Hveragerdi	(Geothermal energy for house and greenhouse heating)	17	17	1960
U.S.S.R.[e] Kamchatka				
Pauzhetsk	5	7.5	12.5	1966
Paratunka	0.75		0.75	1968
Bolshiye Bannyye	25		25	1968
Total	30.75	7.5	38.25	
Grand Total	828.25	296.5	1,124.75	

Sources: [a]Facca and Ten Dam, 1964. [b]Donald E. White, U.S. Geological Survey, June 1969, personal communication. [c]Julian W. Feiss, 1968, personal communication. [d]Icelandic Embassy, Washington, D.C., July 1969. [e]Donald C. Alverson, Foreign Geology Branch, U.S. Geological Survey, July 1969, personal communication.

energy for power was at Larderello, in the Tuscany province of Italy, in 1904. The capacity of power plants in this locality has been increased to about 370 megawatts as of 1969. Recently two new thermal fields in the Monte Amiata region about 70 kilometers southeast of Larderello have been discovered, and smaller power plants installed. The Bagnore field has two generators of 7 Mw each, and the Piancastagnaio field, one station of 5 Mw. This gives a total geothermal power capacity for Italy of just under 400 Mw.

After Italy, the largest development of geothermal power is at Wairakei,

New Zealand. There, drilling for steam was begun about 1950 and the first power plant began operation in November 1958. The plant has been expanded to a capacity of 290 Mw in 1969.

The third largest project is in the United States at The Geysers in northern California. Here, power production began in 1960 with a 12.5 Mw unit. The plant capacity has been expanded to 82 Mw and an additional capacity of 100 Mw is planned for the near future.

In Japan, geothermal-power production was begun at Matsukawa in 1966 and at Otake in 1967. The total 1969 capacity of these two plants is 20 Mw and 13 Mw, respectively, with planned increases to 60 Mw each. These, plus a planned 10 Mw plant at Goshogate, will give Japan a total capacity of 130 Mw by the early 1970's.

Mexico now operates a small pilot plant of 3.5 Mw capacity at Pathé, about 200 kilometers north of Mexico City. A much larger thermal field has been drilled at Cerro Prieto, in Baja California, about 25 kilometers southeast of Mexicali on an extension of the San Andreas fault system. Two of the wells in this field are said to have the largest steam production of any in the world. Two power units of 37.5 Mw each are due to begin operation in 1970 or 1971.

Iceland has large geothermal fields. The steam from one of these is used for space heating of almost the entire town of Hveragerdi, and for large greenhouses nearby. No geothermal-electric power is yet produced (1 July 1969), but a plant of 17 Mw capacity at Hveragerdi is expected to begin operation before the end of 1969.

In the Soviet Union, the only geothermal power produced is at three small plants in Kamchatka (Pauzhetsk, Paratunka, and Bolshiye Bannyye) with a total present capacity of 30.75 Mw and a planned increase to 38.25 Mw.

The relevant data are summarized in Table 8.9, according to which the present installed geothermal-electric power capacity of the world amounts to 828 Mw with planned increases to 1,125 Mw by 1971–72. With regard to the ultimate world capacity of geothermal power, only an order-of-magnitude figure can be given. Basic information on geothermal installations and estimated potential power capacities of various countries is summarized by Baldwin and McNair (1967). By far the most comprehensive compilation on thermal springs, however, is that by Waring, Blankenship, and Bentall (1965), who give basic geologic data on flow rates and temperatures but do not interpret the data in terms of potential geothermal power.

A better appraisal of the quality of energy involved is given by Donald E. White (1965). For most of the better-known geothermal areas of the world, White has estimated the rate at which heat is discharged to the surface of the earth, and has also estimated the amount of stored heat above surface temperatures to depths of 3 kilometers and 10 kilometers. From the areas studied, he estimates that the world's total natural heat flow from all hydrothermal areas is of the order of 3×10^{10} cal/sec, or about 1.3×10^{11} thermal watts. He also estimates that the total stored heat of all hydrothermal systems to a depth of 3 kilometers amounts to 2×10^{21} cal (8×10^{21} thermal joules), while to a depth of 10 kilometers it amounts to 1×10^{22} cal (4×10^{22} thermal joules). Of the world's hydrothermal energy, White estimates that about 5–10 percent occurs in the United States, mainly in the western states.

To obtain an order of magnitude for geothermal power, White assumes that about 1 percent of the hydrothermal energy can be converted into electrical energy. For the depth of 10 kilometers, 1 percent of the estimated thermal energy would be 1×10^{20} cal, or 4×10^{20} thermal joules. For a 0.25 conversion factor, this would represent 1×10^{20} joules of electrical energy, or about 3×10^6 Mw-yrs. Then, if this amount of energy were to be withdrawn during a period of 50 years, the average annual geothermal-electric power would be

$$\frac{3 \times 10^6 \text{ Mw-yrs}}{50 \text{ years}} = 60,000 \text{ Mw},$$

or about 60 times the present installed capacity. This agrees with White's conclusion that the world's geothermal energy resources could sustain a rate of withdrawal of 10–100 times that of the present for at least the next 50 years.

It thus appears that the ultimate magnitude of geothermal power production will probably be in the tens of thousands of megawatts. While this is a significant amount of power, a better idea of just how significant can be obtained by comparison with other sources of power. A figure of 60,000 Mw for geothermal power is about the same as that of 64,000 Mw given in Table 8.8 for the world's potential tidal power, but only 2 percent of the 2.8×10^6 Mw given in Table 8.8 for the world's potential water power from conventional sources. It is only about a third larger than the present hydroelectric power capacity, or only about 20 percent of the present total installed electric power capacity of the United States. Hence, while geothermal energy is capable of sustaining a large number of small power plants in a limited number of localities, it still represents only a small fraction of the world's total energy requirements, and this for only a limited period of time.

NUCLEAR ENERGY

For a final source of energy appropriate for large-scale generation of power, we now direct our attention to nuclear energy. For this purpose, our present concern will be limited to the controlled release of energy from two contrasting nuclear processes, *fission* and *fusion*.

Energy from Atomic Fission

In its initial stages, the fission reaction is dependent solely upon the isotope uranium-235. Uranium, as it occurs naturally, consists of three isotopes, uranium-234, uranium-235, and uranium-238, with abundances of 0.006, 0.711, and 99.283 percent, respectively. Of these, uranium-234 may be regarded as negligible. Natural uranium would then consist of uranium-235 and uranium-238, with the former constituting only one part in 141 of the whole.

The significance of uranium-235 lies in the fact that of the several hundred naturally occurring atomic isotopes, it is the only one that is spontaneously fissionable by the capture of slow or thermal neutrons. This isotope is accordingly, of necessity, the initial fuel for all subsequent power development based on the fission reaction. The average amount of energy released by uranium-235 per fission-event is approximately 200 million electron-volts (Mev), or 3.20×10^{-11} joules. One gram of uranium-235 contains 2.56×10^{21} atoms. Hence, the energy released by the fissioning of 1 gram of uranium-235 is 8.19×10^{10} joules. This is equivalent to the heat of combustion of 2.7 metric tons of coal, or of 13.7 barrels of crude oil. It also is approximately equal to 1 thermal megawatt-day. Accordingly, a nuclear power plant with a capacity of 1,000 electrical megawatts, and a thermal efficiency of 0.33, would consume uranium-235 at a rate of about 3 kilograms per day.

Burner, Converter, and Breeder Reactors. A physical assembly in which a controlled chain reaction occurs is known as a nuclear reactor. For fission reactions, these reactors are divided into three principal types, *burners*, *converters*, and *breeders*.

A burner reactor is one that consumes the naturally occurring fissile isotope, uranium-235, in the manner indicated in Figure 8.29. However, despite the enormous amount of thermal energy per gram released by the fissioning of uranium-235, a severe limitation is imposed upon the amount of energy obtainable from this source by the facts that uranium is a comparatively rare chemical element, and that uranium-235 represents only 1/141 of natural uranium. A way out of this difficulty, however, is afforded by the fact that is it possible to convert both nonfissionable uranium-238, comprising 99.28 percent of natural uranium, and thorium-232, comprising essentially the whole of natural thorium, into isotopes which are fissionable.

FISSION POWER REACTION

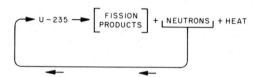

FIGURE 8.29
Schematic representation of nuclear-power-
reaction from the fissioning of Uranium-235.
(From Hubbert, 1962, Figure 56, p. 109.)

In each case, this is accomplished by exposing uranium-238, or thorium-232, to neutron bombardment, producing the following respective reactions:

$$^{238}_{92}U + n \rightarrow {}^{239}_{92}U \rightarrow {}^{239}_{93}Np \rightarrow {}^{239}_{94}Pu,$$

$$^{232}_{90}Th + n \rightarrow {}^{233}_{90}Th \rightarrow {}^{233}_{91}Pa \rightarrow {}^{233}_{92}U.$$

In this notation, the superscript denotes the total number of protons plus neutrons in the atomic nucleus, which also is approximately equal to the atomic mass; the subscript, which also is the atomic number and determines the chemical element, denotes the number of protons.

Thus, uranium-238 absorbs a neutron and is converted to uranium-239. The latter, by two short-lived radioactive transformations changes spontaneously to neptunium-239 and thence to plutonium-239. Similarly, thorium-232 absorbs a neutron and is transformed into thorium-233. This, in turn, changes radioactively into protoactinium-233 and thence into uranium-233. A flow diagram for the breeding reaction is shown in Figure 8.30.

Both plutonium-239 and uranium-233 are fissionable in a manner similar to uranium-235. The isotopes uranium-233, uranium-235, and plutonium-239, are accordingly known as fissile isotopes. Uranium-238 and thorium-232, on the other hand, which are not themselves fissionable, but are capable of being converted into previously nonexistent isotopes which are fissionable, are known as *fertile* materials. The process of converting fertile into fissile materials is known as *conversion*, or, in special cases, as *breeding*.

The thermal energy produced per fission by either plutonium-239 or uranium-233 is approximately the same as that produced by uranium-235, about 200 Mev. Since the atomic masses of uranium-238 and thorium-232 are very close to that of uranium-235, the numbers of atoms per gram are also very nearly the same. Hence, the thermal energy per gram obtainable from natural uranium or thorium by means of conversion or breeding is approximately the same as from the initial fissile material, uranium-235, namely about 8.2×10^{10} joules per gram.

The neutrons required for conversion or breeding are those produced in a reactor whose initial supply of fuel is uranium-235. If uranium-238, or thorium-232, is placed in such a reactor, some of its atoms will absorb neutrons and become converted into its respective fissle isotope. The basic difference between conversion and breeding, is that by means of a conversion reactor, only a fraction of the fertile material can be converted into fissile material before the supply of the latter is completely exhausted. Whereas, for the breeder reactor, more fissile material is produced than is consumed, and it is possible, in principal, to utilize the entire supply of fertile material. provided that sufficient uranium-235 is available to start the process initially.

For the discussion of conversion or breeding, a significant quantity is that known as the *conversion ratio*. If Q_o be the initial amount of fissile material in the fuel inventory of a reactor, including its auxiliary fuel-processing equipment, and if Q be the amount of fissile material remaining after one cycle during which an amount of fuel Q_o has been consumed, the conversion (or breeding) ratio is defined by

$$K = Q/Q_o. \tag{9}$$

If $K = 0$, the reactor is a pure burner; if K is greater than 0, but less than 1, the reactor is a converter; and finally, if K is greater than 1, the reactor is a breeder.

Development of Nuclear Power.   The foregoing principles are essential for an appraisal of the present status and future prospects of nuclear-power development based on atomic-fission reactors.

Historically, the technological evolution from the first experimental

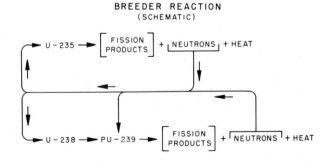

BREEDER REACTION
(SCHEMATIC)

FIGURE 8.30
Schematic representation of breeder reaction for Uranium-238.
(From Hubbert, 1962, Figure 57, p. 109.)

achievement of atomic fission to the present design and construction of nuclear power plants of 1,000 electrical-megawatt capacities occurred in an incredibly short time. Fission was first achieved experimentally in 1938, and the first controlled chain reaction on 2 December 1945. The first electric power was produced in 1951, and the first large-size nuclear-electric power plant—that at Shippingport, Pennsylvania, with an initial capacity of 60 electrical megawatts—went into operation in 1957.

However, in the United States, until about 1963, the development program was largely experimental, with emphasis on alternative designs and cost reduction, in an effort to make nuclear power economically competitive with that from fuels and water power. The latter achievement was reached in 1963 when a contract was let to the General Electric Company for the Oyster Creek plant of the Jersey Central Power Company. This was to have a capacity of 515 electrical megawatts and a guaranteed cost of power production below that of a comparable fuel-powered plant.

Following this, further contracts for additional plants in the 500 to 1,000 electrical megawatt range have followed in such profusion that they can best be considered statistically rather than individually.

As a consequence of this acceleration, the U.S. Atomic Energy Commission (AEC) has recently been obliged to increase significantly its earlier forecasts of the growth of nuclear power. According to this latest estimate (U.S. AEC, 1967b, Table 5, p. 8), the median forecast for the nuclear-power capacity of the United States was for an increase from 1,800 electrical megawatts at the end of 1966 to 145,000 electrical megawatts by the end of 1980. This represents a mean exponential growth rate of 31 percent per year, with a doubling period of only 2.4 years. The corresponding forecast (ibid., Table 1, p. 3) for total U.S. electrical-power capacity for the same period was for an increase from 233,000 electrical megawatts at the end of 1966 to 579,000 by the end of 1980—a mean growth rate of 6.5 percent per year, with a doubling period of 10.6 years.

However, according to the AEC Annual Report for 1967 (U.S. AEC, 1968, p. 93, with the exception of two gas-cooled reactors, all of the central-station nuclear power plants ordered by utilities since 1958 are light-water reactors (as contrasted with heavy water). For present purposes, the distinctive characteristic of these reactors is that they consume uranium-235 as fuel, having such low conversion ratios that they are essentially burners. In the foregoing report (ibid., p. 86) it is stated that such reactors are capable of consuming only 1 to 2 percent of natural uranium or thorium. According to Milton Shaw (1968, Fig. 4), Director of the Division of Reactor Development and Technology, the cumulative production of plutonium by the light-water reactors up to any time between 1968 and 1980 will be approximately one-third of cumulative consumption of uranium-235 to that date. This corresponds to a total consumption of only 1 percent of natural uranium.

The significance of this is that these light-water reactors will effect a heavy drain on the lower-cost resources of uranium-235 if not soon supplanted by high-ratio converter or breeder reactors. As stated by Milton Shaw (ibid., p. 1), ". . . the phenomenal number of orders for nuclear power plants over the last three years . . . emphasizes the increasing importance of the timely introduction of breeder reactors into the utility environment. . . . It becomes more evident each day how dependent we are going to become on the successful introduction of breeders in order to be assured of practically limitless economic electric power and process heat."

The reason for this concern is clear when the magnitude of uranium resources is measured against the requirements between now and 1980. This situation has been succinctly reviewed by Rafford L. Faulkner, Director, Division of Raw Materials, U.S. Atomic Energy Commission, in his opening remarks before the Conference on Nuclear Fuel—Exploration to Power Reactors, Oklahoma City, Oklahoma, on 23 May, 1968. Using the AEC's most recent forecast of nuclear-power capacity to the end of 1980, Faulkner points out that, in addition to year-by-year current requirements, it will be necessary to maintain an 8-year forward reserve of uranium supply; that is, the total requirement to the end of 1980 must comprise not only the amount actually consumed to the end of 1980, but also the additional amount to be consumed during the next 8 years. This total figure he estimates to be about 650,000 tons of uranium oxide, U_3O_8.

To be compared with this requirement figure, Faulkner gives reserve estimates of uranium in three price ranges: (1) less than $10/lb of U_3O_8, (2) $10–15/lb, and (3) $15–30/lb. For each price range, two categories of reserves are given: those that are reasonably assured, and estimated additional reserves. A composite of the price estimates of both producers and buyers of uranium is $7.10/lb of U_3O_8 by 1970, and increasing to $7.80 by 1973. The reserves of less than $10/lb are accordingly the ones of principal interest at present. For this category, Faulkner gives for the United States:

Reasonably assured reserves	310,000 tons U_3O_8
Estimated additional	350,000
Total	660,000 tons U_3O_8

In the same category, the figures for the noncommunist countries of the world (including the United States) are:

Reasonably assured reserves	835,000 tons U_3O_8
Estimated additional	740,000
Total	1,575,000 tons U_3O_8

Against this world figure, however, allowance must be made for the fact that the growth of nuclear power outside the United States will probably be at a comparable rate to that in the United States.

From these figures, it is apparent that a very tight situation in uranium supply at anywhere near current prices is likely to develop within the next two decades. This surmise is confirmed by the U.S. Atomic Energy Commission in its report on civilian nuclear power (1967a), wherein, on page 14, the statement is made:

> With reactors of current technology, the known and estimated domestic resources of uranium at prices less than $10 per pound of uranium oxide (U_3O_8) are adequate to meet the requirements of the projected growth of nuclear electric plant capacity in the U.S. for about the next 25 years.

However, since that report was issued the estimate of nuclear power-plant capacity for 1980 has been increased from 95,000 to 145,000 electrical megawatts without a corresponding increase in the estimates of uranium reserves.

An even further restriction arises from the rate at which these reserves can be mined and processed. According to Faulkner, of the reasonably assured reserves of 310,000 tons of U_3O_8 in the United States, only about 210,000 tons can be produced by 1980. His corresponding estimate for cumulative world production is about 500,000 tons. This alone could force the low-priced reserves into a higher-price category in case, as appears likely, it should be necessary to double the rate of production.

Breeder-Reactor Program. This situation has forced the breeder-reactor program out of a state of lethargy into something more nearly resembling a crash program. A recent account of the program has been given by Milton Shaw, Director, Division of Reactor Development and Technology, U.S. Atomic Energy Commission, in his paper on "The U.S. Fast Breeder Reactor Program" given before the American Power Conference, Chicago, Illinois, on 23 April 1968.

According to Shaw, experimental work was begun by the U.S. Government as early as the late 1940's on the possibility of utilizing the almost limitless energy tied up in uranium-238 and thorium-232. This led to the experimental breeder-reactor program and to the construction and operation of several experimental breeder reactors of different designs, culminating in 1955 in the construction of the Enrico Fermi Atomic Power Plant in Michigan, the first large sodium-cooled fast breeder.

Nevertheless, on the whole, the program was diffuse and characterized by an atmosphere of complacency. The growth rate of nuclear power was seriously underestimated, and no scarcity of uranium resources was forseen.

During the 20-year period from 1948 through 1967, the budget for the entire AEC breeder program amounted to but $12,000,000 per year. "There was much less substance than image" according to Shaw, "in the industrial breeder program for there appeared to be ample time."

With the belated realization of the possibility of a crisis in the fuel supply, the breeder-reactor program is now being pushed with great vigor. A series of technical reviews concerning the status of the advanced breeder program was begun in 1965. About the same time, the unprecedented series of orders by the utilities for light-water reactors emphasized the need for a change of approach to the whole breeder-development program. Consequently, the development and introduction into utility usage of safe, reliable, and economic breeder-reactor power plants became the highest priority in the AEC's reactor-development program. In this program, the highest priority was given to the development of a liquid-metal cooled, fast-breeder reactor (LMFBR) utilizing the uranium-238–plutonium-239 cycle.

Accordingly, in 1966, the LMFBR Program Office (staffed currently with about 50 professional scientists and engineers) was established at the Argonne National Laboratory near Chicago to assist with the detailed planning and technical evaluation of various aspects of the LMFBR program. The time schedule on this program involves getting an initial power plant into operation by the early 1980's, and large commercial plants into operation between 1985 and 1990.

The program of breeder-reactor development is also reviewed in the 1967 annual report of the AEC (U.S. AEC, 1968, pp. 77–86), in which it is confirmed that the highest priority has been given to the development of the liquid-metal cooled, fast-breeder reactor, with the goal of achieving a safe, reliable, and economic 1,000 Mwe LMFBR plant in the 1980's.

In parallel with this, but of secondary priority, studies are being initiated on other types of breeders. The principal of these is the molten-salt breeder reactor (MSBR). This would be based on the thorium-232–uranium-233 cycle, and hence, as a user of thorium as a raw material, would be a highly desirable complement to the LMFBR using uranium-238.

The projected doubling times—the time required for the doubling of the initial fuel inventory—which it is hoped to achieve by these two types are about 10 years for the LMFBR, using the uranium-238–plutonium-239 cycle, and between 10 and 20 years for the MSBR, using the thorium-232–uranium-233 cycle. A doubling period of 10 years, assuming no uses of fissile material for nonbreeding purposes, would permit a maximum rate of growth of breeder-power production of about 7 percent per year; a doubling period of 20 years would allow a maximum growth rate of about 3.5 percent per year.

Another breeder, or possibly converter, program involves the modification of the present type of light-water reactors by means of adding blankets of fertile materials to increase the conversion ratio. In this manner, it is hoped to increase the energy obtainable from natural uranium or thorium from the present approximately 1 percent to possibly as high as 50 percent. For natural uranium, 50 percent burnup would correspond to a conversion ratio of about 0.98.

Long-Term View of Nuclear-Fission Energy.   Taking a view of not less than a century, were electrical power to continue to be produced solely by the present type of light-water reactors, the entire episode of nuclear energy would probably be short-lived. With the growth rates now being experienced, the inexpensive sources of uranium would probably be exhausted within a fraction of a century, and the contained uranium-235 irretrievably lost. With the use of more costly uranium, the cost of power would increase until nuclear power would no longer be economically competitive with that from fuels and water.

This unhappy conclusion cannot be evaded by improvements of conversion ratios by any amount short of breeding, because for any conversion ratio less than 1, the initial supply of uranium-235 as well as all new fissile material generated by conversion will eventually be consumed completely, leaving only the inert fertile materials. Hence, the only long-time benefit from conversion is to multiply by some finite amount the initial quantity of fissile material, and to increase somewhat the length of time for the exhaustion of the initial supply. If such a consequence is to be avoided, it can only be done by the supplanting, at the earliest date possible, of all power reactors having conversion factors less than unity by true breeder reactors.

Since this is technologically possible, as well as necessary, we shall now assume that the present episode of burner and converter reactors is but a temporary developmental phase, and that probably before the end of the present century they will be almost entirely superseded by breeder reactors. When this occurs, as Alvin Weinberg has pointed out repeatedly (e.g., 1959, 1960), the problem of raw materials for energy will be drastically modified. For under these circumstances, it will become possible and practicable to utilize truly low-grade ores of uranium and thorium which cannot at present be given consideration.

A couple of examples will suffice to illustrate this point. For a low-grade source of uranium, we may consider the Chattanooga Shale of Devonian age which crops out along the western Appalachians in eastern Tennessee and neighboring states, and underlies at minable depths a sizable fraction of the total areas of the states of Tennessee, Kentucky, Ohio, Indiana, and Illinois. According to Vernon E. Swanson (1960, p. 4) of the United States Geological Survey, the Gassaway Member of this shale is about 15 feet thick, extends over an area of hundreds of square miles, and contains about

0.0060 percent by weight of uranium. Let us consider the amount of energy which this represents, assuming the use of breeder reactors operating on the uranium-238–plutonium-239 cycle.

Here we deal with a layer of rock 5 meters thick having a density of 2.5 grams/cm³, or 2.5 metric tons per cubic meter, and a uranium content of 60 grams per metric ton, or 150 grams per cubic meter. Hence, for each square meter of surface area there are 5 cubic meters of rock containing 750 grams of uranium. As we have seen heretofore, the energy released by the fissioning of 1 gram of uranium is equivalent to that of the combustion of 2.7 metric tons of coal or of 13.7 barrels of crude oil. Therefore, the fuel equivalent of the uranium in 1 square meter of surface area would be 2,000 metric tons of coal or 10,000 barrels of crude oil. Per square kilometer, this would represent 2 billion metric tons of coal or 10 billion barrels of oil.

Rounding our previous estimates to 1,500 billion metric tons as the ultimate U.S. resources of producible coal, and about 200 billion barrels for producible crude oil, the areas for equivalent amounts of uranium are found to be 750 square kilometers for coal, and 20 square kilometers for oil. The area of 750 square kilometers for coal is about 300 square miles, or an area roughly 17 miles square. The 20-square kilometer area equivalent to the ultimate crude-oil resources would be only about 8 square miles, of an area somewhat less than 3 miles square.

For a similar calculation with regard to the energy obtainable from low-grade thorium deposits, using breeder reactors, we may consider the Conway Granite in New Hampshire. This is a granite which crops out over an area of about 300 square miles, or 750 square kilometers, and extends probably to some kilometers in depth. According to studies by John A. S. Adams and associates (Adams, Kline, Richardson, and Rogers, 1962), this granite has a remarkably uniform thorium content, averaging 56 grams per metric ton. In this case, 1 cubic meter of rock has a mass of 2.7 metric tons and contains 150 grams of thorium. Since the energy released by fissioning of 1 gram of thorium is substantially the same as for uranium, the fuel equivalent of the thorium contained in a cubic meter of rock is equivalent to about 400 metric tons of coal, or 2,000 barrels of crude oil.

Should the whole area be quarried to a depth of only 100 meters (330 feet) and the thorium used in breeder reactors, the fuel equivalent of the energy produced would be 30×10^{12} metric tons of coal, or 150×10^{12} barrels of crude oil. This would be 20 times the coal resources of the United States, or 750 times the resources of crude oil.

These are only illustrative examples. The energy potentially obtainable by breeder reactors from rocks occurring at minable depths in the United States and containing 50 grams or more of uranium and thorium combined per metric ton is hundreds or thousands of times larger than that of all of the fossil fuels combined. It is clear, therefore, that by the transition to a complete breeder-reactor program before the initial supply of uranium-235 is exhausted, very much larger supplies of energy can be made available than now exist. Failure to make this transition would constitute one of the major disasters in human history.

Energy from Fusion

In 1939, H. A. Bethe (1939a; 1939b) published the results of theoretical studies of the preceding year in which he derived from primary data the sequence of nuclear reactions whereby the enormous amounts of energy radiated from the sun and the stars are produced by the fusion of hydrogen of atomic-mass 1 into helium of atomic-mass 4[1]. Since that time, the question of whether controlled fusion may also be achieved in the laboratory has been a continuing challenge.

The chemical element hydrogen has three isotopes of mass numbers 1, 2, and 3, which have now come to be known by the separate names of *hydrogen* with the chemical symbol H, *deuterium* with the symbol D, and *tritium* with the symbol T, respectively. The problem of achieving controlled fusion reduces to that of fusing two or more of these isotopes of hydrogen into helium, the next higher element in the atomic scale. Helium also has two isotopes of present interest, helium-3 and helium-4.

The fusion of deuterium and tritium into helium in an uncontrolled explosive manner has already been achieved and is the basis for the so-called hydrogen, or thermonuclear bomb. Research in an effort to achieve a controlled fusion reaction has been under way in several laboratories in the United States during the last two decades, and comparable work is being conducted in several other countries. However, the British government has recently announced its intention of discontinuing the fusion work being conducted there. Although progress toward the achievement of controlled fusion is gradually being made, it still is not possible to estimate when, or even whether, the development of power from the fusion reaction may ever be accomplished. However, since the possible fusion reactions and their associated energy releases are known, it is possible to estimate the amounts of energy potentially obtainable from these reactions in terms of the earth's resources of the primary isotopes involved.

According to Samuel Glasstone (1964) of the U.S. Atomic Energy Commission, the most hopeful approaches to the achievement of controlled fusion are those that involve the fusion of two deuterium atoms, or of one deuterium and one tritium atom. Of these two, the latter appears to be the one more likely to be successful, at least initially.

---

[1] For this work Bethe was awarded a Nobel Prize in 1968.

The reactions of interest, and their associated energy releases, are the following:

$$_1^2D + _1^2D \rightarrow _2^3He + n + 3.2 \text{ Mev,}$$

$$_1^2D + _1^2D \rightarrow _1^3T + H + 4.0 \text{ Mev.}$$

Here, in addition to the chemical symbols already defined, n is a neutron and Mev signifies a million-electron volts, which is equal to 1.60×10^{-6} ergs or to 1.60×10^{-13} joules.

These two reactions are about equally probable. In the first, a stable product is produced, but in the second, the tritium atom reacts with another deuterium in the following manner:

$$_1^2D + _1^3T \rightarrow _2^4He + n + 17.6 \text{ Mev.}$$

Therefore, the net result of these three reactions can be written in the form

$$5_1^2D \rightarrow _2^4He + _2^3He + H + 2n + 24.8 \text{ Mev.}$$

Hence, the energy released per deuterium atom in these fusion reactions would be 4.96 Mev.

Further interest attaches to the deuterium-tritium reaction in view of the fact that another way exists for producing tritium atoms. When lithium-6 is bombarded with neutrons the following reaction occurs:

$$_3^6Li + n \rightarrow _2^4He + _1^3T + 4.8 \text{ Mev.}$$

When this is combined with the tritium-deuterium reaction,

$$_1^3T + _1^2D \rightarrow _2^4He + n + 17.6 \text{ Mev,}$$

the net result is equivalent to the reaction

$$_3^6Li + _1^2D + n \rightarrow 2_2^4He + b + 22.4 \text{ Mev.}$$

In this reaction, the limiting condition depends on the relative abundance of lithium and deuterium. The magnitude of total energy potentially obtainable will be limited by whichever isotope is the more scarce.

Let us now consider the amounts of energy that would be made potentially available in each case should the deuterium-deuterium, or the lithium-deuterium fusion reaction be achieved.

Energy from D-D Fusion. In the case of deuterium fusion, we have already seen that the release of energy per deuterium atom would amount to 4.96 Mev which is equivalent to 7.94×10^{-13} joules. The relative abundance of deuterium in water (including sea water) is 1 deuterium atom for each 6,500 hydrogen atoms. From these data, together with the respective atomic weights and Avogadro's number, it may be determined that 1 cubic meter of water contains about 1.028×10^{25} atoms of deuterium having a mass of 34.4 grams, and a potential fusion energy of 8.16×10^{12} joules. This is equivalent to the heat combustion of 269 metric tons of coal, or of 1,360 barrels of crude oil.

Since a cubic kilometer contains 10^9 cubic meters, if follows that the fuel equivalents of 1 cubic kilometer of sea water are 269 billion tons of coal, or 1,360 billion barrels of crude oil. The latter figure is approximately equal to the lower of the two estimates of ultimate world resources of crude oil. Since the ultimate world coal resources as estimated by Averitt are about $7,600 \times 10^9$ metric tons, the volume of sea water required to be equivalent to this would be about 28 cubic kilometers. The total volume of the oceans is about 1.5×10^9 cubic kilometers. Should enough deuterium be withdrawn to reduce the initial concentration by 1 percent, the energy released by fusion would amount to about 500,000 times that of the world's initial supply of fossil fuels.

Energy from Lithium-Deuterium Reaction. Consider now the energy potential obtainable from the lithium-deuterium reaction. The amount of this energy will be limited by whichever of the two isotopes is in shortest supply. From our previous calculations, we found that there are about 1025 atoms of deuterium per cubic meter of sea water. This would be 1034 deuterium atoms per cubic kilometer, or a total of about 1.5×10^{43} atoms in total volume of the oceans. And a large fraction of this could readily be extracted at low cost by methods now in use.

Lithium, on the other hand, is found in readily extractible concentrations only in restricted localities on land. The geochemical abundance of lithium in sea water is only about 1 part in 10 million, and recent estimates (Parker, 1967, Table 20) for the average abundance of lithium in the crustal rocks of the earth all fall within the range of 20–32 parts per million. However, the isotope, lithium-6, required for fusion constitutes only 7.42 percent of natural lithium. Hence, lithium-6 is present in a concentration of but 7 parts per billion in sea water, and about 2 parts per million in the crustal rocks of the earth.

Minable deposits of lithium occur principally in the mineral spodumene in igneous pegmatites, and in concentrations of natural brines. As recently as 1965, the sum of the measured, indicated, and inferred reserves of Li_2O in the United States, Canada, and Africa, were estimated by James J. Norton of the U.S. Geological Survey, (unpublished) to be about 1.6 million metric tons. Comparable estimates have been published by Thomas L. Kesler, Chief Geologist of the Foote Mineral Company, the largest lithium producer in the United States (Kesler, 1960; 1961). These estimates include about 2 million metric tons for the United States, 390,000 for Canada, and 180,000 for Africa.

The Foote Mineral Company has begun exploitation of a brine deposit near Silver Peak, Nevada, which is reported (Foote Mineral Co., 1967) to contain reserves of 2.5 to 5 million short tons of lithium. This deposit alone would correspond to about 5 to 10 million metric tons of Li_2O. In addition, the brine of Great Salt Lake, Utah, with a lithium content of 0.006 percent, is beginning to be processed for this element by the Lithium Corporation of America.

In view of the large but only roughly known magnitudes of the lithium reserves in the Silver Peak and Great Salt Lake brines, Norton considers 10 million short tons of elemental lithium to be a good order-of-magnitude estimate of the presently known resources of lithium in the United States, Canada, and Africa. Using this figure and the previous estimates for Canada and Africa, revised lithium reserves of these three areas are shown in Table 8.10. Also, in each instance, the amount of the isotope lithium-6 is given in metric tons. From the latter figures, the number of lithium-6 atoms can be obtained from the relationship,

$$\frac{\text{Avogadro's number}}{\text{Atomic weight, } {}^6Li} = \frac{6.0225 \times 10^{23}}{6.015 \text{ grams}}$$

$$= 1.0 \times 10^{23} \text{ atoms per gram.}$$

Then, since 1 metric ton $= 10^6$ grams, there are 1.00×10^{29} lithium-6 atoms per metric ton.

From the fourth column of Table 8.10, it is seen that the number of atoms of lithium-6 in the known lithium reserves of North America and Africa is about 7×10^{34}. Since this number is of the order of a hundred-millionth of the 1.5×10^{43} deuterium atoms in the oceans, it follows that the amount of energy potentially obtainable from the lithium-deuterium fusion reaction will be limited by the scarcity of lithium-6 rather than of deuterium. Accordingly, we may ascribe the total energy of 22.4 Mev, or 3.58×10^{-12} joules, obtainable from each atom of lithium-6 consumed, to the lithium-6 alone. On this basis, the energy potentially obtainable by the consumption of the amounts of lithium-6 shown in column 4 is given in column 5 of Table 8.10. This amounts to a total of about 2.4×10^{23} joules,

TABLE 8.10
Estimated lithium reserves of the United States, Canada, and Africa.

Location	Li_2O Measured, indicated, and inferred[a] (10^6 metric tons)	Lithium metal (10^6 metric tons)	Lithium-6 (10^4 metric tons)	Number of lithium-6 atoms (10^{33} atoms)	Equivalent fusion energy (10^{21} joules)
United States	19.0	8.8	65.4	65.4	234
Canada	0.4	0.2	1.4	1.4	5
Africa	0.2	0.1	0.7	0.7	2.5
Total	19.6	9.1	67.5	67.5	241.5

[a] Figures based on data from James J. Norton, U.S. Geol. Survey, Thomas L. Kesler (1961), and Foote Mineral Co., (1967).

which is approximately equal to the figure of 2.6×10^{23} joules for the energy obtainable from the combustion of the world's initial supply of fossil fuels.

Hence, unless much larger quantities of lithium of a lower grade than those now mined should be exploited, the scarcity of lithium renders the lithium-deuterium fusion reaction a much less promising ultimate source of energy than the deuterium-deuterium reaction. However, should the controlled lithium-deuterium reaction be the first to be achieved, it is technologically probable that achievement of the deuterium-deuterium reaction would follow.

DISPOSAL OF RADIOACTIVE WASTES[2]

An essential requirement for a nuclear-power industry based on the fission reaction[3] is a system for the safe management and disposal of radioactive wastes.

All common matter on earth is radioactive in some degree. Organisms on the earth are subjected continuously to a low level of damaging radiation from the radioactivity inside their tissues, from that of their immediately surrounding environment, and from cosmic rays. Men and other animals have evolved physiological systems able to repair tissue damage from "background" radiation at about the same rate the damage occurs. However, if the radiation rate is significantly increased, such repair is no longer possible, and permanent injury results. Depending on the nature of the exposure, radiation injuries take many forms, ranging from small and long-delayed effects to short-term lethal effects; a subtle and serious consequence of some radiation injuries is genetic transmission of physiological defects.

Radioactive wastes are distinguished from all other kinds of noxious wastes of chemical origin by the fact that there is no method of treating them to counteract their innate biological harmfulness. Radioactivity, a nuclear phenomenon, cannot be changed by any process less drastic than that which occurs inside nuclear reactors. Each radioactive isotope decays at a fixed negative-exponential rate peculiar to itself.

Health physicists and others have determined standards for the maximum concentration of radioactivity from different radioactive materials that is considered safe for human or other biological exposure. These maximum safe concentrations are different for different isotopes, but as a practical generalization the Health Physics Division of the Atomic Energy Commission

---

[2] Prepared by Earl Cook, Texas A&M University, from notes provided by M. King Hubbert.

[3] In the alternative fusion reaction the end product is mainly nonradioactive helium.

has used 20 half-lives[4] as the minimum period a given type of high-level radioactive waste should be permitted to decay before being considered safe for biological exposure. This rule would require that wastes containing the long-lived isotopes strontium-90 and cesium-137, which have half-lives of 28 and 30 years, be isolated at least 600, and possibly as long as 1,000 years, to render them biologically harmless.

Radioactive wastes are produced mainly by the "burning" of the fissile fuel, and to a much lesser extent by neutron bombardment of otherwise neutral materials within the reactor, including reactor metals, coolant fluids, and air or other gases. *The mass of radioactive fission proa ᴢts produced in a reactor is very nearly equal to the mass of fuel consumed.*

Inside a reactor, the fuel elements are encased in metal containers which retain the fission products produced. After a certain percentage of "burnup" of the initial fuel, the fuel elements are removed from the reactors and taken to fuel-processing plants where the fission products are separated chemically from the unspent fuel, which is then refabricated into new fuel elements. As they come from the reactor the fission products represent a wide scatter of isotopes, the composite of which is highly radioactive.

Most radioactive waste is generated in the fuel-processing plants and is in liquid or slurry form; it is stored in tanks of steel, or of steel and concrete, for a preliminary period of "cooling" before disposition as waste. The principal solid wastes are radioactive trash (contaminated boxes, rags, and laboratory apparatus) and reactor and machinery parts that have acquired an induced radioactivity from neutron bombardment. Radioactive liquids or slurries are classified as high-level when their radioactivity is greater than 1 curie[5] per gallon, intermediate-level for radioactivities between 1 microcurie (10^{-6} curies) and 1 curie per gallon, and low-level for less than 1 microcurie per gallon.

In 1955, at the request of the Atomic Energy Commission, an advisory Committee on the Geologic Aspects of Radioactive Waste Disposal was established by the Division of Earth Sciences of the National Academy of Sciences—National Research Council. This committee, which included geologists, ground-water hydrologists, and mining and petroleum engineers, served until 1967, and made a succession of study visits to most of the AEC establishments concerned with management and disposal of radioactive wastes. The committee formulated three general principles on which any long-term program of disposal of radioactive wastes should be based. These principles may be paraphrased as follows:

1. All radioactive materials are biologically injurious. Therefore, all

---

[4] A half-life is the time required for any given species of radioactive material to disintegrate or decay to one-half its original mass.

[5] A curie is a measure of the rate of radioactive disintegration; it equals a rate of 3.7×10^{10} disintegrations per second, about the disintegration rate of 1 gram of natural radium.

radioactive wastes should be isolated from the biological environment during their periods of harmfulness, which for the long-lived isotopes exceeds 600 years.

2. The rate of generation of radioactive wastes is roughly proportional to the rate of power production from nuclear-fission reactors. In the period of its work, the committee regarded the rate of nuclear power and related radioactive-waste production as being on the very low portion of a steep exponential-growth curve. The committee therefore reasoned that no waste-disposal practice, even if regarded as safe at an initially low level of waste production, should be initiated unless it would still be safe when the rate of waste production becomes orders of magnitude larger.

3. No compromise of safety in the interest of economy of waste disposal should be tolerated.

These principles are still valid.

Present practices which satisfy these principles best are those pertaining to the high-level wastes that emerge from the chemical processing of spent reactor fuel elements. These extremely radioactive aqueous-solid slurries generate heat at rates as high as 200 watts per gallon (Zeitlin and Ullmann, 1955), and it is necessary to store them a year or more to dissipate thermal energy before attempting more permanent storage or disposal.[6]

For permanent storage, the AEC has a number of possible procedures under research and development at present (U.S. AEC, 1968; Fox, 1967).

One possibility is to retain the self-dessicated slurries permanently in the original storage tanks. More promising procedures involve reduction of the wastes to solids in the form of glass or ceramic slugs, or calcined granules. These solids can then be buried in natural salt beds or stored in concrete-and-metal bins on or near the earth's surface. In either case, the high-level radioactivity of the solids will be isolated from circulating ground water and from the biological environment. Of the two alternatives, underground storage in salt, which is highly impervious to ground-water flow, appears preferable.

Present practices with regard to intermediate- and low-level aqueous wastes, of gaseous wastes, and of radioactive trash, are less satisfactory. The large amounts of water involved in low-level aqueous wastes make the problem of concentrating the radioactive isotopes difficult. Oak Ridge National Laboratory puts intermediate-level wastes into slurry form and injects the slurry into hydraulically induced fractures at a depth of about 700–1,000 feet in shale, where the slurry "sets" as a solid. In the Oak Ridge locality these fractures appear to be principally horizontal, or parallel to the bedding planes of the shales, and there seems *little* chance that radioactivity will escape upward. In most areas, however, oil-industry experience shows hydraulically induced fractures to be vertical and therefore unfavorable to

---

[6]Storage implies that the material is retrievable; disposal, that it is not.

safe disposal by injection. In consequence, it is questionable whether the Oak Ridge practice can be extended to other areas without going to much greater depths in the interest of safety. In any area, the wastes should be placed below the level of circulating potable ground water.

At the Hanford Works in Washington and at the National Reactor Test Station in Idaho, intermediate-level wastes are either stored in earth ponds or discharged underground through special cribs. At both localities, low-level wastes are discharged through wells into the subsurface body of circulating ground water. In Great Britain and possibly elsewhere, low-level wastes are being discharged directly into the sea.

At most of the AEC localities, and at several sites recently authorized for operation by private industry, solid wastes are buried in trenches 10–15 feet deep and covered with soil. Although these trenches are above the ground-water table, they are within the domain of circulating soil moisture, some of which returns to the surface by evaporation and plant transpiration, and some of which descends to the water table.

Radioactive gases, after removal of most of the longer-lived isotopes and a period of storage of the rest, are discharged through tall dispersion stacks into the atmosphere.

From this brief outline, it can be seen that most present practices in the disposal of radioactive wastes *other than high-level liquid* violate the first of the three principles stated above, and probably the second also. These wastes are not being isolated from the biological environment at present, and it is questionable to what extent the same practices can be continued when the rate of waste production becomes 10 or 100 times larger than it is at present without causing serious hazard.

With regard to the third principle, which deals with the possible com-promise of safety by economy, it should be pointed out that management costs for high-level wastes in the United States at present (Fox, 1967, p. 15) is less than 1 percent of the total cost of nuclear-power production. The cost of the entire waste-management program probably does not exceed 2 percent. In other words, the cost problem is not formidable. Nor is the physical problem intractible, for the rate of production of radioactive isotopes in the United States at present (1968) is only a metric ton or two per year.

It is more than penny-wise and pound-foolish to skimp on budgets for radioactive waste-disposal programs and to adopt *expedient* practices for economic reasons; it is hazardous to the health and genetic security of the nation.

A new monitoring system for radioactive-waste disposal practices is needed. This system must be independent of the agencies and organizations that produce such wastes, and would be somewhat analogous to the system of financial auditing which has been found both essential and effective in monetary affairs. Furthermore, reports generated by the group or body charged with operation of this monitoring system should be public, for every citizen is a shareholder in the common good.

HUMAN AFFAIRS IN TIME PERSPECTIVE

From the foregoing review, it is evident that the fortunes of the world's human population, for better or for worse, are inextricably interrelated with the use that is made of energy resources. Although the human species has always used energy to meet its minimum biological requirements, it is only within recent centuries, with the advent of energy from the fossil fuels and from wind and water power, that mankind has been able to increase its energy utilization per capita significantly above this minimum level. Despite the fact that the exploitation of these sources of energy has had a history extending over a period of several centuries, most of the developments during this entire period have occurred since 1900.

A much better perspective of the state of human affairs, and of the prospects for the future, can be obtained if the events in which we are concerned are regarded on a time scale of some tens of thousands of years. On such a scale, the quantities whose growth with respect to time we have been considering—the world's human population, the consumption of energy per capita, the development of water power, and the exploitation of the energy from fossil fuels—would all plot as curves with such uniform similarities as to be almost indistinguishable from one another. The curve of human population, for example, would plot as a nearly horizontal line just above zero for the entire period of human history until the last thousand years or so. Then a barely perceptible rise would begin and, as the present is approached, the curve would turn abruptly upward and rise nearly vertically to the 1969 world-population figure of about 3.5 billions.

The curve of the rate of energy consumption per capita would behave in a similar manner. Beginning with the biological minimum of about 100 thermal watts per capita represented by food, this curve would rise very slowly as other sources of energy—particularly that of firewood—are added, until it stabilized at about 500 thermal watts per capita. Then, a few centuries before the present when the exploitation of the energy from coal and of the power from water and wind was begun, this curve too would begin a slow and barely perceptible rise until, as the present is approached, it also would turn nearly vertically upward to a height of about 10,000 thermal watts per capita, which is the present average for the United States.

The curves of energy production from the fossil fuels would behave in a similar manner except that in the very recent past these would begin at zero.

Looking into the future on the same time scale, and assuming that a catastrophic event such as the near annihilation of the industrialized world by thermonuclear warfare can somehow be avoided, the physical realities discussed in this book dictate that the curve of human population must follow one of three possible courses: (1) It could continue to rise for a brief period and then gradually level off to some stable magnitude capable of being sustained by the world's energy and material resources for a long period of time; (2) it could overshoot any possible stable level and then drop back and eventually stabilize at some level compatible with the world's resources; or (3), finally, as a result of resource exhaustion and a general cultural decline, the curve could be forced back to a population corresponding to the lowest energy-consumption level of a primitive existence.

The one type of behavior for this curve that is not possible is that of continued and unlimited growth. To see that limits do exist, one need only consider that if the present world population were to be doubled but 15 more times, there would be one man for each square meter on all of the land areas of the earth, including Antarctica, Greenland, and the Sahara Desert. And at the present rate of growth, this would require but 525 more years.

Considering the other curves discussed previously, that of the production of the fossil fuels would continue upward for a brief period, and would then decline about as abruptly as it arose.

To sustain a high-energy-dependent world culture for a period much longer than a few centuries requires, therefore, a reliable source of energy of appropriate magnitude. The largest and most obvious of such sources is solar radiation, the continuance of which at close to present rates may be relied upon for millions of years into the future. The energy from solar radiation, with the exception of that fraction manifested as water power, does not offer much promise as a means of large-scale power production, although future technology may circumvent this difficulty. This leaves us with nuclear energy as our only remaining energy source of requisite magnitude. Although the earth's resources of uranium and thorium, and of deuterium, are finite and therefore exhaustible, the magnitudes of these resources in terms of their potential energy contents are so large that with breeder and fusion reactors they should be able to supply the power requirements of an industrialized world society for some millenia. In this case, the limits to the growth of industrial activity would not be imposed by a scarcity of energy resources, but by the limitations of area and of the other natural resources of a finite earth.

It now appears that the period of rapid population and industrial growth that has prevailed during the last few centuries, instead of being the normal order of things and capable of continuance into the indefinite future, is actually one of the most abnormal phases of human history. It represents only a brief transitional episode between two very much longer periods, each characterized by rates of change so slow as to be regarded essentially as a period of nongrowth. It is paradoxical that although the forthcoming period of nongrowth poses no insuperable physical or biological problems, it will entail a fundamental revision of those aspects of our current economic and social thinking which stem from the assumption that the growth rates which have characterized this temporary period can be permanent.

References

Adams, F. L. 1961 (unpublished). *Statement on water power*. Paper presented at Conference on Energy Resources, Committee on Natural Resources, National Academy of Sciences, Rockefeller Institute, New York, 10 July 1961.

Adams, J. A. S., M. C. Kline, K. A. Richardson, and J. J. W. Rogers. 1962. The Conway Granite of New Hampshire as a major low-grade thorium resource. *Proc. Natl. Acad. Sci. U.S.* 48: 1898–1905.

American Gas Association, Inc., American Petroleum Institute, and the Canadian Petroleum Association. 1967. *Reserves of crude oil, natural gas liquids, and natural gas in the United States and Canada as of December 31, 1966*, vol. 21.

Averitt, Paul. 1961 (unpublished). *Coal reserves of the United States and of the World. Domestic and world resources of fossil fuels, radioactive minerals, and geothermal energy*. Preliminary reports prepared by members of the U.S. Geol. Survey for the Natural Resources Subcommittee of the Federal Council of Science and Technology, 28 Nov. 1961.

Averitt, Paul. 1969. *Coal resources of the United States, Jan. 1, 1967*. U.S. Geol. Survey Bull. 1275.

Baldwin, C. L., and E. McNair. 1967. *California's geothermal resources*. Report to the 1967 California Legislature, the Joint Legislative Committee on Tidelands.

Bernshtein, L. B. 1965. *Tiday energy for electric power plants* [English translation of 1961 Russian edition]. Jerusalem: Israel Program for Scientific Translations.

Bethe, H. A. 1939a. Energy production in stars. *Phys. Rev.* 55: 103.

Bethe, H. A. 1939b. Energy production in stars. *Phys. Rev.* 55: 434–456.

Cabell, J. B. 1926. *The Silver stallion*. New York: Robert M. McBride and Co.

Daniels, F. 1964. *Direct use of the sun's energy*. New Haven and London: Yale Univ. Press.

Dillon, E. L., and L. H. Van Dyke. 1967. North American drilling activity in 1966. *Am. Assoc. Petrol. Geol. Bull.* 51: 973–1003.

Duncan, D. C., and V. E. Swanson. 1965. *Organic-rich shales of the United States and World land areas*. U.S. Geol. Survey Circ. 523.

Facca, G., and A. Ten Dam. 1964. *Geothermal power economics*. Los Angeles: Worldwide Geothermal Exploration Co.

Faulkner, R. L. 1968. *Remarks at the Conference on Nuclear Fuel—Exploration to Power Reactors, Oklahoma City, Oklahoma.* U.S. Atomic Energy Commission Press Release of 23 May 1968.

Feiss, J. W. 1968. *Report of the second joint meeting of the Japanese-American Energy Panel 27 May–11 June 1968.* U.S. Department of the Interior. Washington, D.C.

Foote Mineral Co. 1967. Is there enough lithium? *Foote Prints* 36: 22–23.

Fox, C. H. 1967. *Radioactive wastes.* Understanding the Atom Series. U.S. Atomic Energy Commission. Washington, D.C.

Frey, J. W., and H. C. Ide. 1946. *A history of the Petroleum Administration for War, 1941–1945.* Petroleum Administration for War. Washington, D.C.

Glasstone, S. 1964. *Controlled nuclear fusion.* Understanding the Atom Series. U.S. Atomic Energy Commission. Washington, D.C.

Hendricks, T. A. 1965. *Resources of oil, gas, and natural-gas liquids in the United States and the World.* U.S. Geol. Survey Circ. 522.

Hodgkins, J. A. 1961. *Soviet power: Energy resources, production, and potential.* Englewood Cliffs, N.J.: Prentice-Hall.

Hubbert, M. King. 1962. *Energy resources: A report to the Committee on Natural Resources.* National Academy of Sciences—National Research Council Publ. 1000-D. Washington, D.C.

Hubbert, M. King. 1967. Degree of advancement of petroleum exploration in United States. *Am. Assoc. Petrol. Geol. Bull.* 51: 2207–2227.

International Joint Commission, United States and Canada. 1961. *Report on the International Passamaquoddy tidal power project.*

International Passamaquoddy Engineering Board. 1959. *Investigation of the International Passamaquoddy tidal power project.*

Ion, D. C. 1967. *The significance of world petroleum reserves.* Seventh World Petroleum Congress, Proc. 1B: 25–36. Mexico City, April 1967.

Jeffreys, H. 1920. Tidal friction in shallow seas. *Phil. Trans. Roy. Soc.*, A, 229: 239–264.

Jeffreys, H. 1959. *The earth, its origin, history, and physical constitution*, 4th ed. Cambridge, Eng.: Cambridge Univ. Press.

Kesler, T. L. 1960. Lithium raw materials. In *Industrial minerals and rocks*, Am. Inst. Mining, Metall., and Petroleum Engineers, pp. 521–531.

Kesler, T. L. 1961. Exploration of the Kings Mountain Pegmatites. *Mining Eng.* 13(9): 1062–1068.

McKelvey, V. E., and D. C. Duncan. 1965. United States and world resources of energy. In *Symposium on fuel and energy economics*, 9(2): 1–17. American Chemical Society.

Munk, W. H., and G. J. F. MacDonald. 1960. *The rotation of the earth, a geophysical discussion.* Cambridge Monographs on Mechanics and Applied Mathematics. Cambridge, Eng.: Cambridge Univ. Press.

National Petroleum Council. 1961. *Proved discoveries and productive capacity of crude oil, natural gas and natural gas liquids in the United States.* Washington, D.C.

National Petroleum Council. 1965. *Proved discoveries and productive capacity of crude oil, natural gas and natural gas liquids in the United States.* Washington, D.C.

Parker, R. L. 1967. Composition of the earth's crust. In *Data of geochemistry*, 6th ed., Chapter D. U.S. Geol. Survey Prof. Paper 440.

Potential Gas Committee. 1967. *Potential supply of natural gas in the United States as of December 31, 1966*. Potential Gas Agency, Mineral Resources Institute, Colorado School of Mines, Golden, Colorado.

Pow, J. R., G. H. Fairbanks, and W. J. Zamora. 1963. Descriptions and reserve estimates of the oil sands of Alberta. In *Athabasca oil sands*, K. A. Clark, ed., Research Council of Alberta, Edmonton, Information Series no. 45, pp. 1–14.

Shaw, M. 1968. *The U.S. fast breeder reactor program*. Paper given at American Power Conference, Chicago, Illinois 23 April 1968. U.S. Atomic Energy Commission Press Release of 1 May 1968.

Swanson, V. E. 1960. Oil yield and uranium content of black shales. In *Uranium and carbonaceous rocks*. U.S. Geol. Survey Prof. Paper 356.

Taylor, G. I. 1919. Tidal friction in the Irish Sea. *Phil. Trans. Roy. Soc.*, A, 220: 1–33.

Trenholm, N. W. 1961. Canada's wasting asset—tidal power. *Elect. News. Eng.* 70(2): 52–55.

Udall, S. L. 1963. *The international Passamaquoddy tidal power project and Upper St. John River hydroelectric power development*. Report to President John F. Kennedy. U.S. Department of the Interior. Washington, D.C.

U.S. Atomic Energy Commission. 1967a. *Civilian nuclear power*. 1967 supplement to the 1962 report to the President. Washington, D.C.

U.S. Atomic Energy Commission. 1967b. *Forecast of growth of nuclear power*. U.S. Atomic Energy Commission, Division of Operations Analysis and Forecasting. Washington, D.C.

U.S. Atomic Energy Commission. 1968. *Annual Report to Congress of the Atomic Energy Commission for 1967*. Washington, D.C.

U.S. Federal Power Commission. 1966. *World power data, 1964*. Washington, D.C.

Van Dyke, L. H. 1968. North American drilling activity in 1967. *Am. Assoc. Petrol. Geol. Bull.* 52: 895–926.

Waring, G. A., R. R. Blankenship, and R. Bentall. 1965. *Thermal springs of the United States and other countries of the world—A summary*. U.S. Geol. Survey Prof. Paper 492.

Weeks, L. G. 1948. Highlights on 1947 developments in foreign petroleum fields. *Am. Assoc. Petrol. Geol. Bull.* 32: 1093–1160.

Weeks, L. G. 1950. *Discussion of* "Estimates of undiscovered petroleum reserves by A. I. Levorsen." United Nations Scientific Conference on the Conservation and Utilization of Resources, 17 August–6 Sept. 1949, Lake Success, New York, Proc. 1: 107–110.

Weeks, L. G. 1958. Fuel reserves of the future. *Am. Assoc. Petrol. Geol. Bull.* 42: 431–438.

Weeks, L. G. 1959. Where will energy come from in 2059. *Petrol. Engineer* 31(Aug. 1959): A-24–A-31.

Weinberg, A. M. 1959. Energy as an ultimate raw material. *Phys. Today* 12(11): 18–25.

Weinberg, A. M. 1960. Breeder reactors. *Scientific American* 202(1): 82–94.

White, D. E. 1965. *Geothermal energy*. U.S. Geol. Survey Circ. 519.

Zapp, A. D. 1961 (unpublished). *World petroleum resources. Domestic and world resources of fossil fuels, radioactive minerals, and geothermal energy.* Preliminary reports prepared by members of the U.S. Geol. Survey for the Natural Resources Subcommittee of the Federal Council of Science and Technology, 28 Nov. 1961.

Zapp, A. D. 1962. *Future petroleum producing capacity of the United States.* U.S. Geol. Survey Bull. 1142-H.

Zeitlin, H. R., and J. W. Ullmann. 1955. *Radioactive waste economics; Optimum storage time prior to shipping to disposal site.* Oak Ridge National Laboratory, Tennessee, Central Files No. 55-10-101.

Acknowledgments

We are indebted to so many for help with our work that to acknowledge each as he deserves would be to lengthen disproportionately a book that aims to be brief. We merely list, therefore, with our sincere thanks for services or information on the subjects specified, those who participated in one or more of our four long exploratory conferences,[1] or who contributed significantly in other respects to the evolution of our thoughts or the preparation of this book. They are as follows:

P. H. Abelson
Carnegie Institution of Washington

Critical review of Chapter 8

E. A. Ackerman
Carnegie Institution of Washington

Geography of resources

Francis L. Adams
U.S. Federal Power Commission

Water and tidal power

Aaron Altschul
International Agriculture
Development Service

Nutrition, chemical synthesis
of foods

William M. Armstrong
The University of British Columbia

Metallurgical engineering

Paul Averitt
U.S. Geological Survey

World coal resources

Harold J. Barnett
Washington University

Mineral economics

[1] Conference on Human Ecology, 16–18 Dec. 1966, Tucson, Arizona. Conference on Technological, Political, and Social Factors, 25–27 March 1967, College Park, Maryland. Conference on Renewable Resources, 16–18 June 1967, Cacapon Lodge, West Virginia. Conference on Nonrenewable Resources, 15–18 Sept. 1967, Vancouver, British Columbia.

B. W. Beebe Boulder, Colorado	U.S. and world resources of natural gas
Philip Bethke U.S. Geological Survey	Geochemistry of mineral resources
John R. Borchert University of Minnesota	Discussion of goals and methods as an *ex officio* member of the Committee
Kenneth E. Boulding University of Colorado	Critique of the expanding economy
Albert N. Bove National Research Council	Constructive editing
Harvey Brooks Harvard University	Nuclear reactor technology and economics; review of the typescript
Eugene Callahan Geological Survey of Utah	Mineral resources
Earl F. Cook Texas A&M University	Imaginative staff assistance in early phases of work; preparation of section on "Disposal of Radioactive Wastes" (pp. 233–237)
J. B. Cragg The University of Alberta	Human ecology
Farrington Daniels University of Wisconsin	Solar energy
Henry David National Research Council	Sociology of resource problems; review of the typescript
Robert C. Dean, Jr. Dartmouth University	Technological innovation with respect to energy and mineral resources
Edward S. Deevey, Jr. Dalhousie University	Principles of ecology
John Van N. Dorr, II U.S. Geological Survey	Mineral resources
Matthew Drosdoff Cornell University	Food resources from the land
Harry Eagle Yeshiva University	Review of the typescript
Northcutt Ely Ely & Duncan	Legal aspects of mineral resources
K. O. Emery Woods Hole Oceanographic Institute	Marine mineral resources
Charles Fairhurst University of Minnesota	Rock mechanics and mining

Peter T. Flawn
University of Texas

Aspects of mineral resource
innovation; metal reserves

Frank A. Forward
The University of British Columbia

Metallurgy; mineral resources
policy

Clifford Geertz
The University of Chicago

Social and anthropological aspects
of urbanization

Edwin R. Gilliland
Massachusetts Institute of Technology

Energy storage by means of
synthetic chemical compounds

Jean Gottmann
Oxford University

Geographical factors in the
balance between needs and resources

L. M. Gould
The University of Arizona

Resource policy

M. Grant Gross
State University of New York,
Stony Brook

Marine mineral resources

R. G. Gustavson
Tucson, Arizona

Resource policy

James Harrison
Department of Energy, Mining, and
Resources, Ottawa

Global mineral exploration;
mineral resources policy

Arthur Hasler
University of Wisconsin

Eutrophication; food from inland
waters

George E. Hatsopoulis
Massachusetts Institute of Technology

Electrochemical conversion from
chemical to electrical energy; fuel cells

Walter R. Hibbard, Jr.
Owens-Corning Fiberglas Corp.

Evaluation of mineral resources;
U.S. Bureau of Mines reserve estimates

Werner Z. Hirsch
University of California, Los Angeles

Urban economics and demands

G. Evelyn Hutchinson
Yale University

Energy flow through the biological
complex; review of the typescript

H. L. James
U.S. Geological Survey

Metalliferous geology;
review of the typescript

W. D. Johnston, Jr.
U.S. Geological Survey

Global mineral exploration

H. R. Josephson
U.S. Department of Agriculture

Forestry and forest products

I. R. Kaplan
University of California, Los Angeles

Biological and geochemical factors in the
concentration of metals in the sea

Hiroshi Kasahara
United Nations Development Programme

Productivity of oceans and lakes

Omer J. Kelley Agency for International Development	Water for agriculture
John Kincaid U.S. Department of Commerce	Mineral fertilizers
Eric Lampard University of Wisconsin	Economic and political history of resources
Francois J. Lampietti Ocean Science and Engineering, Inc.	Marine mining and mineral resources
James Laver University of Minnesota	Mining and metallurgy
C. D. McAllister Fisheries Research Board of Canada	Aquatic food chains
J. I. McLelland Ocean Science and Engineering, Inc.	Marine mining and mineral resources
Vincent E. McKelvey U.S. Geological Survey	Resources of fissionable materials; geothermal energy
George Macinko University of Delaware	Urban geography
François Mergen Yale University	Forestry and forest products
Donald E. Michels National Research Council	Staff assistance; detailed review of the typescript
George Miller Rockefeller University	Review of the typescript
E. Max Nicholson International Biological Programme (Nature Conservancy)	Conservation of biological resources
A. G. Norman The University of Michigan	Review of the typescript
Father John O'Brien University of Notre Dame	Religious aspects of population problems
John W. Padan U.S. Bureau of Mines	Evaluation of marine mineral resources
William C. Paddock Washington, D.C.	Food and populations
W. Delano Page Boulder, Colorado	Staff assistance
T. R. Parsons Fisheries Research Board of Canada	Production of organic matter in the sea
W. C. Paynton Texas Instruments, Inc.	Recycling and cladding of metals

Jacques J. Polak International Monetary Fund	Interaction between GNP and resources
W. P. Ryman Standard Oil Company of New Jersey	World resources of crude oil and natural gas outside the United States
M. B. Schaefer University of California, San Diego	Productivity of the sea
Brian J. Skinner Yale University	Review of the typescript
Lawrence B. Slobodkin The University of Michigan	Principles of ecology, human ecology
Perry R. Stout University of California, Davis	Agricultural innovation and technology
James L. Tuck Los Alamos Scientific Laboratory	Nuclear energy from fusion
Alvin M. Weinberg Oak Ridge National Laboratory	Nuclear energy from fission
Walter S. White U.S. Geological Survey	Comprehensive review of the typescript
M. Gordon Wolman The Johns Hopkins University	Geography of resources
William C. Yeomans Victoria, British Columbia	Regional planning and development

The studies that led to this publication were supported by grants from The Population Council; pursuant to Contract No. PH 86-67-252 of the U.S. Public Health Service, Department of Health, Education, and Welfare; and by Funding from the U.S. Geological Survey, U.S. Bureau of Mines, and U.S. Bureau of Commercial Fisheries, Department of the Interior.

Index